GW00655927

A little Osborn & Wallis flotilla in line astern off Battery Point as they leave Portishead on a sparkling summer's day in 1957. *Brandon* is leading, with *Salcombe* and *St. Vincent* behind. This aerial photograph was taken for the Company's updated Tide Book and the story behind it is related in full on page 112. All is not quite as 'ship shape' as would appear, however; *Brandon*'s hatch covers were painted on by the photographer, on the instructions of Mr Osborn. The four chimneys of Portishead 'A' and 'B' power stations were visible, and unmistakable, from the South Wales coast. *Brandon*, on which I was Deck Boy when the photograph was taken, was bound for Newport to load coal but I do not recall the destination of the other two; it may well have been Ely Harbour. By this date, the name Battery Point had been adopted locally instead of the official name Portishead Point, due to the presence of a pair of large coastal defence guns mounted there during the Second World War for the defence of Avonmouth, just three miles further up the estuary. *Author's collection*

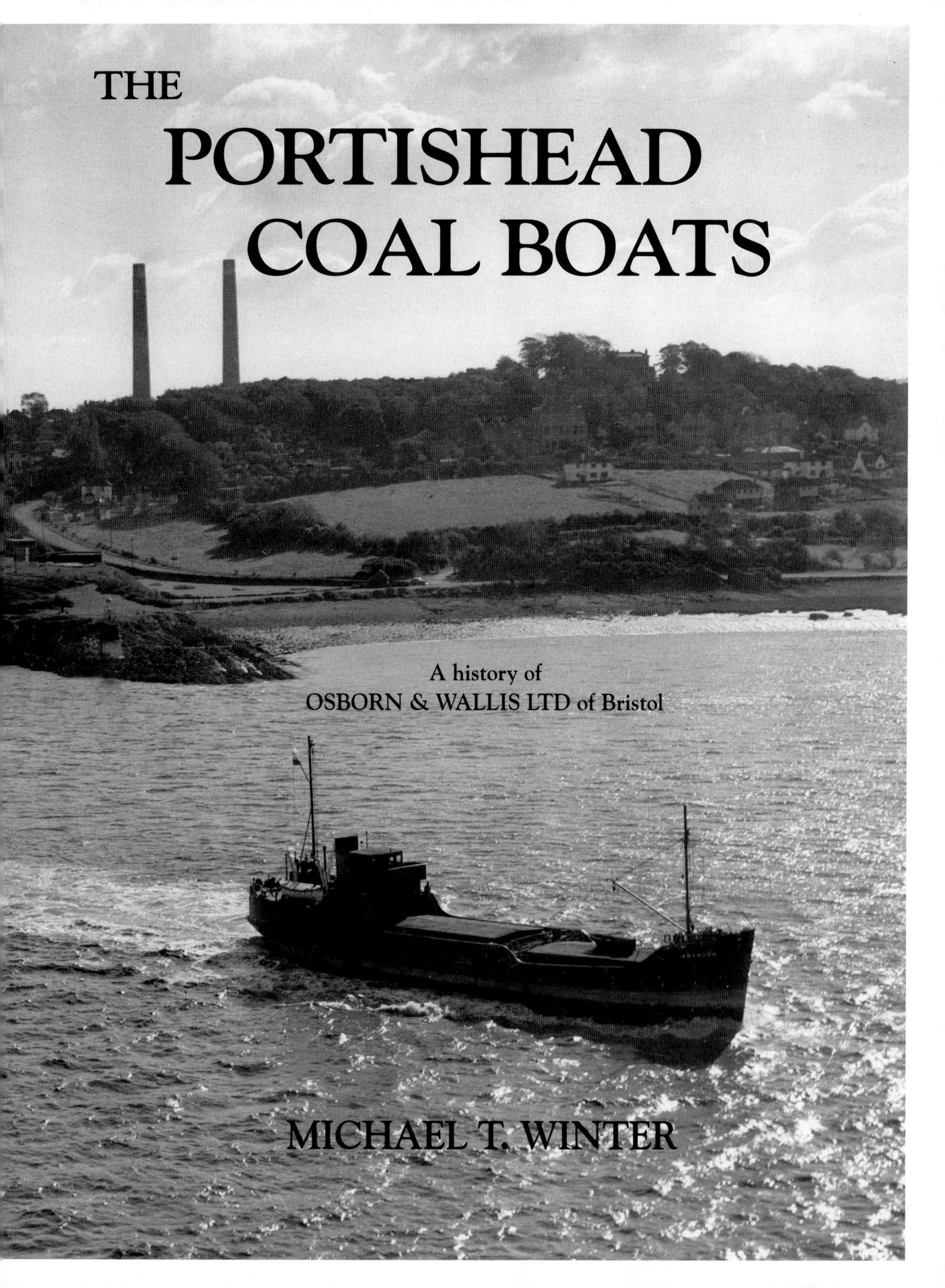

THE PORTISHEAD COAL BOATS

A history of
OSBORN & WALLIS LTD of Bristol

MICHAEL T. WINTER

This is how I remember my time as Deck Boy and this is my favourite view of *Colston*, entering Portishead Lock with Avonmouth Docks in the background. Gordon Richards, the Mate, is on the foc'sle (with his back to the camera) and with him is Jimmy Wong, the Sailor. The Skipper, Captain 'Sammy' Taylor, is on the wheel and Senior Sailor Fred Knight is standing under the wing of the bridge. Chief Engineer Colin Campbell and Second Engineer Arthur Anderson would be 'underground'. No sign of yours truly but my bike is propped up against the forward end of the main hatch coaming. A bike was an essential item of kit for the Deck Boy. The only disappointing feature of this otherwise perfect photograph of *Colston*, is the fact that her Builder's Plaque is missing from the front of the bridge. It had been temporarily removed while the bridge structure was being painted. *Capt. P. Tambling*

CONTENTS

INTRODUCTION .... page 7
WHY & HOW .... page 7
ACKNOWLEDGMENTS .... page 10

PART ONE: THE COMPANY .... page 11
1. ORIGINS, GROWTH & DECLINE .... page 11
2. FLEET HISTORY .... page 23
CHRONOLOGY OF ACQUISITIONS AND DISPOSALS .... page 84
SUMMARY OF O&W HISTORY FOR EACH SHIP .... page 85

PART TWO: THE JOB .... page 87
THE BOY'S JOB... 91 † THE WORKBOAT... 93 † THE SHIP'S PLAQUE... 93 † LOTS OF LESSONS... 94 † THE ROYAL VISIT TO BRISTOL... 95 † HOLIDAY RELIEFS... 98 † THE LEVEL OF EQUIPMENT ON THE SHIPS... 99 † TIDES... 100 † WIND... 100 † FOG... 101 † ICE... 102 † SUNSHINE... 102 † NEWPORT DOCK... 102 † NEWPORT DOCK COAL HOISTS... 106 † DISCHARGING AT PORTISHEAD... 109 † DRYDOCKING AT HILL'S... 113 † PORTISHEAD DOCK... 114 † MOVE TO BRANDON... 116 † BRANDON'S TRIALS... 117 † NEW TIDE BOOKS... 118 † MOVE TO DOWNLEAZE... 119 † LIVING IN DOWNLEAZE... 123 † ELY HARBOUR... 123 † MOORING WITH THE BOAT... 124 † RELIEF ON COLSTON... 130 † MOVE TO DRUID STOKE... 131 † MOVE TO SALCOMBE... 136 † OUSTED BY BIGGER SHIPS... 143 † SUMMARY OF MY TIME WITH THE FIRM... 143 †

PART THREE: SHIPS & PLACES – COLOUR SECTION .... page 145

PART FOUR: THE POST OSBORN & WALLIS YEARS .... page 161
1. THE SHIPS .... page 161
2. CHANGING PLACES .... page 175

PART FIVE: THE MEN .... page 181
CREWMEN... 181 † HOTWELLS YARD... 184 † PORTISHEAD DOCK... 184 † CREWS OF SHIPS... 185 † IN MEMORIAM – LUNAN'S CREW... 188 †

APPENDIX: GENERAL ARRANGEMENT S.S. DRUID STOKE .... page 189
INDEX .... page 191

Designed by Neil Parkhouse

British Library Cataloguing-in-Publication Data. A catalogue record for this book is available from the British Library

ISBN 1 903599 13 X

BLACK DWARF PUBLICATIONS
Black Dwarf Lightmoor
Unit 144B Lydney Trading Estate, Harbour Road, Lydney, Gloucestershire GL15 5EJ
www.lightmoor.co.uk

Printed by The Cromwell Press, Trowbridge

A circa 1930 aerial view of the entrance to Bristol City Docks, with a large steamer locking out at the bottom of the picture. Beyond is the Cumberland Basin, with two of the bonded tobacco warehouses on the right. The basin opens into the Floating Harbour, whilst the New Cut heads off round to the right. Merchants Dock is on the left immediately after the entrance to the Floating Harbour and Osborn & Wallis's wharf and yard is right next to it. Further up the harbour, almost on the apex of the bend, a vessel can be seen negotiating the entrance to Charles Hill's dry dock. *Neil Parkhouse collection*

St. Vincent ashore at Portishead in 1949. A youthful Michael Winter and his younger sister are standing in the foreground. *Author's collection*

Introduction

As a child, I had visited Black Nore Point at Portishead to see the motor vessel ***St. Vincent***, which had run ashore there in thick fog during February 1949. Despite attempts to refloat her, she stayed fast on the rocks and it was not until most of her cargo of coal, destined for Portishead Power Station, had been shovelled over the side by hand that, with the aid of two Bristol tugs, she was pulled free. ***St. Vincent*** had become a local spectacle and she remained a firm favourite of mine as a subject during art lessons at school, until it was suggested that perhaps I had completed enough paintings of the stranded collier.

A few years later, my father worked on the lock gates at Portishead and was able to arrange a trip to Newport for me on this same ship. This was followed later by another trip, this time to Ely Harbour at Penarth, near Cardiff. The voyage this time was aboard one of the steam ships, ***Druid Stoke***, whose Skipper was to become a key figure in my life some years later.

So began my association with 'The Coal Boats' as they were known in Portishead. They were a small fleet of roughly similar sized ships, engaged exclusively in the work of bringing coal from Newport and Ely Harbour to Portishead for the big power station. The fuelling of this important generating facility was supplemented by rail-borne coal but the majority of the fuel for it arrived by ship.

The ships belonged to the Bristol firm of Osborn & Wallis Ltd and Bristol was their port of Registry. However, they were very much Portishead's ships and a large proportion of their crews were Portishead men, with almost everyone else working on them hailing from Bristol. With a crew of seven in each ship – a Skipper, a Mate, a Chief Engineer, a Second Engineer, two Ordinary Seamen (Sailors) and the Deckboy (Boy) – they provided some local employment and few were the tides without at least two of them to be seen passing Battery Point, either inbound with their cargo, or outbound to fetch another one.

The vessels had black hulls with a red lead band of 'boot topping' and brown upperworks. They sported orange coloured funnels with black tops. However, this orange paint was nothing more than simple red-lead and in the case of the steam ships, it soon turned pink from the heat! Despite the unglamorous work, the ships were well maintained and looked after by the company and by their crews.

There was much increased demand for electricity during the winter months and this was thus the busiest time for the little vessels, as the power station worked to its maximum loading, with the result that the ships were constantly scurrying back and forth delivering the coal. Three trips per ship per week was the norm, four was not unusual and, occasionally, even five trips were made. The hours of work did not come into the equation, so it was frequently very intense and made all the more difficult by the weather conditions of the winter months. Dense and long lasting fogs were a feature of the Bristol Channel, as was the wind, rain, snow and ice. The latter created particular difficulties in the loading process, with the result that it took far longer than normal, which in turn increased the pressure to replenish the ever dwindling stocks of coal held at the power station.

Together with many other small vessels earning their living in the busy waters between the Somerset and South Wales coasts, the coal boats and their crews had to deal with these conditions, so there was some envy for the crews of the Bristol Channel 'swans'. These were P & A Campbell's pleasure steamers, which lorded it elegantly over the Channel during the summer months but were safely put away 'in the cupboard' when winter approached!

Following the construction of a second, bigger, power station at Portishead during the early 1950s, the company ordered the building of a further two ships. Larger than the others, these were to be the final new builds for the company and were ordered from Charles Hill's shipyard at Bristol, with whom Osborn & Wallis had had a long working relationship. All of their repairs, their later new builds and the biannual Board of Trade and Lloyds Insurance inspections were carried out at Hill's.

Thus, Osborn & Wallis and their ships and crews were a prominent feature of the Portishead scene. For their work in fuelling the two power stations so faithfully, the ships and the men that worked them are deserving of their small place in the annals of Bristol Channel shipping.

I hope that, in this book, I can do justice to them all.

Why & How

Since leaving the firm of Osborn & Wallis I have had a variety of jobs, none of which have had the slightest connection with ships, and I am at a loss to explain just why I have such an interest in my first employment. Ever since, through all my working life and now in retirement, I have felt a strong desire to know, if possible, where the ships were. To this end, I began to add to my little collection of pictures and memorabilia of the vessels and the company and, whenever the opportunity arose, I bought copies of photographs from other people. I began to feel that I wanted to know about the lives of the ships O&W bought before they belonged to the firm. This opened up a whole new field of enquiry.

In this context, I would say as a word of encouragement to others who feel they want to delve a little into the background of their work, that I have been amazed at how many photographs and items of information have come to light. Ships do not come much less important, insignificant, or lacking in prestige than the little O&W colliers, and yet every now and again, one small chance piece of information will open up a whole new and unsuspected line of enquiry. I have written letters to newspapers asking for anyone's memories and sometimes a reply would come accompanied by a slightly wrinkled photograph which had been lying for years forgotten in the bottom of a drawer somewhere. This book contains so many photographs which have been copied from such sources – with permission of course – and they are only a few of those which have been rounded up over the past forty years. To judge from past experience, I am certain there are still more that I am not aware of.

I have always felt that the work the ships and their crews did was worthy of a small record so that it is not forgotten. It is now over thirty years since the ships left Portishead and I have been waiting patiently for someone, with more knowledge and authority than myself and with longer service with the company, to record it all. It has not happened and, as the years have passed, I have become aware that memories of the ships are fading into oblivion. I have witnessed the departures of the older employees taking their memories with them and realised that, as limited as my own experience was, it was perhaps better I did the best I could to record what little I knew and had experienced. I wish that I had had the good sense to seek and record their memories while they were still with us. This book and the much larger collection from which it has been extracted, is the result of my efforts. Please excuse its shortcomings. There must be many but I baked the best cake I could with the ingredients I had.

It will be noted that throughout the narrative of the section dealing with my years working for the company I have deliberately largely left out names. This is partly because I had no wish to cause offence to the surviving family of men involved in some of the things which happened but largely because the memory can play tricks after 50 years and a particular incident may well have ended up being attributed to the wrong person! However, a separate chapter on the men lists all of those names that I could remember who were connected with Osborn & Wallis during my time with the company, as well as some of the dock workers at Portishead. I have included a selection of personal snapshots of my own and others acquired over time along with this.

This is simply the outcome of a laymans forty-year interest. I cannot claim credit for much of it. It would not have been possible without so much information and photographs obtained from a variety of sources, private and professional, and without so much kindness and willing help from so many people. Much of the material came from such sources and each item in isolation would mean almost nothing. All that I have done is to try to pull these fragments together and add it to my own photographs and memories so that, presented as one, it hopefully makes a reasonably complete tribute to the company, the men, and the ships. Some examples of the kind of enquiry and the generous help that I almost invariably received follow.

When Charles Hill's shipyard was closing, I wrote to them to ask if it was possible to buy copies of the General Arrangement Drawings for either **Colston** or **Brandon** and for either of their Engine Room Layout Drawings. The company generously responded by sending me, at no cost, original drawings from which the ships had been built. Through this, I made contact with Jim Crissup. If ever there was a man with passion, it was Jim. He worked for Hill's and was an absolute oracle on everything connected with the company and, indeed, Bristol shipping generally, and was only too willing to share what he knew. When the yard was closing, Jim sought permission to save all the ships drawings which were to be disposed of. He thus became the custodian of a treasure-mine of priceless information. He later passed all of this material to the National Maritime Museum at Greenwich. However, before it went to London Jim gave me the opportunity to see, and have copied, any O&W material. There is much of it in these pages. Without Jim's contribution, this book would hardly have been worth attempting and I cannot thank him enough. It was Jim who prompted me to try to turn my collection into a book but, sadly, he died before it was finished.

I was fortunate enough to make a trip, as a passenger, on one of the Geest Banana ships to the Windward Islands during 1984. Her Chief Officer, being a local man, knew 'the coal boats' well and listened to my chatter about them with great patience. The Ship's Radio Officer was an enthusiast for the many ex-European small coasting ships which abound in the Caribbean and knew all of the many wrecks there. At that time, I had heard rumours that the **Salcombe** had gone to the Caribbean but had considerable doubts. However, I showed him some photographs to ask him to keep a look out and he recognised her straight away as a small, sad, ship moored in Bridgetown, Barbados. I was delighted to think that I might see her once again but fate took a hand and, very unusually, the ship's orders were changed, as a consequence of which she did not visit Barbados during that voyage. He promised that he would take some photographs of her at the next opportunity. He and the First Officer duly visited **Salcombe** (renamed **Friars Craig**) during the next trip, taking many photographs and buying her port emergency paraffin navigation light for me. Within just a few days of their visit to her, she was taken out to sea and sunk.

Following this, I invented an address by writing to the 'Main Daily Local Paper', Bridgetown, Barbados, enquiring if any photographs had been taken of her sinking; some of the resulting material is included here. Several months later, I was given a leisure magazine in which there was a feature on scuba diving in Barbados and a list of scuba training schools, which included one in Bridgetown. With **Salcombe** in shallow water just outside Bridgetown, I assumed that she would be on their agenda, so writing to them to explain my interest, I asked if some small item could be retrieved. In due course, the Chief Officer of **Geeststar** called on them, and paid for and brought home to me the deadlight featured on page 164. Still later, I contacted the daughter of **Salcombe**'s Chief Engineer with whom I had worked, when she and her husband were due to go on holiday to Barbados. They were friendly with the owner of a diving company there and, on my behalf, they asked if it might be possible to obtain some photographs of the wreck. This was done and I later exchanged them for a history of the ship, which the diving company had asked for in return.

Still with **Salcombe**, I decided to enquire whether any original drawings of the ship might still exist. I assumed that Rotterdam would surely have a Lloyds Maritime Insurance Office, so I again invented an address and asked if they would be kind enough to redirect my letter to an appropriate office. Having had to write in English and given that she was built before the Second World War, I felt it was probably a lost cause but one worth attempting. Some six weeks later and after my letter had passed through four official offices, I received a package from the Prinz Hendrik Maritime Museum, enclosing copies of the drawings and with an apology for not having replied earlier!

For about two years, I lost track of **Colston** and **Brandon**, and despite my best efforts, I could find no information about them or their whereabouts. However, the July 1984 issue of *Ships Monthly* included an item describing the recently completed restoration of the paddle steamer, ***Kingswear Castle*** and in one of the photographs, right in the background, were **Colston** and **Brandon**.

If the photograph had been taken just seconds earlier, they would not have been in the picture. I could not believe my luck. The caption advised only that the photograph had been taken '*on the Medway*', so a letter was immediately sent to Mr R. Shopland, editor of the magazine, who had already helped with previous enquiries, to ask if he would pass on another, enclosed, letter to the photographer. Thus contact was made and the photographer kindly made me an enlargement of just the top right hand corner of the picture, completely ignoring the main subject! In this connection, another 'invented address' came into play. I thought there would be a Pilotage Authority on the River Medway and I wrote to this assumed body enclosing a photocopy of the photograph for identification. Explaining my interest, I asked if they could inform me who were the owners of the two ships. The answer came in a telephone call, advising me to make enquiries of a gentleman at Corveda Marine. This was done and with some follow-up letters, I was able to fill in some very important stages in the lives of the two ships about which I had no previous knowledge.

During the late 1980s, I recalled that very shortly after I joined the ***Colston*** she had been visited by a professional photographer. The ship had been moored on the Albright & Wilson side of the dock and several photographs had been taken with the, as yet, very incomplete 'B' Power Station as a background. I also recalled that photographs had been taken in the Engine Room. Wondering if any prints or negatives still existed, it seemed to me that there must have been some special interest in her machinery and her Ruston & Hornsby engines. Knowing that the firm was based in Lincoln, I wrote to 'Ruston & Hornsby, (Marine Engine Builders), Lincoln, England.' Two weeks later, I received a letter from a Mr R. Hooley, who explained that when the company had been acquired some years ago, all the archive material was to be eliminated, so he obtained permission to save it. He had thus become an unofficial archivist for the company's long industrial heritage. He was able to provide me with copies of those photographs, taken thirty years before, and also details and serial numbers of all of the Ruston & Hornsby machinery fitted to the O&W ships.

During 1987, I learnt that *Colston* was completing her first voyage after her long lay up, by coming to Gloucester with a cargo of fertiliser. Booking a day's holiday from work, I went to Gloucester to find and hopefully visit the ship. I managed to talk my way on board and armed with my photographs of her, soon explained my interest. I spent five hours aboard and was pleased to find that she was in very tidy condition.

In most of the photographs that I had of her since leaving O&W, her bell was absent from the foremast and this was one of the first things I asked about. I was told by her temporary Skipper that it had been lost some time earlier. Having spent several interesting hours aboard (and after many photographs) I was taking my leave and, having thanked the crew for their hospitality, I was on the stern having a few last words with the Skipper, when he told me to wait there for a couple of minutes. Disappearing below, he came back with the scruffy and somewhat battered bell! I am almost certain that if I had pushed just a little, I could, for the price of a decent 'run ashore', have taken it home with me but I did not feel that it was right to take it from the ship whilst she still needed it. For some years after, I regretted having lost the opportunity because of sentiment. Two mementos that I had always coveted, were her bell and Builders Plate, which was also missing from the front of the Bridge.

Several years later, I learnt that she had also made her way out to the Caribbean. By this time, Geest had ceased shipowning but my friend who had been the Chief Officer during my trip with the company – and who later became a Captain – remained with them as their Superintendent, overseeing their interests in connection with the vessels they now chartered. This, of course, meant he had close contact with shipping movements in the region and armed with a photograph which I sent to him, he began to look out for the ***Colston*** for me. In a very short time, I had a telephone call advising that he had found her, had been aboard and taken many photographs for me – oh and did I wish to buy her bell (he was aware of the previous episode)? The ship was in a very shabby state as later photographs were to show, and feeling that she was probably at the end of her life and had also undergone a name change, I felt too many coincidences had come together to turn my back on this second chance. I duly confirmed that he should buy it for me. The bell eventually returned to Portishead as a small cargo package in one of the ships bringing Geest's produce to the UK.

Colston was, and remains, very special to me and whatever happens to her eventually as at fifty years of age (her fiftieth birthday coincides with the publication of this book in 2005) her eventual demise must come at some time. At least her bell is back here, it has visited its old home at Portishead Docks, now looking so very different, as well as Battery Point. All of her sisters have gone. She is the last O&W ship in existence and one of the very last – and probably the largest – Charles Hill ship still earning a living. Her fortunes have picked up. She has undergone close inspection and was found to be basically in excellent condition. A great deal has been spent on her and she is now being well cared for, with some considerable life expectancy ahead of her. As well as 'local work' in and around the Caribbean, she also travels often to South America.

The Caribbean region is noted for hurricane conditions and the likelihood is that, at some time, she will have to try to cope with one. She is only small and now very old. If she is in harbour somewhere she will be safe but if at sea…? I cannot bear the thought of her lost in the absolute darkness and eternal silence of deep water. My hope is that when her time comes, she will either be lost in shallow, sunlit water, or blown ashore on a Caribbean beach somewhere, as have so many old coasters. There she could sit quietly in the sunshine and remember her early life in the cold, damp, often foggy days of the Bristol Channel where she was born half a century ago and where she was once part of a small fleet of ships making their way back and forth with complete reliability across the Bristol Channel, bringing the coal which kept two power stations running.

To finish, I would also like to pass comment on the four paintings presented on pages 148-51 and, in particular, their commissioning. I met Robert Blackwell, the Bristol-based marine artist, during 1986, following an introduction by Jim Crissup. I had said rather wistfully that I greatly wished that someone would paint a picture of ***Colston*** for me and Jim suggested I contact Robert. He agreed to do the painting for me and, a few days later, having had time to think about it, I asked if it was possible to have ***Brandon*** in the background, proceeding down Channel, light ship, passing ***Colston*** in-bound, loaded. In this way, I felt that with them being identical, it would nicely portray them in both conditions. He agreed and the germ of an idea was planted.

I had to visit Robert several times while the painting was developing and at one of these meetings, I tentatively asked if he would be prepared to consider the following proposal. Would he be prepared to do for me a further three paintings, each portraying two of the company's ships, so that when finished, all the ships I had known during my time with Osborn & Wallis would be recorded? Recognising that the request was driven by enthusiasm for the subjects, Robert agreed to produce them at the rate of one per year and I now have a unique memento of the eight ships that comprised the fleet during my own time with the company. They are superb and the reduced scale reproduction necessary here does not do them justice.

Regarding the final compositions, after much consideration, I had decided that as O&W were operating what were three pairs of virtually identical ships, that a one light and one loaded format should apply where there was a pair and the two odd ones could be portrayed in one condition of loading or the other. I decided that ***Druid Stoke*** should be shown laden to illustrate her minimal freeboard when loaded, while ***Salcombe*** should be light ship so that her rather odd hull shape might be seen.

However, three canvasses depicting very similar pairs of ships was rather obvious, so in the event they were split between the paintings and the only pair shown together are ***Colston*** and ***Brandon***. I asked that no false glamour be introduced to the pictures and that they should portray the job as I remembered it. The upper reaches of the Bristol Channel are brown and muddy due to the constant tidal movements and that is how I wished it to be portrayed. Some variations on the weather conditions were asked for and, again, these were to be true, with no false heroics and no mountainous seas, which we never saw running across to South Wales (they came later, down on the Yelland run!).

The finished pictures are superb. Those who worked on the ships and who have seen the paintings, find that they capture the job so exactly. Robert Blackwell drew upon his own experience to get the water exactly right and his skill as a maritime artist is evident. They are, for me, a wonderful memento of all those years ago, more evocative than any photograph could ever be and I am very proud to own them. In compiling this record, I have had so much help, from so many people. My own contribution has really been little more than to collate the information and collect the photographs over the years. Thank you to everyone who contributed and helped me to record those halcyon days.

ACKNOWLEDGMENTS

I would like to thank the following people most sincerely, both private individuals and those with professional connections, for the generous help that they have given. Without their help and interest, this book could never have been compiled. My only contribution to it has been to collect and gather together all of their information and add it to my own memories and photographs. Their names are given below in alphabetical order.

For the idea for this book, my eternal thanks to the late Jim Crissup, Bristol's Oracle on shipping matters.

For information and the use of photographs:
Neil Burns, Dave Caple, C. Catt, John Clarkson, Chris Collard, Dave Corner, Micky Cooling, Rick Cox, Capt. Chris Flanagan, M.J. Gaston, Bill Griffiths, Hector Hamer, Mike Hawkins, Ray Hooley, John Hill, Frank House, David Hunt, Richard Jolliffe, J. Knott, Viv Llewellyn, Bernard McCall, Neil Parkhouse, Ian Pope, Capt. Chris Reynolds, L. Robinson, Denis Shone, Robert Shopland, Tony Sutcliffe, Capt. Peter Tambling, Alan Thorne and Chris Witts.

For memories and information:
Mrs K. Colenso, Mrs K. Farmer, Chris Rendle, Stanley Robinson, Harry Sellick, Mrs J. Taylor, Miss G. White, Wesley Windows.

My thanks to the following persons who have helped in their professional capacities and have dealt with my enquiries with the utmost courtesy and patience:
Ed Bartholomew at the National Railway Museum; Peter Bennett at the Welsh Industrial & Maritime Museum; Mrs. Kay Kays at the National Museums & Galleries of Wales; Andy King, at the Bristol Industrial Museum; Mr P. Neumann of Fotoflite; Mr R. Petre and staff at the Bristol Records Office; Mr D. Stribling of Metso Minerals; Mr A. Strong of Strachan & Henshaw; Graham Thompson, Curator of Historic Photographs and Ship Plans at the National Maritime Museum; Lucy Waite, Picture Librarian at the National Maritime Museum.

To anyone I may inadvertently have forgotten to mention, my sincere apologies and grateful thanks for your help.

My thanks are due as well to the men with whom I worked on the ships, most of them sadly no longer with us. They, the company and the ships themselves have had a profound influence on my life since those early days.

I need to say a special thank you to Robert Blackwell, whose superb paintings of the ships have given myself and other old O&W employees endless pleasure.

My warmest thanks to Neil Parkhouse, of Black Dwarf Lightmoor, my publishers, for his advice and guidance, which has made this little tribute to the company, the men and the ships so much more than I ever hoped it could be. He has put up with my clumsiness, lack of experience and the occasional tantrum with great patience.

Roy Fenton has made his own unique and very necessary contribution to the book by checking, and correcting where required, the histories of the O&W ships, in particular, the larger vessels and one or two of the more unusual craft from the company's early days. I owe him a special debt of gratitude for his interest and expertise.

My good friend Mike Shackleton has proof read the book for me and his contribution is greatly appreciated.

Finally, Capt. C. Flanagan has gone to extraordinary lengths to keep me in touch with ***Colston*** and her exploits in the Caribbean. Based in the Caribbean for his work and with a personal interest in maritime history, he has been kind enough to take the trouble, whenever possible, to visit the ship and 'report back' to me. I have been so fortunate that, through his interest and efforts, I have been able to follow ***Colston***, literally the last of the line.

Finally, I would be very interested in making contact with anyone who might be able to add to my collection of Osborn & Wallis memories in any way and can be contacted through the publishers.

Michael T. Winter
Portishead
April 2005

Part One
THE COMPANY

1. ORIGINS, GROWTH & DECLINE

During the latter part of the 19th century, Humphrey Wallis held considerable influence in the coal and shipping industries in South Wales. Based in Cardiff, he was a founder member of the Cardiff Coal & Shipping Exchange and was engaged in the shipment of coal to Spain and the importation from Huelva, in the same country, of copper pyrites, in deep-sea vessels which he had chartered for the purpose.

On arrival at Cardiff, this ore was off-loaded into small coastal trading vessels for delivery to destinations around the Bristol Channel, leaving the main ship to load her next outgoing cargo of coal. One of the destinations for the copper ore was the United Alkali Company, which had a chemical manufacturing plant at Netham, Bristol, where it was used in the manufacture of sulphuric acid. Netham was beyond the area covered by the City Docks and was reached via the Feeder Canal, necessitating the use of very small craft to complete the delivery of the ore.

At least one of the craft used for this onward shipment, the small steamer ***Enterprize***, belonged to William Osborn, whose business was in the sale of South Wales coal to domestic customers and factories in Bristol. He also owned and maintained a barge-mounted steam crane at the chemical works, which was used to off load the incoming cargoes of copper ore. It was then used to load spent ore into the ships for return to Cardiff for further processing. William Osborn was a cousin of Humphrey Wallis and he maintained a small yard at Temple Back, which was the hub of his business. The yard was stocked with coal brought in by various small and elderly sailing vessels, which Osborn may have either part-owned or been chartering. In addition to the coal cargoes, these ships were engaged in such other work as they could find, an important part of which was the transportation of copper ore.

The fact that Humphrey Wallis and William Osborn were cousins must have meant that the small Osborn-owned or chartered ships were given preference in this regular and reliable work. There was no doubt that the two enterprises, though vastly different, could slot together well. Thus, in 1880, they decided that it would be beneficial to amalgamate their interests, so that the shipment of copper ore might be properly co-ordinated. Accordingly, they set up a partnership, the intention being that Osborn & Wallis would manage the purchase and use of their own vessels.

A programme of acquisition of new large ships was initiated and, during the early 1880s, the large ship operation flourished whilst the small ship part of the firm remained static. The Cardiff office of Humphrey Wallis had become the partnership's headquarters, whilst William Osborn also established a small branch office at 37 Queen Square in Bristol and he continued to maintain his yard.

Around this time, the City of Bristol was experimenting with electricity generation and distribution. Despite a hesitant start, in 1891 Bristol set about the construction of

Bristol Corporation Electricity Department's first power station at Temple Back, circa 1900, showing the street frontage, *left*, and the Engine Room, *above*. It was initially equipped with six generating machines but these had multiplied to eighteen by the turn of the century. The pictures are from a BCED booklet issued in 1902.

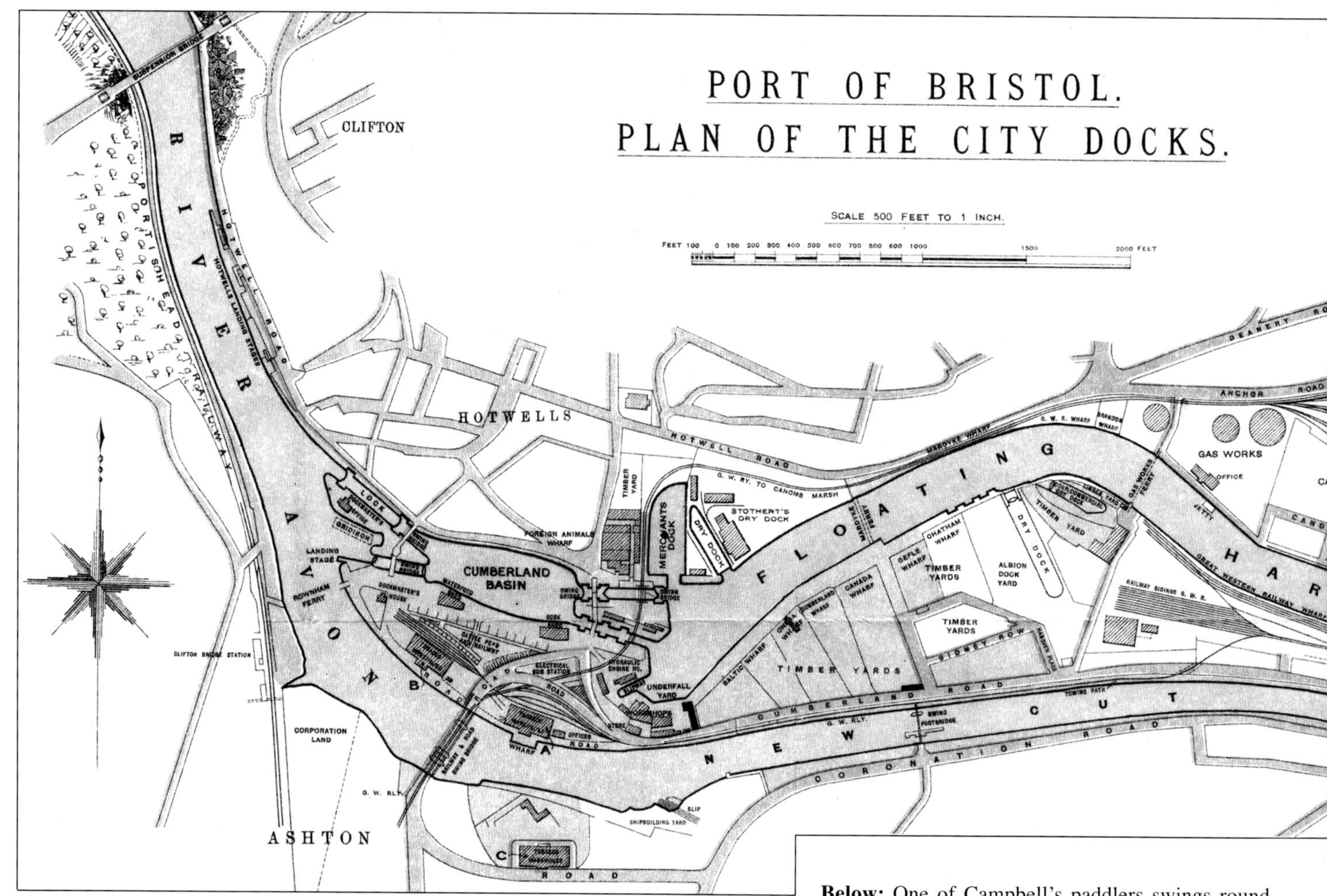

Above: Bristol City Docks circa 1920. The 2½ mile Floating Harbour was formed from the courses of the rivers Avon and Frome in the early part of the 19th century, whilst the Avon was diverted along the New Cut, dug at the same time. Both routes met on the eastern side of the city centre (adjacent to Temple Meads station), forming a junction also with the Feeder Canal. Stothert's dry dock, which Osborn & Wallis bought for their new base in 1933, was handily situated right next to the entrance to the Floating Harbour from Cumberland Basin. Charles Hill's premises and dry dock (and the old SS *Great Britain* dry dock) were on the opposite side just a little further up the harbour. *Neil Parkhouse collection*

Below: One of Campbell's paddlers swings round outside the entrance lock to the Cumberland Basin in this circa 1910 view, prior to pulling alongside Hotwells landing stage, just out of view to the left. Once through the basin and past the second lot of swing bridges, there was a sharp turn to port for ships heading up the Floating Harbour. On the right are the bonded tobacco warehouses and the New Cut heads off to the right of them. *Neil Parkhouse collection*

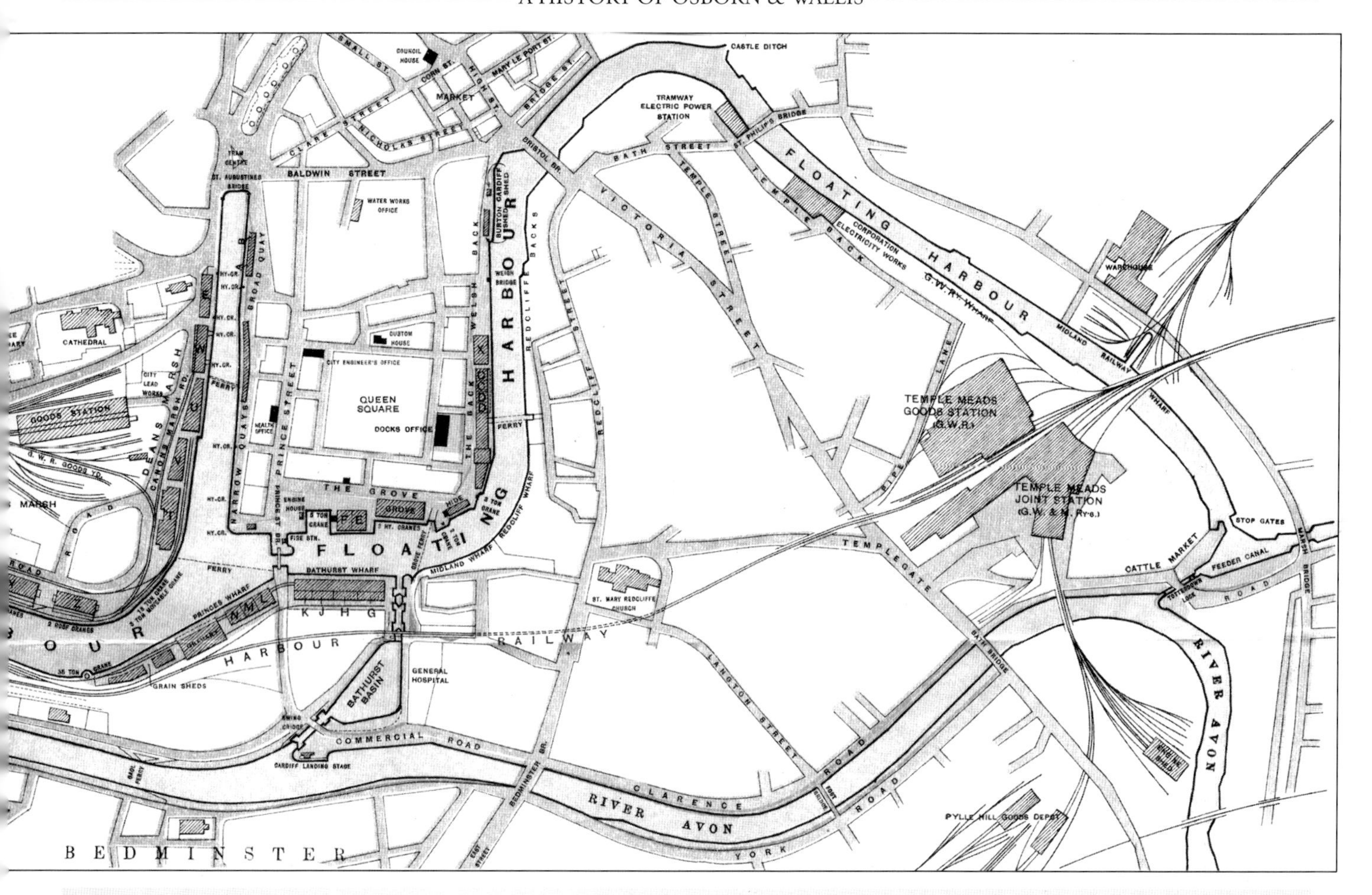

This busy scene looking up the Floating Harbour also dates from around 1910 and was taken from the roof of one of the tobacco warehouses. The group of ships just to the left of the chimney are alongside the entrance to Stothert's dry dock, whilst the White Funnel paddler visible in the centre right distance is moored just outside Charles Hill's yard. *Neil Parkhouse collection*

Left: A turn of the century view of Avonbank Electricity Works, with the Feeder Canal in the foreground. From a BCED booklet, 1902.

Below: John Lysaght's St. Vincent Ironworks, as seen from the Feeder Canal circa 1905, with construction of an extension to the works in progress.
Neil Parkhouse collection

its own power station at Temple Back at a cost of £66,000, to be managed and run by Bristol Corporation Electricity Department. The early ventures into the exploitation of this new power source were largely confined to domestic customers, with very little use made of the facility by business and manufacturing.

However, in 1895, a private company, the Bristol Tramways & Carriage Company Ltd, introduced electric tramcars to a small part of the city. Unable to agree with the City Council about the supply of electricity for the trams, the company built its own power station outside the city boundary. As the trams gained in popularity, and their number and the system expanded, further generation capacity was required. Again the company sought permission to build a power station within the city but, as before, the Council's agreement was not forthcoming, the view being taken that electricity generation on this scale should be a municipal undertaking.

After intense negotiations permission was finally granted in 1898 for the BT&CC to build its additional plant within the city with the proviso that, at some future date, the Corporation had the option to purchase the company. In the meantime, the demand for electricity within Bristol had increased to the point where the Temple Back generating station was no longer adequate and the building of a further power station, known initially as Avonbank Electricity Works, began on the Feeder Canal.

Clearly, this was a growing industry and from his office in Queen Square, as well as from his yard sited so close to all of this activity, William Osborn could not fail to have noticed the opportunity which it presented. Coal, in quantities never before envisaged, was going to have to be brought right into the heart of the city and along the Feeder Canal for the power stations. It was work for which his business was ideally suited. He had the ships and he had the contacts in

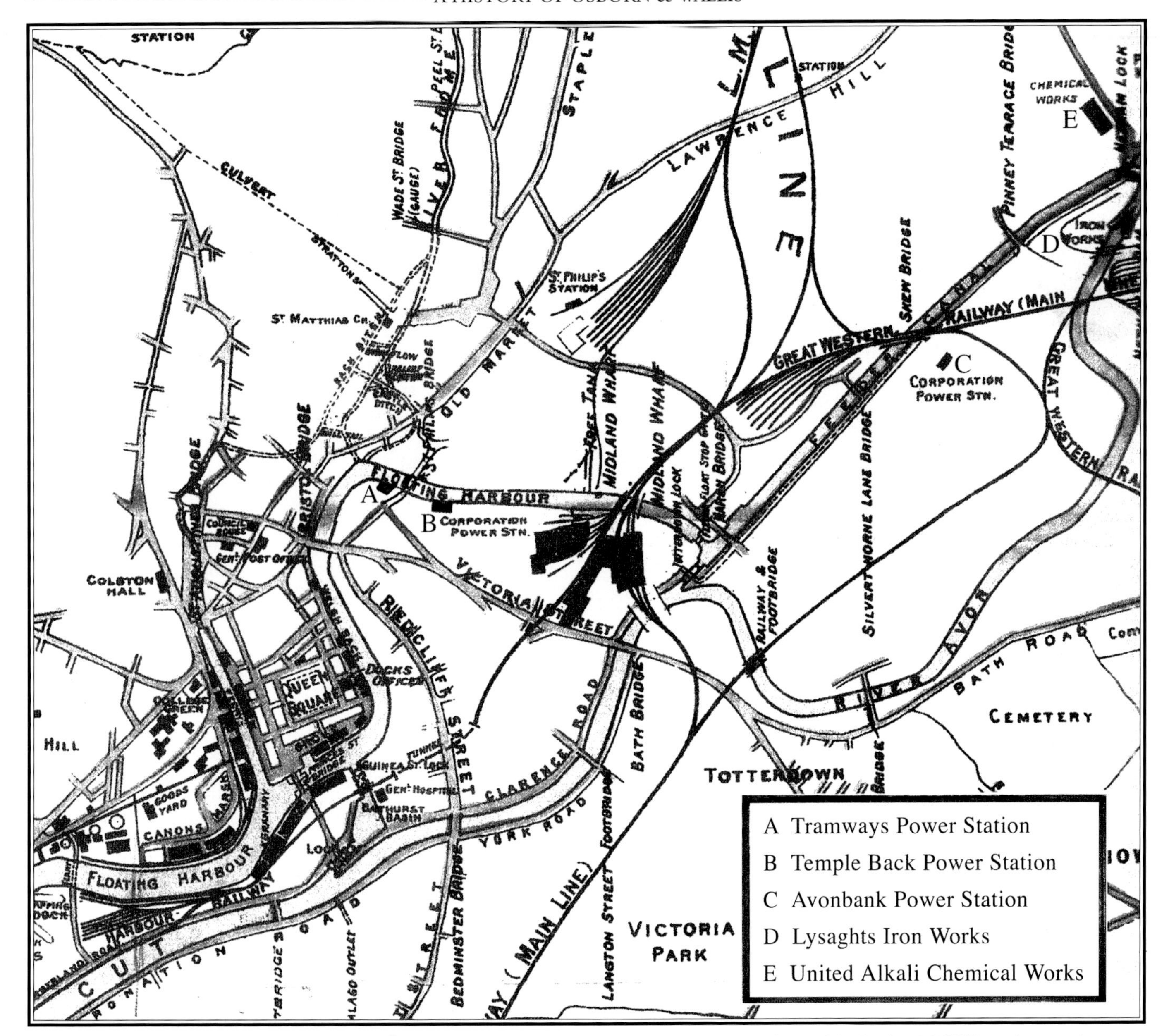

The locations of the various industrial installations on or near Bristol's Feeder Canal, which formed the basis of O&W's early growth.

South Wales, the source of the precious coal. However, it was soon realised that the small fleet of tiny sailing ships and steam barges would not be adequate to keep pace with the demand if this new and reliable work was to be tendered for. Thus, around the turn of the century, a programme of acquisition began of further steam-powered ships, small enough to negotiate the Feeder Canal.

These small vessels, all acquired second-hand, were the seed from which Osborn & Wallis and its link to the electricity industry was to grow. With the now regular and predictable runs transporting coal from South Wales to Bristol, further work was sought to make the empty outward voyages useful. Thus, the company came to be engaged by John Lysaght Ltd of Bristol, ironfounders and constructional engineers. Lysaghts employed Osborn & Wallis to carry sheet steel which had been galvanised at their St Vincent's Ironworks in Bristol, to their Orb Ironworks at Newport, for further manufacture and distribution. This connection with Lysaght's and the work it provided was obviously extremely important for the company, a fact which was to be acknowledged in the naming of one of the ships in their fleet – *Orb*, built in 1911. However, whilst two other O&W vessels carried names which appear to link them with Lysaght's works in Bristol, *St. Vincent* and *Netham*, these names seem to pre-date the working arrangement between the two concerns.

Such was the stability offered by this work, which fully occupied the smaller ships in the Osborn & Wallis fleet that, by 1914, all but one of the large ships had been disposed of and the company's efforts were now concentrated completely upon the task of fuelling the power stations. In order to accomplish this with the level of reliability demanded, the company bought further vessels and, crucially, began placing orders for new ships specifically matched to the requirements of the task.

In 1916, with the loss of *Euterpe*, which sank after striking

Inset right: Portishead Pier in the early 1920s. The pier was for many years Great Western Railway property and, at one stage, according to the dock plan, a railway line ran out onto it but there is no sign of it here. A number of tugs are clustered here awaiting work. *Neil Parkhouse collection*

This circa 1930 view, looking towards the sea lock, shows almost the whole extent of the dock. On the left, alongside the two electrically driven cranes, is Osborn & Wallis's *Druid Stoke*, which was quite new when this picture was taken, having been delivered to the company from Charles Hill's Yard in 1929. Astern of her is the O&W steam barge *Ferric*, built by Hill's in 1912 and the ship which began the long association between the two companies. Neither of the two ships on the right are identifiable, although it can be seen that the nearer one has brought in a cargo of timber. The vessel in the foreground is the Portishead Dock fire float *Denny*, which was permanently moored in this position, as indicated on the map opposite. *Neil Parkhouse collection*

This acrial view showing the landward end of the dock dates from the late 1920s. Timber and grain were the two main cargoes coming in at this time, with the area in the foreground occupied by more timber sheds. The three-masted barque has probably brought in a cargo of timber from the Baltic. Note there was also a thriving business in scrapping old warships at this end of the dock, with three vessels in various stages of dismantling.
Neil Parkhouse collection

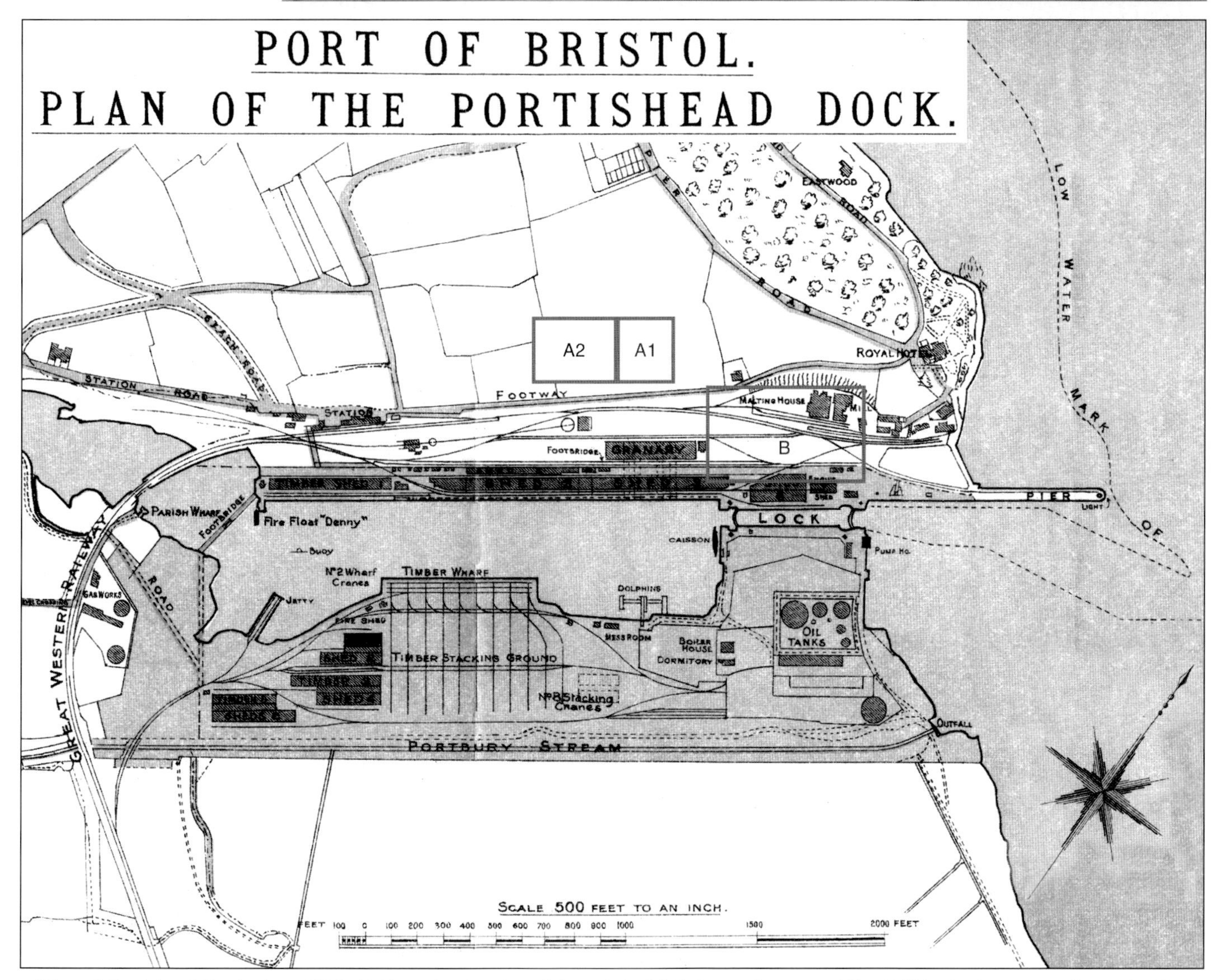

Plan of Portishead Dock circa 1920. 'A1' marks the site of the original 'A' Power Station, whilst 'A2' is the later extension to it. The rectangle 'B' shows the site of 'B' Power Station. The area occupied by the unloading plant and coal stores for both stations is not shown but it eventually took over the whole of that side of the dock, the granary and timber sheds being demolished. *Neil Parkhouse collection*

A circa 1930 aerial view of Portishead Docks which shows, top left, an extension to the original power station underway. The later 'B' Station was built to the left of the entrance lock, on the site of Baily's Mill, which is the building with tall chimney top left of the picture. The associated grain berth, unloading conveyors and warehousing were also demolished. *Neil Parkhouse collection*

a mine, the company's involvement with big ships came to an end. Despite this, the head office remained in Cardiff and Bristol continued as a branch office. William Osborn and Humphrey Wallis were the sole partners in the company and the Superintendent Engineer's Office was also located at Cardiff.

Sometime around the end of the First World War, Humphrey Wallis seems to have departed the partnership, either having retired or died. With his going, the Wallis connection remained hereafter in name only. In 1921, Osborn & Wallis became a registered limited company, financed almost entirely by W. A. Osborn and his son, I.D. Osborn. There was, at the time of registration, a further minority shareholder, a G.A. Dearlove, and he ran the company's Cardiff office.

The next major development to affect the newly incorporated company occurred in the early 1920s, when the Bristol Corporation Electricity Department again found itself stretched for capacity. Accordingly, a decision was taken to build a significant new generating station at Portishead, two miles downstream from the mouth of the River Avon. Thus was to begin Osborn & Wallis Ltd's long association with the town of Portishead and its dock.

The company, now almost completely locked into the supply of coal for Bristol's power stations, realised that it too was going to have to upgrade its capacity significantly to cope and a further programme of new build and second-hand ship acquisitions began in 1926. The commissioning of the new Portishead Power Station in 1929 resulted in further expansion of the fleet.

By this time also, the Queen Square establishment in Bristol had become the head office, which was a far more practical arrangement, whilst the Cardiff premises had become a branch office. There was also another branch office at Immingham, on Humberside. The directors of the company were now listed as W.A. Osborn, I.D. Osborn, H.K. Mower and W.T. Hutchings. The Superintendent Engineer at this time was R.G. Paynter.

In 1933, a further significant change occurred when the company bought and occupied the offices and dock in Hotwells which had once been the shipbuilding and repair yard of G.K. Stothert & Co Ltd. This had been a dry dock and the characteristic stepped sides remained to the end but as vessels were unloaded with the aid of a Telfer crane, this made little difference to its operation.

As the Second World War loomed, plans to further extend

Portishead Power Station around 1930, shortly after completion of the extension seen underway in the previous view. It later became designated Portishead 'A', following the construction of a second power station, Portishead 'B', in the 1950s. *Author's collection*

Two advertisements taken from the *Port of Bristol Authority Handbook* for 1931. Osborn & Wallis are shown at Queen Square, Bristol, with Branch Offices at Cardiff and Immingham. The second advert is interesting in that it indicates the scale and importance of the new Portishead Power Station – '*the Base Load Station for the South West*' – and thus emphasizes the vital nature of reliable coal deliveries. *Neil Parkhouse collection*

OSBORN & WALLIS
LIMITED.

37, Queen Square,
BRISTOL.

COAL, BUNKERING and
FREIGHT CONTRACTORS

Also at CARDIFF, NEWPORT
& IMMINGHAM DOCKS.

Telegraphic Addresses—
"Osborn, Bristol."
"Wallis, Cardiff."
"Osborn, Immingham-Dock Station."

Telephone Numbers—
4090-4091 Bristol.
5 Cardiff.
44 Immingham.

CHEAP ELECTRICITY
FOR
POWER

POWER INSTALLATIONS ALREADY
SUPPLIED EXCEED

100,000 H.P.

THE CORPORATION'S
PORTISHEAD GENERATING STATION
IS THE BASE LOAD STATION FOR
THE SOUTH WEST OF ENGLAND

For Information apply—
Bristol Corporation Electricity Dept.,
Colston Avenue,
BRISTOL.

This aerial view shows Osborn & Wallis's yard at Hotwells in the late 1930s; the white line marks the boundary of their premises and two of the company's ships can be seen moored in the dock. To the left of the wharf are two White Funnel paddle steamers in their winter berths.

This advert for Osborn & Wallis is from the *Port of Bristol Authority Handbook* for 1936 and shows the company at their new Hotwells location. *Neil Parkhouse collection*

The entrance to O&W's Dock at Hotwells, circa 1960. *Author's collection*

the power station at Portishead were put on hold. However, recent ship acquisitions, including the company's first ever motorship, delivered in 1940 and the second vessel in the fleet to carry the name ***St. Vincent***, had been made in anticipation of this expansion. Despite this, the company and its ships were stretched to the limit as Portishead Power Station, at that time one of the largest in the country, was in production at maximum load day and night to compensate for generating capacity lost by enemy action and to cover the demands of industry involved in war production. The company suffered a heavy loss in 1941 with the destruction of one of its ships, ***Lunan***, when she struck a mine at Penarth. Tragically, she was lost with all but one of her crew.

Replacement capacity was obtained and, additionally, the company was tasked with the management of two new Government-owned ships by the Ministry of War Transport in 1943. These were to be used for fuelling Gloucester Power Station, as well as assisting the rest of the fleet with the supply of coal to Portishead Power Station. However, two of the company's steamships found themselves seconded to help in the Normandy landings a year later, an adventure from which both returned relatively unscathed.

Following the cessation of hostilities in 1945, the planned expansion of Portishead Power Station was commenced almost immediately and a further increase in tonnage was ordered in the form of a near sister to the 1940 motorship. This was to be ***Hotwells***, delivered by Charles Hill's in 1950.

However, no sooner was the extension to the power station completed, when the construction of a completely new and even larger generating facility at Portishead was begun. This was to be the giant Portishead 'B' Power Station, with the original plant then becoming Portishead 'A'. To service their coal requirements, a further two ships, larger than the one just completed, were ordered. These identical sisters, ***Colston***, delivered during 1955, and ***Brandon***, in 1957, were to be the Company's final acquisitions.

By 1963, all but one of the steamships had gone. The company now owned just five motorships, whilst the final remaining steamer, ***Druid Stoke***, was laid up in the yard at Hotwells awaiting scrapping. At this period, the O&W directors were D.C. Osborn (I.D. Osborn's son), G. Incledon-Webber, F. Skuse and R.G. Paynter; the Superintendent Engineer was M. Goodacre.

With the changes taking place in the generating industry, the company found that its long relationship with Bristol's electricity providers counted for naught and, just four years after the second new ship was delivered, the local power stations began to take deliveries of coal from larger ships run by other companies. Osborn & Wallis remained engaged on coal shipments but on a greatly reduced scale and, inevitably, the company had to seek other work for the ships. The two newest vessels began to trade further down Channel to East Yelland Power Station, on the River Taw estuary near Barnstaple, and to Hayle Power Station on the north Cornish coast. They were still delivering coal from the South Wales ports but even this work was shared with ships of other owners.

Osborn & Wallis's fate was finally sealed with the closure of the old Portishead 'A' Station and the planned conversion of 'B' Power Station to oil firing. During 1969, the decision was made to close the company and, accordingly, the ships were sold off to various owners and the yard at Hotwells was disposed of the following year.

The company, its ships and their crews had given long and reliable service to the electricity supply industry of the Bristol area in its various guises but had been overtaken by change and events over which they had no control. In the increasingly competitive industry in which they were engaged, they became just another minor and un-noticed casualty in the list of Britain's expiring merchant marine.

The departure of ***Colston*** from the City Docks during August 1970 marked the end of the link between the City of Bristol and Osborn & Wallis Ltd.

Finally, it is worth noting that throughout the company's 90-year existence, the Osborn family had remained at the helm. Mr Denis Osborn, the Managing Director at the time of the company's closure, was the grandson of one of the founding partners.

An original surviving Osborn & Wallis company houseflag. *Courtesy Bristol Museums & Art Gallery*

With her paintwork looking spruce, probably following a recent dry-docking, *Stakesby* is seen approaching the entrance lock to the City Docks around 1900. Note the crossed 'O' and 'W' emblem just visible on the funnel and the davits for handling the anchors. Her saloon windows, just underneath her bridge are quite curious, there are manholes in the semicircular plate at the point the ratlines are attached to the foremast and the construction of the topmasts is also unusual.
Courtesy Bristol Museums & Art Gallery

2. FLEET HISTORY

The decision by Humphrey Wallis and William Osborn to merge their separate shipping interests in 1880 seems at first sight to have been an odd one, such was the apparent disparity between their two operations. As previously mentioned, Humphrey Wallis was a founder member of the Cardiff Coal & Shipping Exchange which, as its name suggests, was set up in order to bring together colliery proprietors, ship owners and coal and shipping agents in South Wales, to improve and facilitate the whole process of shipping coal for export. Wallis's business lay in the shipping of Welsh coal to Spain in large, deep-sea ships, which usually then backloaded cargoes of copper pyrites. No evidence has so far been found of Wallis owning any vessels prior to 1880, so the likelihood is that he was chartering vessels belonging to other owners through the auspices of the Exchange.

The deep-sea ships brought their cargoes of Spanish pyrites into Cardiff, where it was then transshipped into smaller craft for transportation across the Bristol Channel and up the twisting, tidal, mud-riven River Avon to Bristol Docks. The final destination for the copper pyrites, the United Alkali Works at Netham, lay on the Feeder Canal, beyond the upper limits of the docks, so that although the large ships themselves could and indeed did, on occasion, make the passage into the City Docks, this was not the regular procedure. Transshipment into smaller craft was still required for delivery along the Feeder Canal and the larger vessel then had to return to Cardiff to reload with coal for Spain.

It was obviously more efficient if the copper pyrites were unloaded at Cardiff, where the vessel could immediately reload with coal. The saving in both dock dues and time made it more viable to transship the copper pyrites into much smaller craft there and so reduce the time that the big ships spent in harbour. At this time, Humphrey Wallis's Bristol-based cousin, William Osborn, owned a small steamer named ***Enterprize***, trading across the Channel and probably up the River Avon as far as Bath. He may also have owned one or two wooden sailing ships at this time. It is quite likely that amongst the cargoes carried were regular shipments of copper pyrites, transshipped from Wallis-chartered vessels at Cardiff and this almost certainly was the catalyst for the partnership between the two cousins. The smaller vessel handled the short voyage to Bristol and beyond, while the bigger ships were free to carry on with the deep sea work.

As the partnership's business developed, the smaller craft were often able to make two-way trade voyages, backloading sheet steel from John Lysaght's Works in Bristol for their Orb Works at Newport. However, it was not until 1921 that Osborn & Wallis was registered as a limited company, after the two partners had deceased. A certain amount of supposition is involved regarding the original partnership. What seems to be the case is that the two men set up a ship management business, with the intention also of using their combined assets to purchase new ships.

It was quite normal for the ownership and management of vessels to be kept completely separate, even if the personnel involved were the same. A limited company would be set up to purchase the vessel, whether new or second-hand, and the management was then handed over to another concern, which would generally look after the vessel and find work for it. There were two main reasons for this. Firstly, if the owning company got into financial difficulties or the vessel was lost, it would be unlikely to bring about the ruin of the whole company. Secondly, in the days of sail, the ownership of vessels was split into sixty-four shares. This conveniently divisible number allowed ownership to be split in many different ways, whether equally or not. However, with the advent of larger, steam powered, iron-built vessels, even one sixty-fourth could involve quite a large sum of money, so the setting up of a limited company permitted the issue of a greater quantity of shares at a much more affordable individual price. Thus, throughout the history of the shipping industry, there is a proliferation of single ship-owning limited companies.

In 1880, shortly after founding their partnership, Osborn & Wallis took control of their first large vessel, the newly built ***Alverton***, owned by a separate limited company they set up themselves. The wisdom of having a separate limited company owning the ship was to quickly become apparent to the partners when ***Alverton*** was lost in 1881. Rather than bring down the fledgling concern, in 1882 Osborn & Wallis bought two new ships through two new companies, no doubt following settlement of their insurance claim on the first vessel. This was to establish a pattern for their operations during the rest of the 19th century, although they also continued to maintain an interest in smaller craft as well.

During the life of the partnership, William Osborn either owned or part-owned a number of wooden sailing craft. Most – if not all – have been identified but it is quite likely, given the paucity of records for many of these small vessels, that one or two more still wait to be found. The proliferation of similar names can also confuse matters further. It is known, for instance, that there were at least four sailing craft named ***Charlotte*** trading in the Bristol Channel in the 19th century. It is quite possible that Osborn had an interest, at least, in one or two other sailing ships before the partnership was formed but, to date, none have been positively identified and the only vessel he definitely owned in 1880 was the steamer *Enterprize*. Osborn was taking ownership of these small ships after the partnership had been set up, so they must have agreed there was little point in their both having a financial interest in them. Their management, however, was a part of the Osborn & Wallis business.

The predominance of the large ships and their trade was such that, at this period, the company's heart lay in Cardiff and, as a result, the head office was based there too. Cardiff was also where Humphrey Wallis had considerable influence. The Bristol office at this time was merely a branch, at Queen Square, operated by William Osborn. There was also a yard, located at Temple Back, where a number of other coal shippers were based and from which coal was sold.

This also leads on to another facet of the partnership's business at this time. It is known that in the period from January 1888 to December 1896, Osborn & Wallis were hiring coal wagons from the Gloucester Railway Carriage & Wagon Company Ltd. For much of this period, they had a total of 51 wagons on hire, which suggests a considerable trade being done in the supply of coal around the Bristol area, probably both for domestic and industrial use. Following cessation of the hire contracts, it may be that O&W sold this part of the business to another local coal merchant, in order to concentrate on their developing coal shipping business for Bristol's embryonic electricity industry. Alternatively, they may have bought their own wagons in order to carry on the trade, although no record of any such purchases has yet been discovered.

Finally, it is perhaps worth noting that, seemingly, Osborn & Wallis were not a 'lucky' company for ships. All seven of the large deep-sea tramps they owned were eventually lost at sea, in varying circumstances, although four of them were no longer in O&W ownership when they met their demise. Of the thirty-nine vessels the company owned during their existence, ten were lost, with 1901 being a particularly bad year – *Blanche*, *Wye* and *Herschel* (one of the deep-sea ships). It certainly makes for sobering reading of the fleet list.

ENTERPRIZE Official No. 29213

The first vessel known to have been acquired by William Osborn was the iron screw steamer *Enterprize* (sometimes miss-spelt *Enterprise*), built in Bristol by Stothert & Marten in 1860. She was of 97 tons gross (71 tons net), with a length of 84 feet 1 inch, a beam of 16 feet 9 inches and a depth of 8 feet 4 inches. She was registered in Bristol on 19th November 1860, jointly by her builders George K. Stothert and George P. Marten. Three days later, she was sold to George Greenvell, Stephen Steeds, Thomas Pilditch and Alfred Palmer, who took equal (16/64ths) shares in her. On 12th April 1878, she was bought by Osborn. This small ship was able to negotiate the Avon as far inland as Bath (except during exceptionally low water conditions), whilst during 1866, she is recorded as having made no less than 57 voyages between Cardiff and Bristol with cargoes of coal.

On 12th December 1895, whilst on a voyage from Cardiff to Bristol with a cargo of 141 tons of coal and making only 3.5 knots across Cardiff Grounds in heavy seas, *Enterprize*'s engine broke down when the shoe in the bottom slide valve spindle broke. She hove to under her mainsail and the paddle steamer *Devonia* took her in tow. At 17.30 the tow broke, the hatches were washed off and the forecastle and engine room was flooded. The crew of four managed to get off in the boat before she sank.

FLOATING CRANE

This was used to discharge and load small ships at the United Alkali Works. It is likely that it belonged to William Osborn before the foundation of the partnership. No other details are known, although the photograph below indicates that it was in the ownership of Osborn & Wallis until around the turn of the century at least.

O & W's floating crane is seen here in a photograph taken circa 1900, at Gas House Yard, Bristol. Also in view is the trow *Dolphin*, of 41 tons and built at Bristol in 1835. At this date, she was in the ownership of Alfred Smith & Co, coal merchants of Bristol. Behind her is the wooden screw steamer *Jessie & Emily*, built at North Shields in 1870 and of 86 tons gross.
Courtesy Bristol Museums & Art Gallery

The pier alongside the entrance lock, with the Clifton suspension bridge forming a dramatic backdrop, was a favoured vantage point for photographing vessels trading to the City Docks. *Dolcoath* is seen here about to lock in circa 1900. *Courtesy Bristol Museums & Art Gallery*

THOMAS & MARIA Official No. 26709

Thomas & Maria was a trow of 65 tons net, built at Gloucester in 1841 and owned by James Longney of Hotwells, Bristol, for most of the 1870s. William Osborn acquired her in 1889 from George Nurse of Bristol and had her until 1904, when she was deleted from the MNL. She may have survived for a few more years as a hulk.

ALVERTON Official No. 83810

Alverton was built in 1880 by A. Stephen & Sons, Linthouse, for the Alverton Steam Ship Company Ltd, a single-ship company which was floated and managed by Osborn & Wallis. She cost £19,000. Registered at Cardiff, she carried the newly adopted black funnel with the white interlocked 'O' and 'W' monogram. Her dimensions were 240 feet long by 34 feet beam by 17 feet depth and her gross tonnage 1,321. Like the company's other ocean-going tramps, she was propelled by a two-cylinder compound steam engine.

Alverton's career was very short. On 13th November 1881, she was wrecked near Cape Finisterre whilst carrying a cargo of pig iron from Bilbao to Sete, France.

EUREKA Official No. 86485

Eureka was built in 1882 at the Sunderland yard of the Strand Slipway Company. Osborn & Wallis registered the new ship at Cardiff in the name of the Eureka Steam Ship Company Ltd. The vessel's dimensions were 244 feet by 34 feet and her original gross tonnage was 1,344.

Eureka was sold to Sunderland owners without change of name in 1908 and in 1911 went under the Norwegian flag as *Vaarli*. She was mined and sunk in the North Sea on 9th February 1916.

DOLCOATH Official No. 86498

Dolcoath was also built in 1882 at Sunderland but by James Laing. Owner from new was another single ship company managed by Osborn & Wallis, the Dolcoath Steam Ship Company Ltd. Her dimensions were 266 feet by 37 feet by 19 feet and her gross tonnage was 1,706.

After 23 years with Osborn & Wallis, *Dolcoath* was sold to Dundee owners in 1913 without being renamed. She was mined off the North Foreland on 19th May 1916.

EUTERPE Official No. 87498

Built of iron like all the company's ocean tramps, *Euterpe* was completed on the Clyde by A. Stephen & Sons in 1883. Her owners were the Euterpe Steam Ship Company Ltd and it appears she may have been originally managed by Humphrey Wallis alone. However, by 1886, Osborn & Wallis are recorded as managers and it is possible the earlier listing may not have been correct. Her dimensions were 260 feet by 36 feet by 17 feet and her gross tonnage was 1,522.

Euterpe in the River Avon on the approach to Bristol around 1900, with the road up to Clifton just visible behind. The O&W logo can be clearly seen on her funnel. *Courtesy Bristol Museums & Art Gallery*

Euterpe was the last of the ocean-going ships to survive with the company. On 7th January 1916, she passed Great Yarmouth on a voyage to Middlesbrough with Spanish iron ore and disappeared, presumably sunk by a mine.

WYE Official No. 19071

Wye was a tiny trow built at Bristol in 1860 and registered at the Port of Chepstow. Much is known of *Wye*, for her history is documented in some detail in Grahame Farr's *Chepstow Ships* (Chepstow 1954). Originally of 23 tons, she was 58 feet 5 inches in length, 13 feet 4 inches breadth and 4 feet 2 inches depth. She was built for a Llandogo timber merchant, John Morgan. Sold in 1874 to John Knight of Trelleck, near Monmouth, she was re-registered in February 1877 as being of 36 tons, having been lengthened to 66 feet 3 inches, her other dimensions being increased to 14 feet 2 inches and 5 feet 4 inches respectively.

In 1882, she was bought by John Wyld, general dealer of Bristol and in 1887 he sold her to George Nurse, a coal merchant also of Bristol. Nurse sold half her ownership (32 shares) to another local coal merchant, William Galbraith. Finally, on 20th January 1890, Nurse sold his 32 shares in the vessel to William Osborn, whilst Galbraith sold his 32 shares to Humphrey Wallis. *Wye* was one of the last ten vessels to be still registered at Chepstow. However, she was altered once more and re-registered at Gloucester on 16th May 1895. She was lost on 22nd December 1901 when she was wrecked near Lavernock Point, near Penarth. *Wye* appears in the photograph of *Netham* on page 29.

STAKESBY Official No. 81215

After having four steamers built in the 1880s, Osborn & Wallis relied on second-hand purchases to expand their fleet in the 1890s. ***Stakesby*** had been built by J.L. Thompson & Sons at Sunderland for Whitby owners in 1880. She was purchased by O&W in 1891 and it was not until 1900 that she was registered under a single-ship company, the Stakesby Steam Ship Company Ltd. Her dimensions were 243 feet by 34 feet by 18 feet and her gross tonnage was 1,370. ***Stakesby*** was sold in 1910 and worked for a number of Italian owners as ***Perseveranza*** and later ***Eugenia***, until 19th October 1921 when she foundered in the Mediterranean.

ECLIPSE Official No. 27229

Eclipse was a sloop of 64 tons. Her origins are obscure but she may have been Dutch as her previous name is given in MNL as *Vrouw Mary*. An earlier owner was William Vincent of Wapping Coal Wharf, Bristol, then John Hurley of Bristol from 1889. William Osborn bought her in 1891 and she is recorded as having struck a quay wall at Bristol on 18th October 1892. She does not appear in the MNL for 1893, so possibly her collision with the quay proved terminal.

SALTWICK Official No. 86636

Saltwick had a very similar pedigree to the slightly smaller ***Stakesby***, having been built in 1882 also by J.L. Thompson and again for Whitby owners. She joined the Osborn & Wallis fleet in 1893. Her dimensions were 261 feet by 36 feet by 18 feet and her gross tonnage was 1,618. In 1897, O&W registered her under the Saltwick Steam Ship Company Ltd.

When sold to Norwegian owners in 1911, ***Saltwick*** was first renamed ***Tornyvore*** and later ***Fredavore***. Ownership in neutral Norway did not preserve her from the attentions of

German submarines, however, and she was captured and sunk by UB 39 off Ouessant on 11th September 1916.

CHARLOTTE Official No. 26742

Charlotte was a sloop of 69 tons net, built at Neath Abbey in 1848. She was bought by William Osborn on 14th May 1895 and was used chiefly in the Penarth to Bristol coal trade. The vessel was lost on 2nd November 1898, when she foundered approximately one mile from the Upper Hook Buoy in the Bristol Channel.

SUNSHINE Official No. 45373

Sunshine was a very different vessel, built at Hull in 1862 by M. Samuelson as a paddle tug and originally named *Phoenix*. Samuelson also built her two-cylinder, 80 HNP, diagonal engine. Of 178 grt, she was registered in the ownership of the New Steam Tug Co Ltd, Liverpool, on 15th October 1862. *Phoenix* had a length of 126 feet and a beam of 20 feet. She was renamed *Sunshine* in 1870.

She changed hands several times during the 1880s, on each occasion to other Liverpool owners, before she was sold to John Hurley of Bristol on 31st March 1890. Seven months later, her register was closed when she was dismantled to become a hulk. This was not to be the end of her story, however. On 12th October 1898, she was re-registered as a ketch in the ownership of William A. Osborn.

Osborn ran her until 1907, when he sold her back to Liverpool, to William Hill. Her final owner, from 1909, was George Nicholson. She was probably used as a lighter in Liverpool Docks and her multi-faceted career continued until 1930, when she was finally deleted from the MNL.

YAN YEAN Official No. 83820

Yan Yean was built by Edward Finch & Co Ltd, of Bridge Works, Chepstow in 1880. She was an iron screw steamer, 98 feet long by 19 feet beam and of 134 grt, 91 tons net.

She was registered in 1881 and was certainly in the ownership of Humphrey Wallis that year but her oriental name suggests she was built for service in the Far East. This may have been for an owner who would not or could not take delivery of her, so that a despairing builder sold her to Wallis, who kept her name. He did not, however, keep the vessel for long. In 1882, she was sold to an owner in Montrose and she left the MNL in 1887.

Her builders were also an interesting concern. In 1851-2, Edward Finch had built the tubular bridge, designed by Brunel, which carried the South Wales Railway over the River Wye at Chepstow and had then continued at the works established for its construction. Specialising initially in fabricating bridges and manufacturing boilers, *Yan Yean* was only the third vessel completed by Finch & Co, who then went on to build many more, up until the closure of the company just after the First World War.

SNEYD (1) Official No. 62240

This vessel was built in 1872 at Northam, Southampton, by Day, Summers & Co for their own account and was named by them *Itchen*, after one of the local rivers. She was of 193 grt, with a length of 106 feet 1 inch and a beam of 22 feet 3 inches. Her compound engine was manufactured by her builders. In 1888, *Itchen* was sold to Osborn & Wallis, who renamed her *Sneyd*. She remained as part of the fleet until late 1927 when, on 28th October she became stranded on

Sneyd at Ilfracombe harbour circa 1920, an unusual location for an O&W vessel. *Courtesy Bristol Museums & Art Gallery*

The s.s. Sneyd, a small coasting steamer wrecked in Swansea Bay. The crew escaped by jumping ashore when the vessel crashed into the pier.

Newspaper cutting showing the *Sneyd*'s inglorious end. The angle at which she came to rest at least provides a good view of her deck layout. *Courtesy Bristol Museums & Art Gallery*

the breakwater at Swansea during heavy weather, while on passage in ballast from Briton Ferry to Bristol. Her crew of five got off successfully. ***Sneyd*** was re-floated on 11th November and towed to Bristol, where she was broken up.

Some details of the vessel have been discovered in a letter published in *Sea Breezes* in May 1954:

> The steamer *Sneyd*, in which I was then serving, possessed a unique telegraph. I have never seen one like it before or since. The dial in the engine-room was a large brass fitting with the orders, in an unusual style, around the edge, thus: 'stop her'; 'ease her'; 'half speed'; 'full speed' and 'ahead' inscribed in large letters, as was 'astern' with the 'full' in either direction being almost in the vertical position.
>
> This indicator was connected to a horizontal shaft which led inside the boiler casing where there was a crown and pinion with the vertical shaft leading to the bridge. The instrument on the bridge had an horizontal face on a basin-like top and two handles, one at either side of the dial.
>
> Orders were cut out of solid brass, which permitted a light inside to shine through the letters. I never saw the lamp lit however. I mention this telegraph because I understand it was once fitted to a vessel chartered by H.M. Stanley when going in search of Dr. Livingstone in 1871. I think she was one of the baggage ships and at that time bore the name *Governor Albercurk* [sic]. But of this, I am not sure. In after years she was the *Agra* and was in the Bristol Channel trade; she was afterwards converted into a barge for T.R. Brown.
>
> In about 1925 the *Sneyd* was driven ashore and wrecked in Swansea Bay and another coaster now bears her name.
>
> Charles Phillips
> Long Ashton, Somerset

The ***Governor Albuquerque*** was also briefly a part of the Osborn & Wallis fleet in 1891-2 and details of her are given a little further on.

NETHAM Official No. 78453

Netham was purchased by Osborn & Wallis during 1889. She was built by G.K. Stothert & Co for Richard C. Ring in 1878 and was fitted with a compound steam engine manufactured by her builders. With a grt of 113, she was 97 feet 7 inches long, with a beam of 17 feet 7 inches. In 1885, Richard Ring sold the vessel to George Nurse of Bristol, who kept her for four years, until he in turn sold her to William Osborn. In 1896, the ship was re-engined with a compound engine built by Lobnitz & Co of Renfrew. On 29th December 1898, while loaded with a cargo of coal, she sank off Goldcliffe near the mouth of the River Usk, when her cargo shifted during exceptionally heavy weather. Three of her crew were lost. Newspaper reports of the time gave a graphic account of the disaster and of the subsequent inquest. They are worth reproducing in full, not least because of the extra information they contain about the vessel and the crew. The second extract reporting the inquest is from the *South Wales Argus,* Monday 13th February 1899:

LOSS OF A BRISTOL STEAMER

BODIES CAST UP AT NASH.

During the gale on Sunday morning the SS *Netham*, of Bristol, was wrecked near the Nash Lighthouse at the mouth of the Usk, apparently with the loss of all hands. Wreckage was seen in the vicinity on Sunday, and the steamer's masts were above water at low tide. On Sunday evening a man named Albert Bennet found three bodies near the spot and gave information to Police Constable Fripp of the Monmouthshire Constabulary. The two went together wading through deep water, but as there were miles of floods between them and the dry land, and in the face of the rising tide, which threatened their lives, they were compelled to secure the bodies and leave them. There appears to be no doubt that the men were the ill-fated crew of the SS *Netham*, of Bristol, which left Newport on Saturday night laden with coal, in the company of the SS *Clifton*, another small collier belonging to the same owners. On one of the bodies was found a receipt made out to the captain of the *Netham* for overtime for finishing loading; while there were also some Building Society papers made out to 'J. Harris'.

INTERVIEW WITH THE OWNERS

A representative of the *Argus* had an interview with Mr Osborn of the firm Osborn and Wallis, Queens Square, Bristol, who owned the vessel. Mr Osborn said the *Netham* and the *Clifton*, which were colliers trading between Bristol and the South Wales ports, left Newport together on Saturday night. The *Clifton* made the passage, but when they had no news from any member of the crew of the *Netham* this morning, while hoping against hope, they feared the worst. There were four men aboard – the master, John Harris of Bristol, the engineer James Hodge also of Bristol, and two men whose names were not certain as there had been changes aboard, though one was believed to be a Chepstow man, named Williams. There is thus one man missing.

WHEN THE WRECK OCCURRED

On one of the bodies was found a watch which had stopped at seven o'clock, from which it appears that the *Netham* was wrecked and her crew drowned at seven o'clock on Sunday morning at which time the gale was blowing furiously from the south-west.

DESCRIPTION OF THE VESSEL

The *Netham* was registered at Bristol in 1873. She was of iron, 97ft. long, and 17ft. in breadth. Her nett tonnage was 74 with a gross tonnage of 121. She was owned by Messrs Osborn and Wallis of Bristol.

The O&W collier *Netham* approaching the entrance lock to the City Docks in the 1890s, with the company's wooden sailing trow *Wye* in tow. *Courtesy Bristol Museums & Art Gallery*

THE REMOVAL OF THE BODIES

As it was practically impossible to convey the bodies from Nash to Lisweny as the whole district was under water, it was determined to take them by boat to the West side of the river and convey them to Pill Mortuary.

Note the vessel's dimensions and tonnage as given above differ from those in the official register. The writer of the next account got a little carried away with the dramatics of this unfortunate tragedy in his opening paragraph:

THE WRECK OF A BRISTOL STEAMER

INQUEST AND VERDICT

THRILLING EXPERIENCE OF RESCUERS

The wreck of the Bristol steamer *Netham*, off the Nash lighthouse, in the mouth of the river Usk, forms a thrilling story of the loss of life, the terrific effects of the storm, and the exciting experiences of the police-constables and others who, on Monday, recovered the bodies of three out of four of the crew of the ill-fated vessel. The bodies, which had been reverently laid out in the belfry of Nash Church, were yesterday afternoon viewed by the jury summoned for the inquest held by Mr. M. Roberts Jones, coroner for South Monmouth.

The inquiry took place in the National Schoolroom, Nash. The names of the deceased were John Harris, the captain; Williams, the mate; James Hodges, the driver; and Pickford, a seaman, all of Bristol, except Williams, whose home was at Bedminster. Supt. Parry of the Monmouthshire Constabulary was present.

Robert Pickford ... said he was a brother of one of the deceased seamen. The captain, Harris, lived at Totterdown, Bristol, and Williams at Bedminster. Witness last saw his brother alive on Thursday morning at Bristol, which port he left the same evening in the SS *Netham*. Witness had never heard him complain of the vessel being unseaworthy.

The Coroner: Do you think there is anyone to blame for his death? – Witness: Well, I shouldn't like to say that.

The Coroner: If you think so, it is your duty to say so. However, you will have an opportunity of asking the witnesses any questions.

Joseph Blacker ... foreman stevedore to Messrs. Osborn and Wallis ... deposed that he last saw the deceased men on Thursday night, at 8.30, going under St. Phillip's Bridge, Bristol. They were walking towards the vessel, which was proceeding to sea by that evening's tide. Witness knew all the crew, four in number. Capt. Harris was 61 years of age, and lived in King William Street, Totterdown, Bristol. He had been master of the *Netham* for about three years, but witness had known him for about 30 years as captain of different vessels. He was a thoroughly experienced man. Williams, who was 42 years of age, had been in the *Netham* for about three months, but had been working for the owners for many years. The *Netham* was a steam barge, 100 feet long, 17 feet beam, and 5 feet in depth. She was 78 tons net register, and was built in Bristol 20 years ago. She had been a very unfortunate ship. Eight years ago she was stranded on the English and Welsh Ground sands. Only one of the late crew was on board at that time, and he was the driver. His body was still in the wreck.

The Coroner: Do you know that the body of the fourth member of the crew, who is missing, is still there? – Witness: Yes, I have just been searching the vessel, and felt the body.

Proceeding, the witness stated that on the 29th December last the *Netham* met with an accident nearly at the same spot where she now lay, and filled. That was caused by bad weather, which washed her companion away. The captain saved her on that occasion by reversing her under the lighthouse. She underwent repairs, and was duly passed by the Board of Trade at Bristol. Three weeks ago she was towing a vessel, when the weather became thick. She struck the sand and swung broadside, and the vessel she was towing came up and cut her through.

The Coroner: Was she stopped by the Board of Trade three weeks ago? – Witness: No. Sir.

The witness, continuing, said the *Netham* left Bristol for Cardiff, for coal, on Friday morning, and arrived at Cardiff at about eleven o'clock. There was no coal at Cardiff, and she remained there until Saturday morning's tide, when she proceeded to Newport, arriving at the latter port between seven and eight o'clock. She loaded 153 tons of coal at the Alexandra Dock jetty, finishing loading at six o'clock on Saturday evening. Witness felt sure that all the crew were competent, and in a fit condition to go to sea, because the vessel proceeded immediately after she was loaded. Captain Harris was a sober, reliable man, and he would have the wheel from Newport across to Avonmouth. He (witness) felt sure the crew were in no way responsible for the wreck. His opinion was that, after the captain started, he found the weather was bad and determined to put back. The *Clifton*, another boat belonging to the same firm, was on ahead about a mile, and her crew suddenly lost sight of the *Netham*'s lights, and came to the conclusion that she had turned back. The night being dark and stormy, the captain must have misjudged the distance between the buoy and the shore in turning, and came too close. The result was the *Netham* struck the bottom, and immediately the sea swept over her and washed the deceased men overboard. She evidently 'jumped' three times on the sands, as there were three distinct marks thereon. The driver's name was James Hodges, and his body was still on board. The vessel could be approached from land, and outwardly appeared alright, though she was full of water.

George Bassett, labourer, West Nash, gave evidence as to the finding of two bodies fifty yards from the bank. The water was four feet deep in his house, and he had to swim out of it.

P.C. Fripp, stationed at Goldcliffe, said he heard of the accident from the last witness at 4.30 on Sunday. He procured assistance, and, accompanied by the last witness, and other men, proceeded to the wreck. He examined two bodies. The first was that of Williams, and they found on him two clay pipes and a knife. The second was that of Harris, and on him they found a silver watch – which had stopped at 7.18 – a knife, 5s. 4d. in money, a pair of spectacles, and some keys. He afterwards found the body of Pickford, lying a couple of hundred yards away in the mud. On him were found 4d., two clay pipes, and a knife. Before removing the bodies he proceeded to the wreck, and boarded the vessel. It was quite filled with water, and they could not discover any other bodies. The hatches were off the coal, and were exposed. He found three lamps in the mud and one at the masthead. There was no outward sign of damage to the vessel, but the gearing &c. looked as if it had been badly knocked about. The flood had been the heaviest in the recollection of anyone living about the district. Witness and those who helped him tried to get the bodies to the shore, but failed, and secured them to the lighthouse. The tide came up, and they were up to their necks in water. He and the five other men were nearly drowned. They were caught by the incoming tide, which washed over the sea wall. On Monday, accompanied by Superintendent Parry, a couple of constables, and several men, they removed the bodies to Nash Church. The small boat belonging to the vessel had been smashed to pieces.

This was all the evidence, and the Coroner having summed up, the jury returned a verdict of "Accidentally drowned", fixing the time as Saturday evening.

The Coroner added that he thought the police were deserving of great praise for their bravery in securing the bodies at such risk.

The Jury: Hear, hear.

The bravery of these men in attempting to rescue the bodies of the crew was indeed remarkable. A few further details regarding ***Netham*** appear in another account of the inquest. Apparently her engines and boilers were new, whilst it was stated that the intention was to pump her out and bring her back to Bristol as soon as possible. It may have been thought at this stage that the damage to the vessel was repairable but in the event she appears to have been scrapped and nothing more is heard of her.

GOVERNOR ALBUQUERQUE Official No. 76366

This iron steamer was built by T. Wingate & Co of Glasgow and registered at Liverpool on 15th February 1876 in the ownership of Isaac Zagury, Liverpool and Loanda, as ***Governor Albuquerque***. In 1877, she was re-registered under the Portuguese flag and renamed ***Governador Albuquerque***. On 14th February of that year, she was recorded as arriving at Loanda and she then traded along the West African coast for about a year, before transferring to the Cape Verde islands. This was unsuccessful and she quickly transferred again back to Angola. In August 1881, she went ashore at Palmeirinhas, south of Loanda, where she remained for 10 months. She was refloated in June 1882 with the aid of the Portuguese gunboat ***Bengo*** and was repaired at Loanda. There are claims that during her time on the West African coast, she was employed by Henry Stanley in his quest to find the explorer Dr. Livingstone but these have been disputed.

In 1885, she returned to British registry for the Congo & Central African Company, Liverpool, who changed her name back to its original spelling. In 1891, she was sold to William Osborn. She was badly damaged in a waterside fire in May of the following year and rather than repair her, O&W had her engines transferred to ***Blanche***, subsequently using her hull as a floating warehouse.

The bare hull of ***Governor Albuquerque*** was sold to Jefferies, a local shipyard owner, and she was used as a floating store hulk. Her registry had been cancelled after the fire but, in 1902, Jefferies fitted an engine and boiler made in his own workshops and re-registered her in the name of ***Agra***. Soon afterwards she was sold to Pockett's Bristol Channel Steam Packet Company (W.G. Tilton, manager) and was employed coasting until 1925. She was then again stripped to a hull and sold to the local stevedores, T.R. Brown & Sons. The hulk was eventually scrapped in the early part of the Second World War by Cashmore's of Newport.

It was remembered that, as a hulk, the vessel had a strange cut away section at the base of her stem. This was where she had originally been fitted with an hydraulic outlet pipe, so that if she got stuck on a bank during her river trading days, a jet of water could be sent forward to disperse the mud and refloat her.

BLANCHE Official No. 45963

The next addition to the fleet was ***Blanche***, bought in 1891. She was of 246 grt and had a length of 121 feet, with a beam of 20 feet, being built of iron. She was nearer to the small end of the fleet in terms of tonnage and size but, with her midships bridge, superstructure and machinery, she was of large ship configuration. Her engines were positioned amidships and, like many small steamers of the period, she also carried sail, being schooner rigged.

Blanche was built in 1863 by A. & J. Inglis of Point House, Glasgow, for Seligmann, also of Glasgow. They built her compound engine too, while her boiler was built by Newall & Co of Bristol. In 1865, she was sold to Matthew Langlands of Glasgow, who sold her on to Joseph Weatherley of London in 1867. In 1875, the owners became Weatherley, Mead, & Hussey of London. In 1877, she was again sold, this time to

Blanche, unladen and outward bound from Bristol, in the late 1890s. *Courtesy Bristol Museums & Art Gallery*

Ocean under repair in Charles Hill's dry dock in Bristol. This dock has a long and illustrious history, having been built originally for the construction of Brunel's famous steamship *Great Britain*. After nearly a century of use as a dry dock by Hills, it once again plays host to the fully restored *Great Britain* today. The large building on the right, now demolished, was the workshop where *Great Britain*'s engines were built. *Courtesy Bristol Museums & Art Gallery*

John McDowall of London who kept her until 1888, when she was sold to Christopher Furness of West Hartlepool. Finally, in 1891, she was purchased by Osborn & Wallis.

The following year *Blanche* was re-engined using the engine from *Governor Albuquerque*. This engine, like the vessel it came from, had been built by Wingate & Co of Glasgow. *Blanche* met her end on 7th July 1901, when she was wrecked and lost at Lescoril, Isle of Tudy, while on passage from Cardiff to Quimper, in France, with a cargo of bran.

OCEAN Official No. 102484

The next acquisition was to be something of a landmark for the company, as they took delivery of their first new, built to order, small ship, *Ocean*.

Ocean was completed in 1893 by the Executors of T.A. Walker, who had operated from the tiny shipyard at Sudbrook, in Monmouthshire, until his death in 1891. The vessel was of 140 grt and was 95 feet in length, with a beam of 19 feet 1 inch. She was a steel screw steamer, built to Walker's Yard No. 36. This shipyard was originally established as an engineering works by Thomas Walker, a railway engineer, who was called in by the Great Western Railway to assist with the severe water incursion problems they were experiencing during the construction of the Severn Tunnel in 1879. It lay within the confines of the old Port of Chepstow, being situated on the west bank of the Severn estuary, a few miles south of the town.

Unusually for such a small ship, she had a triple expansion engine, built by Newall & Co of Bristol. *Ocean* also had a permanent wooden wheelhouse and although she was equipped with a lowerable funnel and mast, as were most of the other ships in O&W's fleet at this time, this prevented her from negotiating some of the very low bridges to reach the Feeder Canal in Bristol. Beyond these lay the later Avonbank Power Station, as well as Lysaght's Ironworks and United Alkali's plant. However, *Ocean* was probably never intended to reach the latter two in any case, as this trade was becoming less important to O&W. Consequently, *Ocean* was used chiefly for coaling the Bristol Tramways generating station near Bristol Bridge. The company's connection with the fledgling electricity industry had begun.

During the 1920s, the ship was altered by giving it a raised, and closed focs'le. *Ocean* remained with the company for the whole of her life and was regarded with some affection by old hands in later years. During August 1951, the little ship arrived at John Cashmore's yard, at Newport, South Wales for breaking up, after a remarkable one-owner career which had lasted 58 years.

MARION Official No. 81267

In 1895, two years after the acquisition of *Ocean*, another small ship was purchased reflecting the growing work for this part of the fleet in connection with the generation of electricity. The vessel was built in 1879, coincidentally also as Yard No. 36, by the Abercorn Shipbuilding Co Ltd of Paisley and was named *Marion*. Of 139 grt, with a length of 90 feet 5 inches and a beam of 19 feet 7 inches, she was completed for R.W. Murray of Warrington, who traded as

Ocean alongside the company's wharf at Hotwells, probably in the late 1930s and showing the raised foc'sle fitted during the 1920s. The vessel lies fairly heavy in the water, so was probably partly unloaded when this view was taken. *Courtesy Bristol Museums & Art Gallery*

Marion at the entrance to Bristol Docks around the turn of the century. *Courtesy Bristol Museums & Art Gallery*

the Whitecross Wire & Iron Co Ltd. Registered at Liverpool, she was fitted with a compound engine built by Dunsmuir & Jackson of Glasgow.

In 1881, when she was just two years old, ***Marion*** was sold to the Mississippi & Dominion Steamship Co Ltd, to serve as a baggage tender for ships of the Dominion Line at Liverpool. In 1886, she was re-engined by D. Rollo & Sons, of Liverpool, whilst in 1889, the management of her was taken over by Flinn, Main & Montgomery.

Osborn & Wallis acquired the vessel during 1895 and kept her name. ***Marion*** remained with the company until 1932, when she was broken up.

HERSCHEL Official No. 89801

Yet another Sunderland-built tramp, ***Herschel*** was completed by Bartram, Haswell & Co in 1884 for Wilkie & Turnbull of North Shields. She joined the Osborn & Wallis fleet in 1898, the last ocean tramp to be bought and was registered as usual under a single ship company, the Herschel Steam Ship Company Ltd. Her dimensions were 260 feet by 36 feet by 19 feet and her gross tonnage was 1,693.

Herschel was lost on 17th November 1901. Entering the Mersey bound for Manchester with pyrites from Spain, she sank following a collision with the steamer ***Ardeola***.

ST. VINCENT Official No. 55202.

The next purchase, during 1900, was another small vessel bought second-hand. ***St. Vincent*** was built by J. Batchelor of Cardiff in 1866 for James A. Ware, also of Cardiff, where the ship was registered. With a length of 99 feet 3 inches and a beam of 19 feet, she was of 141 grt. Her machinery was supplied by Stothert's of Bristol, probably a simple single-cylinder steam engine. During 1912, she was transferred to Bristol registration.

At an unknown date, ***St. Vincent*** sank in the River Avon following a collision with a tug but she was raised, repaired and put back into service. Then, on 2nd November 1929, she was one of several vessels which became stranded on the mud in dense fog in the River Avon. Despite this calamity prone career, she lasted with the company until 1936, when she was finally broken up.

In 1898, Osborn & Wallis had suffered a heavy loss when ***Netham*** had sunk with the loss of three of her crew. This run of misfortune continued in 1901 with the loss of ***Blanche*** and their latest large ship acquisition, ***Herschel***. Although a loss to the company, ***Blanche*** was not an integral part of either of the core activities of the merged firm and she was not replaced. No attempt was made to replace ***Herschel*** either. The company was taking stock of where it was and in which direction it was likely to be going.

Herschel photographed at Bristol Docks probably shortly after her purchase by O & W in 1898; her funnel still sports the colours of her previous owners Wilkie & Turnbull of North Shields. *Courtesy Bristol Museums & Art Gallery*

An unladen *St. Vincent* photographed chugging rather smokily along an unidentified waterway, probably in the 1920s. Note her workboat is here seen in tow rather than stowed aboard. *Courtesy Bristol Museums & Art Gallery*

Above: The funnel and mast of *St. Vincent* projecting from the waters of the River Avon following her sinking as the result of a collision with a tug. The funnel in the foreground is presumably that of the tug. The tug and dumb barge on the right appear to have just manoeuvred between the twin obstacles of the sunken vessels. The date of this incident is not known. **Left:** In trouble again! *St. Vincent* stranded on the mud in the River Avon after she ran aground in early November 1929, one of several vessels to get into difficulties as a result of a thick fog. *Both courtesy Jim Crissup*

CLIFTON Official No. 19290

Clifton was bought during 1903 and had a most unlikely background. She had been built in 1857 for John Symers of Dundee by T.D. Marshall of South Shields, as the iron paddle tug, *Samson* (a popular name, incidentally, for tug boats). As built, the vessel was of 126 grt, and was 81 feet 5 inches long, with a beam of 18 feet 3 inches. Her single cylinder engine was by Stothert & Co of Bristol, with a boiler by Chapman & Co.

In 1870, *Samson* was sold to the Governor & Company of Copper Miners in England, based in London. They in turn sold the ship during 1877 to James Shaw of Taibach, Glamorganshire. In 1882, the vessel underwent a complete transformation when it was lengthened to 103 feet 2 inches, its beam increased to 19 feet and it was converted to screw propulsion. This work was carried out by G.K. Stothert & Co of Bristol. Shortly afterwards, in 1884, the vessel was sold to the Bristol-based coal merchant George Nurse, who was presumably responsible for her change of name.

Nurse had her re-engined and re-boilered during 1903, following which, on 30th June that year, she was bought by W.A. Osborn. It would seem likely that Nurse had the work carried out in order to sell her.

The last chapter of her life comprised a period of stability working back and forth across the Bristol Channel in the colours of Osborn & Wallis until, on 21st May 1920, she made her final journey over, in the tow of *Ocean*, to John Cashmore's yard at Newport for breaking.

NEW ZEALAND Official No. 93086

Built during 1886 by Cochrane, Cooper, & Schofield of Beverley, Yorkshire for the Hull Steam Fishing & Ice Co Ltd, of Hull, as Yard No. 13, *New Zealand* had a length of 117 feet and a beam of 22 feet 1 inch, giving a grt of 179. She was fitted with a triple expansion engine manufactured by C.D. Holmes & Co of Hull.

In 1891, she was sold to HM Government and re-named *Sir Howard Elphinstone*. She was sold during 1907 to Osborn & Wallis who immediately had her lengthened to 155 feet 2 inches (a considerable increase), which then gave her a

grt of 309. The company also returned the ship to her original name, *New Zealand*.

She was by far the largest of the O & W 'small' ships and, like ***Blanche***, was something of an oddity in the make up of the fleet. This seems to have been recognised as her stay with the company lasted for only four years. During 1911, Osborn & Wallis sold the ship to the Mahe Syndicate Ltd, of London, who renamed her ***Cigale*** and, in 1912, her owners changed their name to the Mahe Steamship Co Ltd, of London.

During 1921, she was sold again to a company calling itself Cigale Ltd, no doubt formed specifically to buy the vessel. The manager of this undertaking was one Augusti Esnouf, based at Port Louis, Mauritius.

On 3rd December 1925, this colourful career came to a sudden and tragic end when the ship suffered an explosion in her cargo, which consisted of barrels of petroleum motor spirit and other general goods, and caught fire. The vessel sank and twenty three

Above: *Clifton* outside the entrance lock to the City Docks circa 1900, in a view which emphasises her diminutive size. She has a rope ashore from her bow and appears to be in the process of tying up, perhaps indicating that she was waiting for the lock to clear before making her passage through. She appears to be carrying a cargo of copper ore.
Below: A snapshot from the Portway capturing *Clifton*'s last voyage down the River Avon in May 1920, to the breaker's yard at Newport in the tow of *Ocean*. Her funnel and mast have already been removed and can be seen laying along the port side of her Engine Room casing. *Both courtesy Bristol Museums & Art Gallery*

passengers and crew were lost with her. Thirty six others escaped in lifeboats and on life rafts.

To date, no photographs of ***New Zealand*** have been unearthed.

By now, Osborn & Wallis were heavily engaged with the work of delivering the coal to Bristol's growing electricity supply industry and, apart from the recently built ***Ocean***, the company was operating a motley collection of old and tired ships to carry out the task. With the prospect of steady and reliable work, which in turn necessitated reliable shipping capability, Osborn & Wallis set about upgrading their small ships. In 1910, ***Stakesby*** was sold, followed the next year by the sale of ***Eureka*** and ***Saltwick***. The sale of three 'large' ships and the consequent reduction on this side of the company's business, marked a recognition that the operation of the small ships in the reliable local trades, of which the electricity supply industry was chief, was where the future lay.

ORB Official No. 127089

Completed for Osborn & Wallis as Yard No. 174 in 1911, this was a further new addition to the fleet and the second of the company's vessels to be built at Sudbrook Shipyard, which since 1902 had been in the operation of C.H. Walker & Co Ltd. Of 202 grt, ***Orb*** was 116 feet 7 inches long, with a beam of 20 feet. She was powered by a compound engine built by Plenty & Sons of Newbury and was registered at Bristol on 8th November 1911. Her name obviously reflected Osborn & Wallis's close business links with the John Lysaght Company and, in particular, that concern's Orb Steelworks at Newport.

Orb remained with Osborn & Wallis for her entire life and, in the company of ***Ocean***, her earlier consort from the same builders, went to John Cashmore's yard at Newport for demolition in August 1951.

Below: *Orb* photographed in 'the usual spot', probably around 1912 when the vessel was still quite new. The malevolent sky is actually a result of 'fogging' on the original glass plate, most likely due to poor storage conditions prior to its rescue for posterity.
Courtesy Bristol Museums & Art Gallery

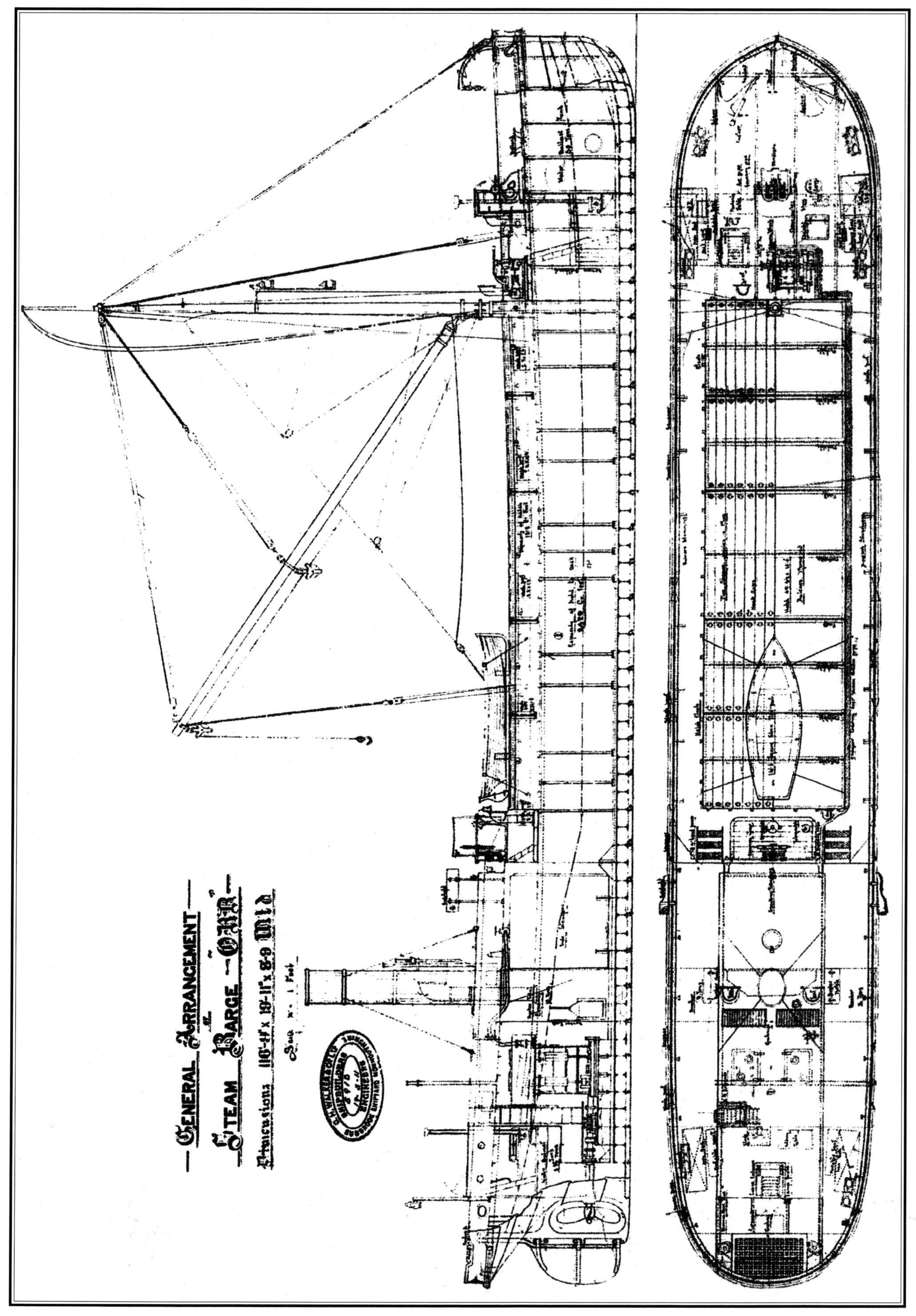
General Arrangement
Steam Barge

Orb at rest moored in the Company's dock at Hotwells. The lack of activity suggests a Sunday view, which was taken sometime in the 1930s. *Courtesy Bristol Museums & Art Gallery*

FERRIC Official No. 134697

A further order for a new ship was placed with Charles Hill & Sons Ltd of Bristol in 1911. *Ferric* was registered (and hence almost certainly delivered) in December 1911. Significantly, it was the first order for a new build that Hill's had received for twelve years. Not only did the vessel bring this famine to an end, her delivery began a long association between O&W and the shipbuilder. This was to result in all further work for Osborn & Wallis, both repairs and new builds, being placed with Charles Hill's Yard, up until the shipping company ceased trading in 1970.

Ferric was built to Hill's Yard No. 121 and, with a length of 116 feet 9 inches, and a beam of 20 feet, she was of 191 grt. Her compound engine, built by Plenty & Son of Newbury, was powered by a boiler built by I. Neilson & Son of Glasgow. *Ferric* represented a loss to her builders, however, having been built to a contract price of £4,350, whereas her actual building cost was £4,952 – 7 - 0½d.

This ship too remained with Osborn & Wallis for her entire life, arriving at John Cashmore's yard for scrapping on 22nd March 1955.

The launch of *Ferric* from Charles Hill's Yard in 1912. The twelve-year gap in new-build orders for the yard ensured that this was something of an event, even though it was a relatively small vessel and the majority of the workforce have assembled to watch. Note she was built and is being launched 'bow down' the slipway, which was most unusual. Much fitting out still remains to be done, with the vessel, as was normally the case, being launched into the harbour minus her masts, funnel, engine, boiler and other equipment. *Courtesy Bristol Museums & Art Gallery*

During 1913, ***Dolcoath*** was sold, leaving O&W with just one large ship, ***Euterpe***. The elimination of the operation of large ships by the company was now almost completed and, with the loss of ***Euterpe*** in 1916 when she was mined, the era of the large ships bearing Osborn & Wallis colours came to an end. From now on, the life of the Company and the future make up of its fleet would be governed by its commitment to the supply of coal to the power stations of Bristol and Portishead.

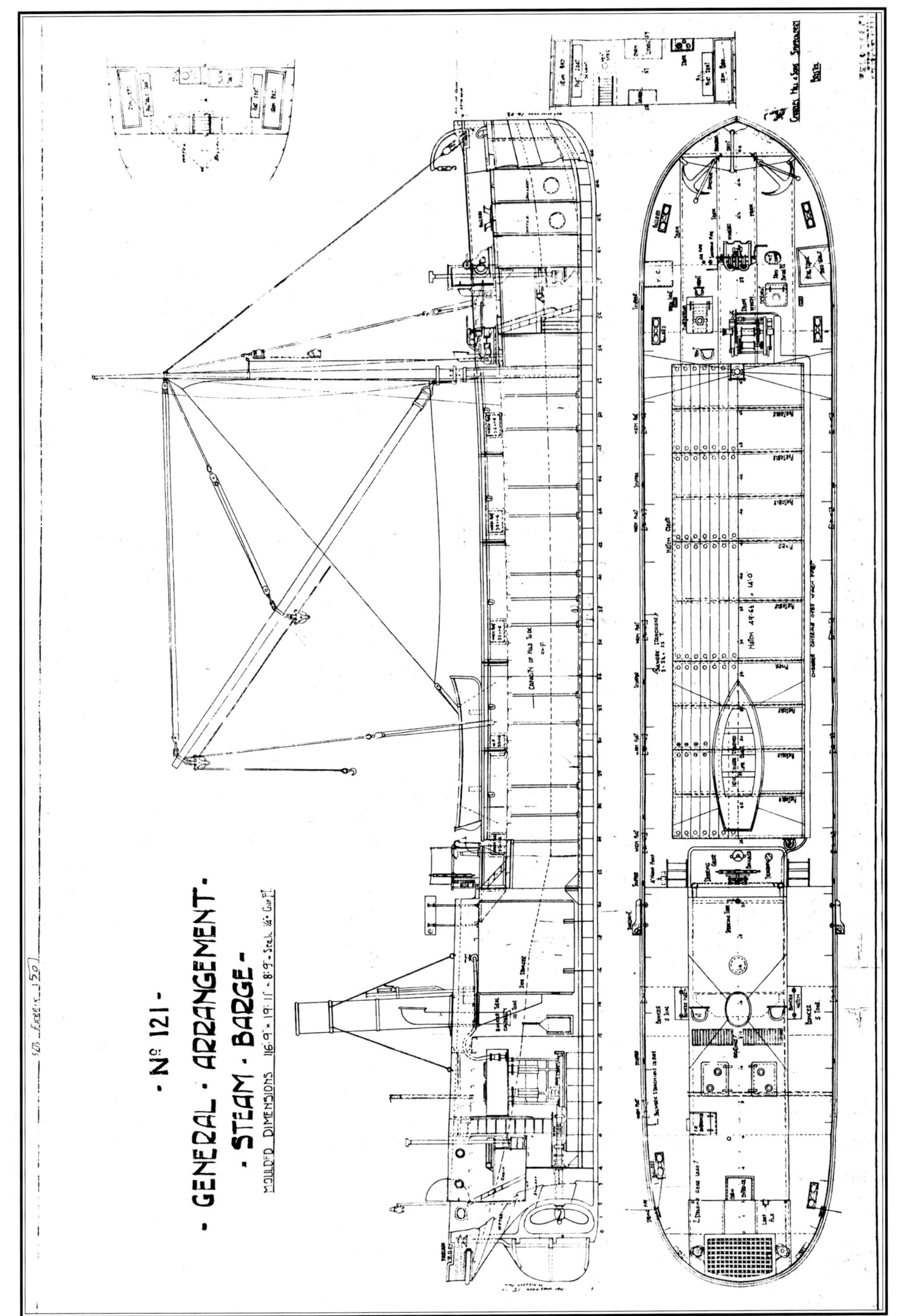
- Nº 121 -
- GENERAL · ARRANGEMENT -
- STEAM · BARGE -
MOULDED DIMENSIONS

Ferric at the entrance to Bristol Docks, probably shortly before the First World War. The vessel looks in tip-top condition and was probably only a year or so old when this photograph was taken. *Courtesy Bristol Museums & Art Gallery*

A1 Official No. 105175

The oddly named *A1* was one of only a handful of vessels to be built at Lydney, in 1895, by C.W. Dodgin. Hailing originally from Bristol, Dodgin took a lease on the tiny ship repair yard alongside the north pier outside Lydney Docks in 1892. Shipbuilding in Lydney had previously been limited to the occasional wooden sailing vessel but Dodgin built four steel vessels here, three in 1895 (*A1* and two barges) and one in 1897, the tiny screw steamer ***Alpha***, destined to be the last ship ever built at the small Forest of Dean port. The following year he relinquished his lease on the shipyard.

A1 was 127 grt (66 tons net), with a length of 96 feet and a beam of 17 feet 6 inches. She was fitted with a single-cylinder engine built by G.K. Stothert of Bristol and was built by Dodgin for the Water Transport Company Ltd, the manager of which was one Robert Johnston. On completion, she was registered at Cardiff.

Her time with WTC Ltd was short for, in 1898, *A1* was sold to John C. Hunt of Bridgwater who ran her until 1921. In that year she was sold to Osborn & Wallis, who retained her name. However, she did not remain in service long, as in 1927 she was dismantled and reduced to a dumb barge.

This acquisition seems to have been completely out of keeping with the need to improve the standard of the ships owned and operated. In age, size and machinery, *A1* was much more closely related to the small ships operated during the company's early years. It is possible that the purchase of this small ship in 1921, at that time clearly out of step with recent acquisitions by O&W, represented a hasty and perhaps ill-judged reaction to the need for increased capacity, to keep pace with the demands for power station coal. Her short life after purchase would seem to confirm this.

MORVAH Official No. 148206

As if to confirm the unsuitability of *A1*, Osborn & Wallis ordered a further new build from Charles Hill & Sons Ltd soon after its purchase. Built during 1926 under Yard No. 158, ***Morvah*** was of 232 grt and 133 feet 8 inches in length, with a beam of 20 feet 3 inches. Her triple-expansion engine was built by Abdela & Mitchell Ltd, who were based on the Thames & Severn Canal at Brimscombe, near Stroud, and her boiler came from Riley Bros Ltd. The boiler worked at 180 lb psi, giving her 270 indicated horse power (ihp).

Morvah was launched on 24th April 1926 and, following final fitting out, was delivered to O&W on 4th June. She remained with the Company all her life, being towed to Cashmore's at Newport for breaking on 22nd March 1955.

This vessel was generally recognised to be the last of the O&W small ships (or 'the barges', as they were referred to within the company). The future demand for coal by the huge electricity generating plant being built at Portishead would require greater capacity, concentrated in larger ships, to make better use of the discharging capability and the time between tides.

The only known photograph of the tiny Lydney-built coaster *A1*. She is seen here in the Severn estuary, heading up-river probably shortly after World War One and a year or two before she was bought by O&W. The exact location of this view is a matter for conjecture but the structures just visible in the left background could well be part of the National Shipyard No. 2 at Beachley. This short lived venture, taken over by the Ministry soon after it was established in order to build standard design transport ships for the war effort, closed in the early 1920s, having only completed one vessel and even that some eighteen months after hostilities had ceased. The larger National Shipyard No. 1 at Chepstow was only marginally more successful. *Courtesy National Maritime Museum*

Preparations in hand for the launch of the *Morvah* at Hill's Yard in April 1926. Either there is still a day or two to go, or such events were more low key at this time than in later years. *Courtesy Bristol Museums & Art Gallery*

Looking considerably smaller than she does on the stocks in the pre-launch view, *Morvah* passes beneath the Clifton suspension bridge as she nears the end of her journey back to Bristol City Docks in this circa 1930 view.
Courtesy Bristol Museums & Art Gallery

With plenty of freeboard on display, an obviously empty *Morvah* makes her way down the River Avon bound for the Bristol Channel, probably sometime during the early 1950s. Note the Bristol to Portishead railway line in the background. Journeys on this route through the Avon Gorge were quite spectacular. It is not possible to make this trip at the present time, although the line has just been re-opened after many years out of use for freight traffic from the Royal Portbury Docks. *Courtesy National Maritime Museum*

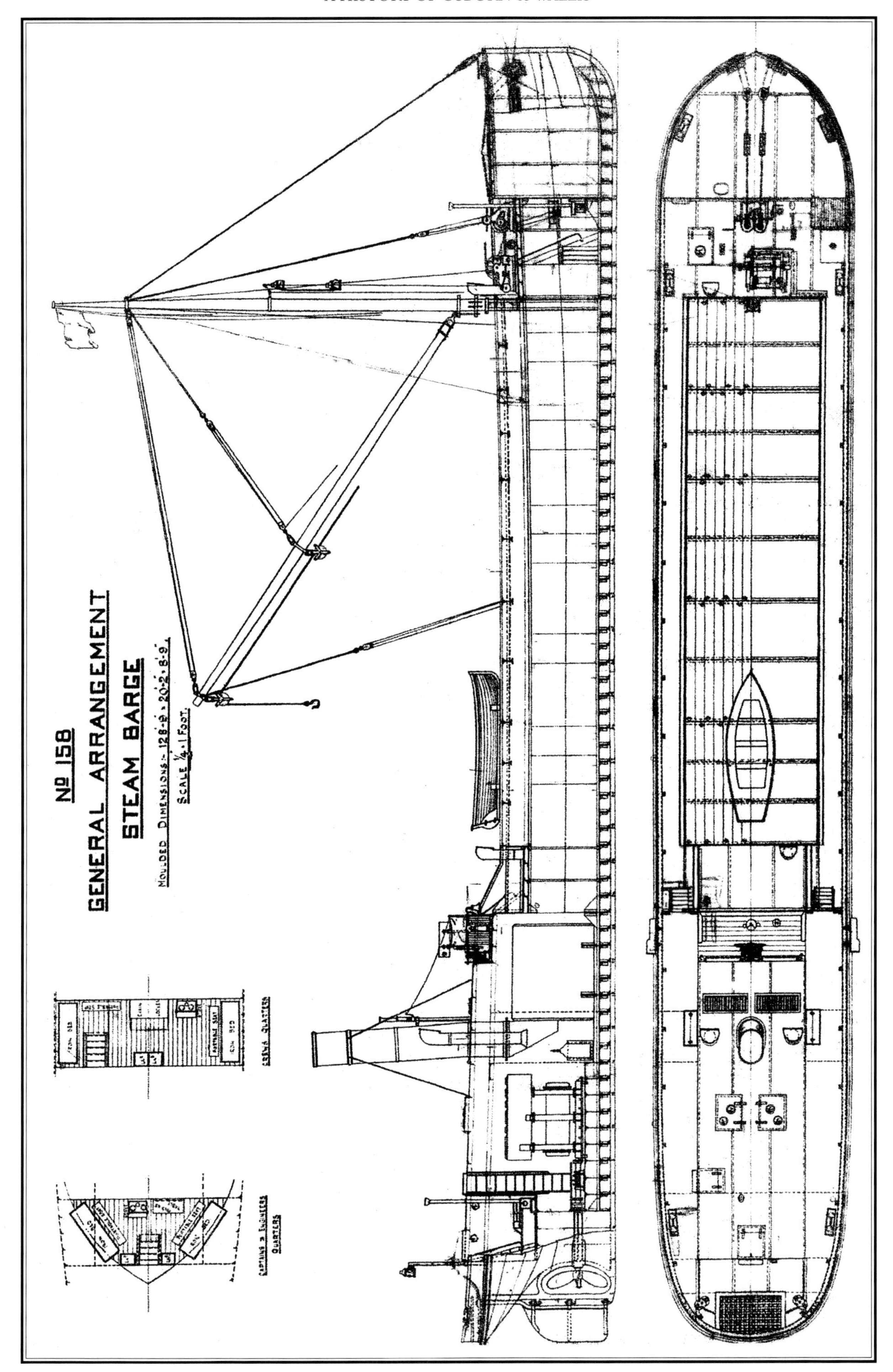
Nº 158
GENERAL ARRANGEMENT
STEAM BARGE
MOULDED DIMENSIONS:- 128'-9" x 20'-2" x 8'-9".
SCALE 1/4" = 1 FOOT.

DRUID STOKE Official No. 149997

Recognising the new demands about to be made upon the Company's capacity, O&W negotiated a further new-build from Hill's during 1928. This resulted in the delivery, late in 1929, of Yard No. 174 ***Druid Stoke***. It is generally recognised that the acquisition of this vessel marked the end of the historical small ship fleet for O&W and the start of its modern era, with the larger vessels needed to supply the new Portishead Power Station.

Freed from the constraints of Feeder Canal trading, the new ship could be much larger and consequently was, at 486 grt, over twice the tonnage of the recently delivered ***Morvah***. She was, at 145 feet, only 17 feet longer but the increase in beam to 26 feet and an increase in hull depth accounted for the doubling in capacity. She was, in fact, of a size comparable to the average coaster of the time.

Without the need to pass under the bridges approaching the Feeder Canal, ***Druid Stoke*** was given a raised foc'sle and raised superstructure at the after end. She was also given a mainmast equipped with its own derrick and winch, in order that the ship would be able to handle its own cargo loading and discharge. While this was not necessary for her intended work, it was presumably done to render the ship more flexible and perhaps more easy to sell later on, should the need arise. On initial appearances, with her foc'sle, raised quarterdeck, superstructure aft carrying two lifeboats in davits and two masts equipped with derricks, she looked almost like a regular small coaster and seemed to represent a new concept for the company.

However, this was but an illusion. In reality, ***Druid Stoke*** was little more than a 'super' ***Morvah***, owing a great deal of her design to the conservatism of Osborn & Wallis and its long association with 'the barges'. She was built without a wheelhouse and her accommodation seemed to have been almost an afterthought. These were, however, only minor items of evidence of her throwback to the barge concept. More importantly, she had no deep-bottom ballast tanks, simply a fore-and-after peak tank. Although appearing to have two separate holds and hatches, as seen from the deck where the bridge across her hold roughly half way along its length gave strength, it was in fact, just one long undivided hold. In this respect, it was a retrograde step from the clear access provided by a barge's large single hatch.

The most positive evidence of her ancestry, however, was in her machinery space. Her boiler was turned round, so that its firing end was in the engine room, instead of the usual arrangement in a ship of this size, where the boiler stokehold was separated from the engine itself by a bulkhead. The initial intention was that the engine and the boiler could be tended and operated by a single engineer. However, not surprisingly, with a 500 ihp triple-expansion engine, requiring appropriate amounts of steam from her boiler operating at 180 lbs psi, this was just too much for one man and a second Engineer or Fireman was found to be necessary. In keeping with the limited range barge mentality, she had a small bunker capacity, which meant frequent bunkering, itself a real problem due to the funnel being so close to the bridge as a result of her back-to-front boiler. The following

Druid Stoke in profile looked very different to O&W's earlier ships but her design was far less radical than it appeared for the reasons outlined in the text. She is here seen unladen and showing plenty of freeboard. However, when laden, she sat very low in the water, which made for very hard work for her crew in heavy weather. *Courtesy Bristol Museums & Art Gallery*

The Queen of the Bristol Channel ... and one of P&A Campbell's paddlers! This snapshot from the summer of 1937 shows a laden *Druid Stoke* inbound to Portishead Docks, whilst PS *Waverley* of the White Funnel Fleet ploughs past, having just taken on board a deck-load of trippers from Portishead Pier. *Alec Pope*

table gives some comparison between the machinery of ***Morvah*** and ***Druid Stoke***:

	MORVAH	DRUID STOKE
HP Cyl.	9 1/2 ins. dia.	12 3/4 ins. dia.
IP Cyl.	15 1/2 ins. dia.	22 ins. dia.
LP Cyl.	26 ins. dia.	34 ins. dia.
Boiler	9 ft. 8 1/2 ins. dia.	13 ft. dia.
	10 ft. long	10 ft. 6 ins. long

These comparatively small increases in dimensions for machinery almost doubled the ihp in ***Druid Stoke*** compared with ***Morvah*** and, ultimately, that power came from the amount of coal burnt in the furnaces, all of which had to be shovelled in by hand.

In many respects, this throwback to the barge mentality, which was obvious in her design and which included the single long well-deck, with the whole length of very limited freeboard exposed to the weather, made her hard work for her crew both on deck and down below in the engine room. She was well known by the people of Portishead and even today, when speaking to any old inhabitant about 'the Coal Boats', everyone remembers the old ***Druid Stoke*** with affection... except those who had to work her and live with her primitive accommodation.

With ***Druid Stoke*** having been built to Osborn & Wallis's specifications, Hill's were probably – and understandably – not very proud of her. However, her hull was built from excellent steel stock and she was always remarkably rust free. When chipping prior to repainting her was carried out thirty years after she was built, the plates were found to be still 'new-blue' and shiny under the many layers of paint.

Druid Stoke remained without a wheelhouse until late in 1939. The addition improved her appearance considerably and enhanced the illusion of her being a proper small ship. No doubt it increased the comfort of the Skipper and the Mate too, as they navigated the little vessel up and down the Channel during the winter months.

The second mast and its attendant derrick was, however, a real blindspot, located as it was directly in front of the steering position. In addition, it was a nuisance to the crane operators while discharging the ship. During the early 1950s, the derrick was removed but the now purposeless mast and winch were left in place. It might as well have been removed, as the ship was just less than the minimum length requiring a second masthead light and the view from the wheelhouse would have been much improved.

No other major alterations were made to ***Druid Stoke*** during her life with the company, although in due course the redundant winch for the derrick in front of the wheelhouse was also removed. She remained a useful and reliable unit of the fleet, though undeniably the 'lame duck'. She was slower than the other ships and could be relied upon to be the one shut out in any race for the locks. Her build and minimum freeboard, along the whole of her working deck length, also guaranteed that, even in the minimum of weather, her hatch boards had to be put up onto the cargo even if it was not properly distributed, to prevent them being washed about by any water coming aboard. This situation was made greatly worse when her washboards were removed in 1960 and replaced with simple bars across the resultant holes, allowing the sea free access onto as well as off the deck!

She was, in every respect, hard work compared with the other ships in the fleet. For good measure, she had winches fitted with open exhausts and when the forward winch or the capstan aft were being used, the ship would become enveloped in a cloud of steam if the weather and wind was from the wrong direction. Many were the occasions when, approaching Ely Harbour and with the need to get the working boat over the side, the exhaust steam from the winch on the foc'sle would blot out the view from the wheelhouse, and the frustrated order to "*Shut that bloody winch off*" would bellow from the wheelhouse, followed very shortly by an agitated suggestion to "*Get the boat over the side, we're nearly there!*"

In 1962, ***Druid Stoke*** tied up in the yard for the last time, shortly leaving for Ireland where, it was rumoured, there were plans to have a diesel engine installed in her for further trading. Certainly her condition would have amply justified further use. However, in the event, she was scrapped at Passage West during 1965.

Inchbrayock, later to become O&W's *Lunan*, in Bristol City Docks. On either side of her funnel, she carries a letter 'O' cut from steel sheet, dating the view to between 1913 and 1922, when she was in the ownership of the Overton Steamship Co Ltd, a Liverpool-based concern. Behind her is the massive bulk of the Corporation Granary on Princes Wharf, which was destroyed by bombing during the Second World War. Note the small foresail rigged on the foremast forestay and the ratlines on both her masts, not unusual for a ship of this period. She was, however, an odd and ill-fated little ship with a peculiar configuration, which is well shown in this view. She had an unusually long foc'sle and a well deck that extended from the foc'sle right aft to the rasied quarter deck. The usual arrangement for ships of this size and type was to have the raised quarter deck extending aft from the after end of the foreward hatch, with the bridge atop this. Instead, on *Lunan*, the bridge was situated virtually in the well-deck, severely restricting the forward view.
Courtesy Bristol Museums & Art Gallery

LUNAN Official No. 124459

Lunan was bought by O&W during 1932 as a direct result of the growing demand for coal shipments to Portishead Power Station. She was already middle aged when the company bought her and, being of only 363 grt, she was considerably smaller than the recently delivered ***Druid Stoke.*** It can be conjectured that her purchase represented a recognition by Osborn & Wallis that it had made very heavy investments in the recent past and, while an increase in shipping capacity was certainly needed, it was necessary to rein in a little and to accomplish this increase with as modest an expenditure as possible.

She was 140 feet in length, with a beam of 23 feet and had been built at Montrose in 1909 for the Grangemouth Steam Ship Company, who named her ***Inchbrayock***. Of an unusual configuration, she was an engines-aft-bridge-amidships type but with the quarter-deck not being raised until the aftermost section. With a long raised foc'sle, this meant that her midships bridge was, in effect, built on the low well-deck, which must have given a good view of the

Right: This silhouette view of *Lunan* in the Bristol Channel shows off her lines well.

Below: With her bow almost rising out of the water, an empty *Lunan* heads down the Bristol Avon sometime in the 1930s, with the Portway visible behind. Note the wheelhouse positioned on the well-deck, not a good arrangement. In this view it can be seen that forward vision when sailing empty was rather restricted by the height of the bow, hence the seaman positioned by the forward mast to keep an eye as they negotiate the navigable channel of the river. The view was even worse when the sail was rigged!

Both courtesy Bristol Museums & Art Gallery

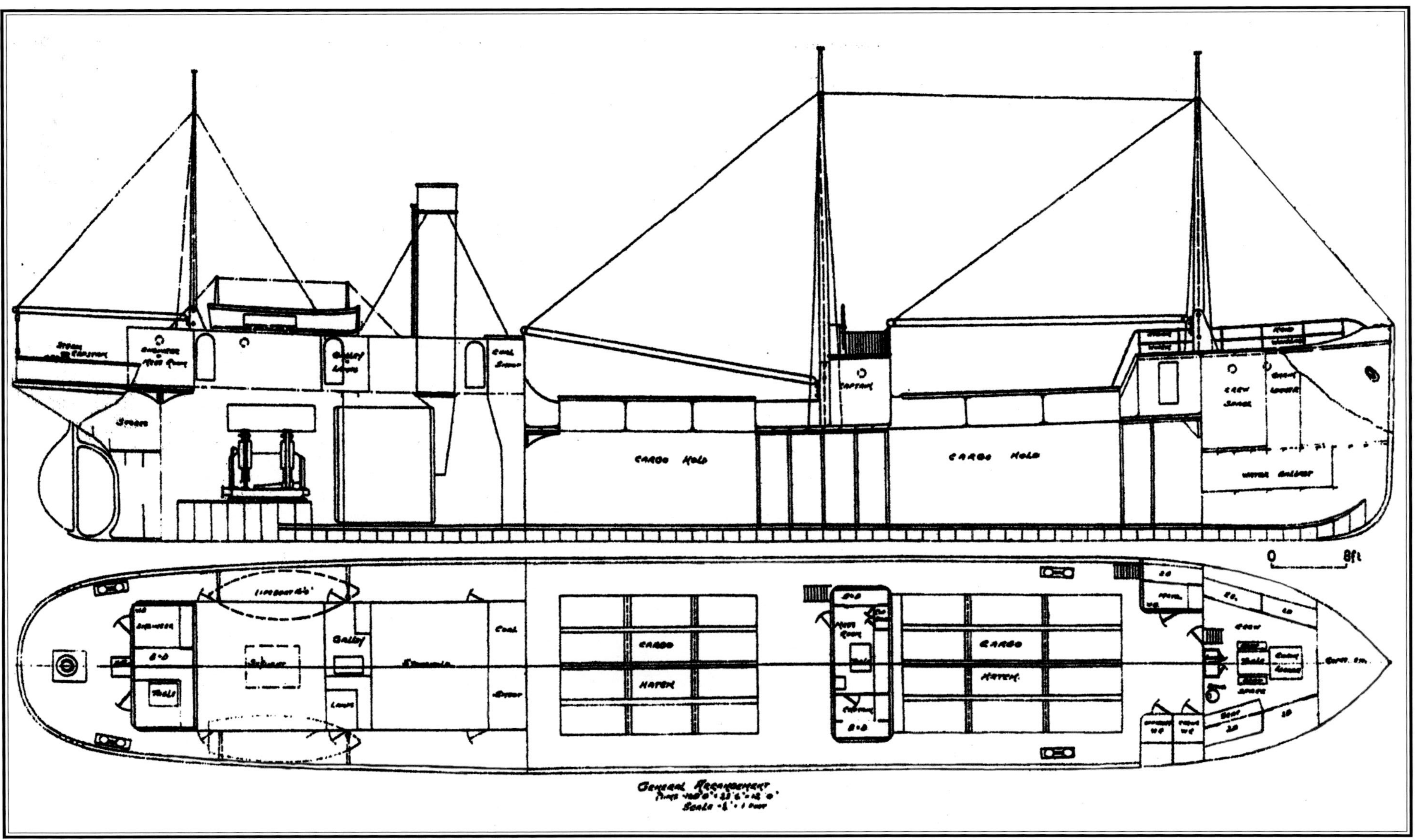

GENERAL ARRANGEMENT DRAWING
S.S. INCHBRAYOCK

foc'sle head deck but little else, especially when the sail on the forestay was rigged. Whether this had any bearing on her frequent changes of ownership, by making her somewhat unhandy, can only be speculated upon.

Inchbrayock was only four years old when, during 1913, she was sold to the Overton Steamship Company Ltd, with whom she stayed until 1920. In that year, she again changed hands, being sold to owners in Bray near Dublin. However, she quickly passed to new Tyneside owners trading as the Inchbrayock Steam Ship Company Ltd. In 1927, she moved to Dundee, where her new owners, Robert Taylor & Sons, renamed her *Lunan*.

Her final move in this rather chequered career occurred in December 1931, when she was bought by O&W who, as they generally did with second-hand vessels, retained her name. She worked steadily for the company and at last seemed settled with an owner, until her career was brought to a tragic end in the early years of the Second World War.

THE LOSS OF THE LUNAN

On 4th July 1941, in the mouth of the River Ely, at position 51. 26. 48 N, 03. 10. 24 W having just left one of the tips in Ely Harbour loaded with coal for Portishead Power Station, *Lunan* struck a German mine. The size of the explosion indicated that it was a landmine, which had probably been dropped out of position during a heavy raid on Cardiff and its docks.

The ship was completely destroyed, being blown into two pieces. The sole survivor of her crew of six was Fred Base, her Chief Engineer, who was found clinging to the wreckage. It was reported that coal from her cargo was found in the streets of Penarth as far as half a mile away.

A tragedy for the families of the men killed, clearly it was also a major disaster for the company and for the crews of the other ships. There were fathers, sons, brothers and other relatives serving as members of the crews in the Osborn & Wallis ships and, as might be imagined, it was a company where everyone was personally known to one another.

The loss of the ship itself created problems for the already pressured company, which had no spare capacity in its task of fuelling the power station at Portishead, as well as helping to supply coal for the power station at Gloucester. In due course, O&W obtained a modern and much larger motor coaster, albeit with a damaged engine. Eventually to be renamed *Salcombe,* this ship was the direct replacement for *Lunan*. The company was also granted the management of two brand new 'Severn Collier' Class ships, in order to cover their Gloucester commitment.

The wrecked *Lunan* lying in the mouth of the River Ely in 1941. The process of cutting the ship into manageable pieces is underway and long cut lines down through the depth of the hull can be seen. Note the work boat carrying oxygen and acetylene bottles near the stern. There is a smashed navigation light to the right of the workboat. The wires running across the mud were used to drag the pieces of the vessel ashore for disposal and many of her fittings, masts, etc, have already been removed. *Courtesy National Railway Museum*

Another view of the wrecked *Lunan*, with the Victoria Oil Farm, the old iron ore wharf and one of the river tips where she had loaded visible in the background. The photographs show clearly how the detached bow section of the ship lay right across the centre of the navigation channel. A temporary warning light can be seen rigged over the wreck. The force of the explosion, sufficient to break the loaded bow section completely off, turn it right over and throw it across the river bed at right angles to the after end of the ship, can only be imagined. It was a wonder that anyone survived the explosion, even more so that the one person who did was her Chief Engineer, who was in the Engine Room, at the bottom of the ship, when the disaster occurred. The explosion would appear to have occurred directly under her mid-ships bridge.
Courtesy National Railway Museum

The transcript of a page from a diary kept by Miss Gwyneth White of Penarth. Miss White maintained her diary right through the Second World War and her description of *Lunan*, made at the time, is the only independent record of the ship's loss. The author was supplied this diary extract in late 2003 by Miss White and although then aged 93, her recollections of the events of those far off years were vivid and completely lucid. Although her account has some errors in it (the number of crew and the incorrect statement that the sole survivor had eventually died), consideration must be given to the fact that she wrote her diary at a time of great secrecy and suppression of bad news. Only the month before, during August, the Government had imposed a total blackout on newspapers and newsreels publishing the statistics of shipping losses so as to avoid further damaging the nation's morale. This explains why, despite considerable effort, it was impossible to find any contemporary mention of the disaster in the local newspapers of the time.

THURSDAY JULY 3RD

Still wonderful weather though I was too busy to avail myself of it outdoors. Tonight, I was fire watching and certainly expecting the warble, when just after coming in from investigating a distant throbbing which might have been a hum, at 1.15am (Friday), there was a colossal explosion which seemed to jolt the whole house. I rushed outside but beyond the sound of wardens and other watchers doing the same, there wasn't a sound to be heard and no siren broke the silence though I stayed up till 4am expecting it. Today (Friday) we were shocked and appalled to learn the origin. A coasting steamer "Lunan", which had been loading coal for the Bristol gasworks had struck a mine in the mouth of the Ely river parallel with Penarth Dock. It must have been the companion of that which landed ON the dock and had been lying in the water and mud since Tuesday, overlooked. We haven't been able to ascertain if it's known whether it was a land or magnetic mine, but the net result was awfully the same. The ship, which is still visible at low tide, sank with the loss of all its crew of 7. One man was rescued but died later of his injuries. It would have been miraculous if anyone at the centre of that terrific blast HAD lived to tell the tale. It was bitter irony to hear on the news that there had been no enemy activity over this country last night. That throbbing I heard must have been the ship's engines. Tonight there was nothing to keep one awake and those who had to probably didn't.

The wreck of ***Lunan*** obstructed the navigation channel and the access to Ely Harbour was already difficult, due to the absence of navigation lights in the river because of the wartime blackout. The ship was clearly not recoverable, so the clearance of the river mouth became the priority. Accordingly, ***Lunan*** was cut up where she lay. Three of her crew, her First Officer, her Second Engineer and one of her Seamen, lie buried in the Penarth UDC Cemetery, just off Lavernock Road (see page 188).

During 1933, a further major acquisition by Osborn & Wallis occurred when they bought and occupied the premises in Hotwells which had once been the ship building and repair yard of G.K. Stothert Ltd. A major site in Bristol's ship building and repair history, it included a large dry dock, although this was of a peculiar curved shape. The existing office block was retained and remained completely unaltered even after Osborn & Wallis sold the yard during 1970. It remains today, largely unaltered, as a listed building. The dry dock itself (also the subject of a preservation order), although never again used as such, was altered in shape at its landward end so that although the curve remained on one side, the other side was straightened to give it an unusual tapered shape. A large span Telfer crane was erected, enabling ships to lie in the ex-dry dock basin for discharge, a service which was not just confined to the company's own ships – the crane provided a source of income by servicing other owners vessels too.

SNEYD (2) Official No. 128966

In 1936, only four years after the purchase of ***Lunan***, O&W were again on the lookout for another vessel and, still with an eye for keeping expenditure down, they purchased a small steamer from John S. Monks Ltd of Liverpool. This was another middle-aged and much travelled vessel, built in 1910 by R. Williamson & Son of Workington and named ***Glanoventa***. Her length of 141 feet and beam of 24 feet gave her a grt of 401. She was fitted with a compound engine built by Ross & Duncan Ltd of Glasgow.

During 1915, the ship was sold to John Harrison Ltd of London, who renamed her ***Horsham***. She was very quickly nominally transferred to the Horsham Steamship Company Ltd of London, managed by H. Harrison. She stayed in this ownership for only two years and was then sold again during 1917 to Thomas Walker & Company Ltd of Hull.

Sneyd, photographed probably not long after O&W bought her in 1936.
Courtesy Bristol Museums & Art Gallery

Main picture: A superb study of *Sneyd*, sitting clear of the water alongside one of the wooden coal tips – probably No. 3 Tip – on the River Ely outside Penarth Docks, taken on 16th April 1938. Some of the crew can be seen sat atop the bridge, enjoying the spring sunshine, whilst waiting for departure on the next tide. *Courtesy Bristol Museums & Art Gallery*
Inset: *Sneyd*'s engine builder's plate. *Author*

In 1924, she was bought by E.G. Wallis of London who, in 1926, floated a new company, Guernsey Coasters Ltd (E.G. Wallis, manager), to which the vessel was transferred or sold. Presumably their trade lay in plying down the English Channel to the Channel Islands. During 1930, she was sold yet again, this time to the St. Baldred Shipping Company Ltd, managed by A. Tate & Co of Newcastle. Two years later, in 1932, she changed hands once more, being purchased by John S. Monks Ltd of Liverpool and renamed ***Crestville***. She was finally bought by Osborn & Wallis in 1936, who promptly renamed her ***Sneyd*** (after another area of Bristol).

Certainly in her O&W days, ***Sneyd*** had an unfortunate tendency to stop her two-cylinder engine in the 'centred' position, necessitating an urgent turning of the engine by hand a short distance to admit steam into one of the cylinders on its working stroke. This was particularly awkward during any manoeuvring and required a prompt response to an "*Astern*" call from the bridge. Like ***Lunan***, she was a retrograde step to ships of a size and type from an earlier era and, with her open bridge, was not a comfortable vessel to work, either for her skipper, her crew or her engine room staff.

After the war, ***Sneyd*** became increasingly unreliable and, as a result, her boiler was given an extensive rebuild and overhaul during the early 1950s. However, she did very little work after that and, during 1953, she was laid up in the yard at Bristol, although officially kept in reserve until the recently ordered new-build vessels were available. The end came in 1957, when she was towed across the floating harbour to Hill's Yard, where the newly refurbished boiler was taken out of her. With this completed, ***Sneyd*** was towed across the Bristol Channel to Cashmore's yard at Newport, arriving there on 7th June 1957 for breaking up.

DOWNLEAZE Official No. 148277

Osborn & Wallis's next acquisition was a vessel built in 1924 by the Goole Shipbuilding & Repair Company, their Yard No. 255, which also was to have several identities. Completed in December of that year for the Miskin Manor Shipping Company (Scriven & Reid) of Cardiff, she began life as ***Southwell***. She was 156 feet 2 inches long, with a beam of 25 feet 6 inches and a grt of 486, and was a well proportioned vessel with bridge amidships but no wheelhouse as was usual, being typical of the size and type of coaster common at this time. Fitted with a triple-expansion engine from C.D. Holmes & Co of Hull, she was capable of 9 knots.

In 1930, she was sold to the Richard England Steam Ship Company (R.P. Care & Co), of Cardiff. In 1936, she was bought by the Ald Shipping Company of Bristol, who renamed her ***Farleigh Combe***. At the same time, the Ald Shipping Co bought another almost identical ship, of the same size and tonnage, the only difference being that the second vessel had a very slightly taller funnel and had a wheelhouse. An exact copy of this wheelhouse was later fitted to ***Farleigh Combe***, making the two vessels virtually indistinguishable.

In 1938, Osborn & Wallis bought ***Farleigh Combe*** from Ald Shipping and changed her name to ***Downleaze***. She also lost the very smart light grey livery of the Ald fleet,

O&W's *Downleaze* seen here in her original guise of *Southwell*, sometime in the early 1930s when in the ownership of the Richard England SS Co. She was more compact in appearance than O&W's earlier coasting colliers and is riding high in the water as she heads off to collect another cargo. Note the lack of a wheelhouse at this stage in the vessel's life. *Courtesy Bristol Museums & Art Gallery*

Left: *Downleaze* in 1946, still carrying the frame for the Carley Float Liferaft, fitted in 1944 when she was on war service running to the Normandy beaches. It can be seen alongside her funnel.
Courtesy Bristol Museums and Art Gallery

Opposite page top: *Downleaze* alongside the tug *Hudson* in the Cumberland Basin, Bristol, in August 1960. Although she looks in fine shape, the tug was about to tow her across the North Sea to the Netherlands for scrapping.
Jim Crissup

adopting instead O&W's black hull with red lead band of boot topping and brown upperworks, along with the red leaded funnel with black top.

As ***Downleaze***, she was involved in the supply shuttle to the Normandy beaches in the weeks immediately following the Allied invasion of Europe in 1944. She was at this time fitted with a Carley Float Liferaft and the launching frame for this was placed adjacent to her funnel on the port side.

Returning to the Bristol Channel, she rejoined the rest of the O&W fleet in bringing coal to the power station at Portishead and she remained a useful and well-liked ship.

During 1957, she was taken across to Hill's Yard, where her by now troublesome boiler was removed and the rebuilt one recently removed from ***Sneyd*** was installed. Once again, however, this boiler was not called upon to do any work, as the ship was laid up in reserve. New build tonnage added to the fleet enabled ***Downleaze*** to be kept as first reserve, just as ***Sneyd*** had been before her.

In August 1960, ***Downleaze*** left Bristol for the last time, looking very smart. Under tow by the tug ***Hudson***, she arrived at Krimpen, Holland, on 22nd August for scrapping. Her boiler, however, finally found useful work, as it was not scrapped but was sold instead to serve as a heating unit for a large glasshouse farm in Holland's flower growing industry.

Downleaze in the Company's dock at Hotwells sometime in the late 1950s, following fitting of her new boiler and when she was in use as 'first reserve' for the O&W fleet.
Capt. C. Reynolds

ROCKLEAZE Official No. 147248

The next vessel to join the Osborn & Wallis fleet, in 1939, was ***Downleaze***'s twin, built in the same year,1924, and by the same company, the Goole Shipbuilding & Repair Co. Built to their Yard No. 253, indicating she was finished slightly before her sister, they were almost identical apart from the choice of engine builders. The vessel was fitted with triple-expansion machinery supplied by William Beardmore & Co Ltd of Speedwell Ironworks, Coatbridge and was built for the Clwyd Steamship Company (R. & D. Jones Ltd) of Liverpool. Launched on 23rd February 1924, she was completed during April of the same year and was named ***Glynconwy***.

The new vessel had the same dimensions as ***Southwell***, being 156 feet long with a 25 feet beam and having an identical grt of 486. Presumably, Goole Shipbuilding were working to a standard small coasting collier design of their own and it would be interesting to know whether Yard No. 254, the vessel completed in between the two sisters, was also of the same type and dimensions.

During 1929, ***Glynconwy*** was sold to R. & W. Paul Ltd of Ipswich, who renamed her ***Goldcrest***. She remained with this company until September 1934, when, in a prelude to the career path that her sister was to follow, she was bought by the Ald Shipping Company Ltd of Bristol. They again changed her name, this time to ***Monkton Combe***.

O&W's *Rockleaze* in one of her previous incarnations as *Goldcrest*. The location is Bristol City Docks and the photograph was taken shortly after she had been bought by the Ald Shipping Co in September 1934 but before her new owners changed her name, which occurred on 29th October. Note the funnel has been repainted, however, and sports the company's large 'A'. *Courtesy Bristol Museums & Art Gallery*

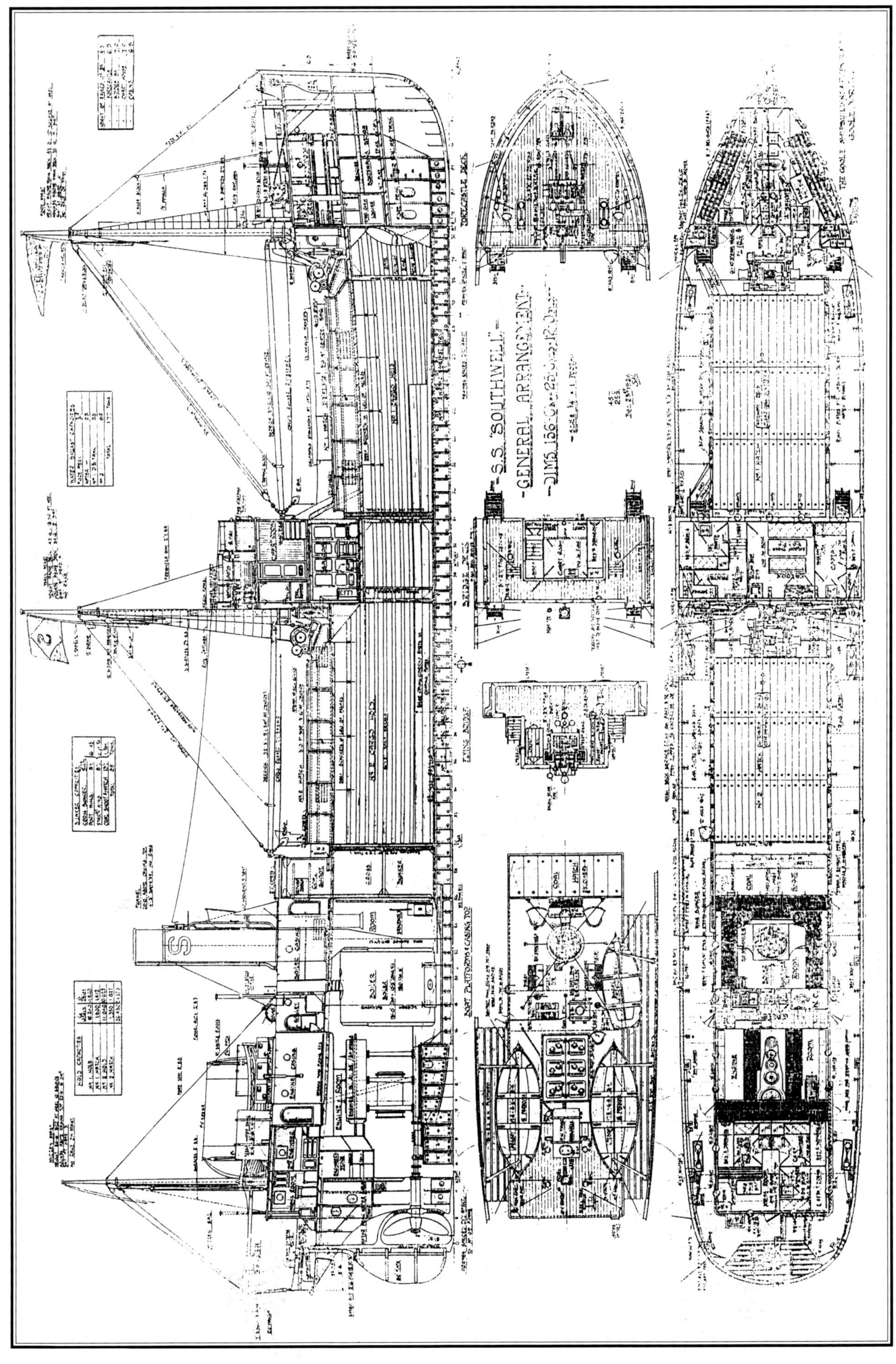
S.S. "SOUTHWELL"
GENERAL ARRANGEMENT
BRIDGE DECK
BOAT PLATFORMS & CASING TOP

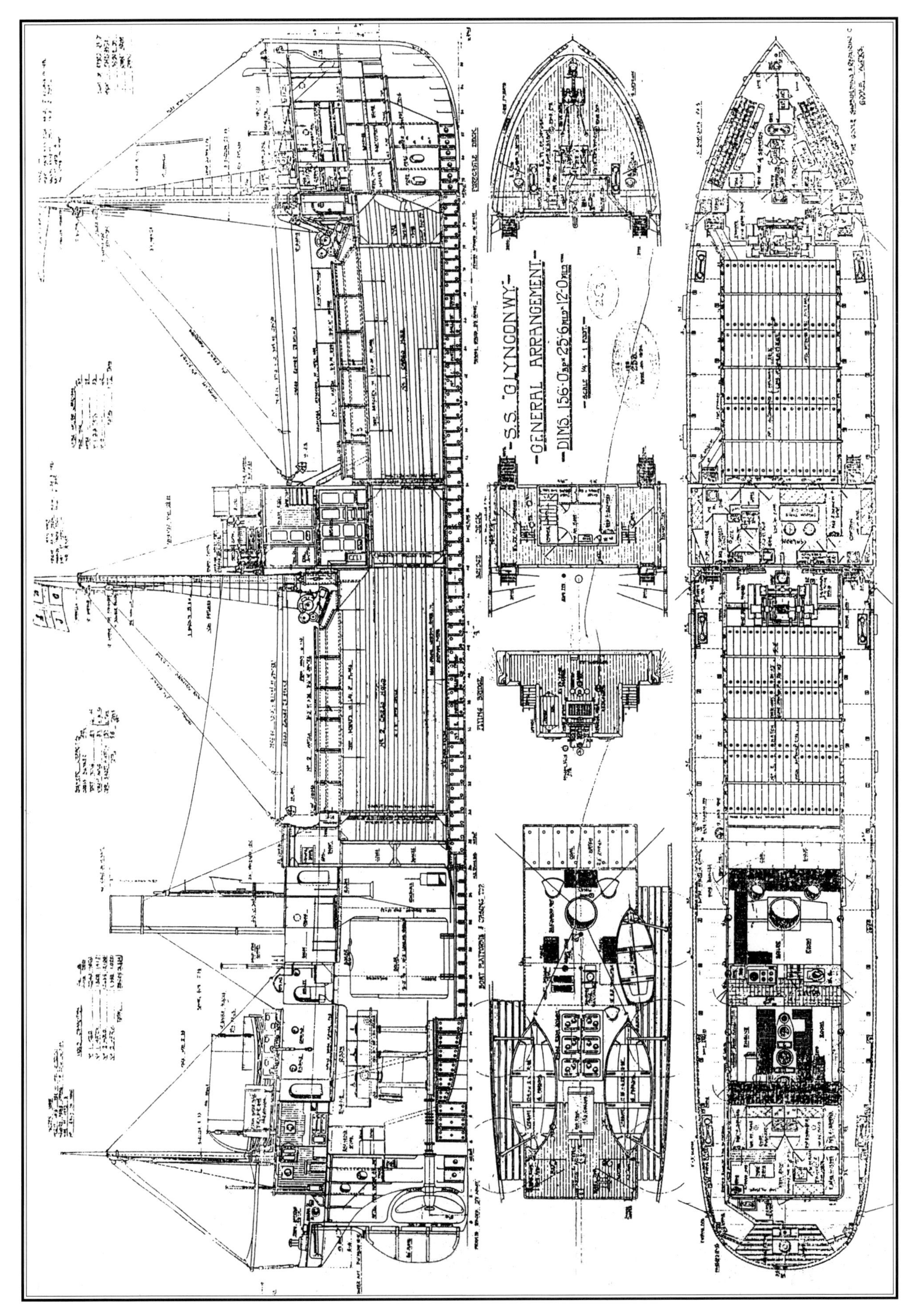
S.S. "GLYNCONWY"
GENERAL ARRANGEMENT

Now renamed *Monkton Combe* and resplendent in the Ald Shipping Co's light grey livery, the coaster was photographed unloading in Bristol City Docks on 2nd July 1936, with one of the goods warehouses of the London Midland & Scottish Railway forming a backdrop.
Courtesy Bristol Museums & Art Gallery

In 1936, she was joined in the Ald fleet by ***Southwell***, which they renamed ***Farleigh Combe***. The two look-alike ships, built in the same yard, at almost the same time but for different owners, were together again. Two years later, in 1938, they were split up once more when ***Farleigh Combe*** was bought by Osborn & Wallis and renamed ***Downleaze***. They were not to be parted for long though, for with O&W's need for extra capacity, they could do no better than to buy ***Downleaze***'s twin sister from Ald Shipping. Consequently, in January 1939, ***Monkton Combe*** also swapped her grey livery for that of the O&W fleet and her name was changed to ***Rockleaze***.

Like her sister, ***Rockleaze*** was a handsome little ship with the same turn of speed when pushed and the twins were well-liked in the fleet. She, too, joined in the supply line to the invasion beaches in Normandy and was also fitted with a Carley Float Liferaft launch frame and this remained in place until late 1947. ***Rockleaze*** returned from her war service with a very sharp and severe kink in her stem bar, caused by her accidentally running into one of the Mulberry Harbour units on the Normandy beaches.

After a long and useful life in the Bristol Channel, she left Bristol Docks for the last time, under tow, on 5th May 1958 and, by now looking extremely woebegone and neglected, was taken to Llanelly for scrapping by the Rees Shipbreaking Company Ltd.

Left: *Rockleaze*, seen here on 27th June 1947, still sporting the Carley Float Liferaft launcher alongside her funnel, which was fitted in 1944 when she was on war service.
Courtesy Bristol Museums & Art Gallery

Below: In sad contrast, the tired and rusting vessel is seen shortly after departing on her last voyage on 5th May 1958. She was bound for Llanelly for scrapping.
Chris Witts

WILLIAM BEARDMORE & CO. LTD
ENGINEERS.
SPEEDWELL IRON WORKS
COATBRIDGE.
Nº 568.

Rockleaze's engine builder's plate.

Author

ST. VINCENT (2) Official No. 166045

Having already invested heavily in ***Downleaze*** and ***Rockleaze*** during 1938 and 1939, and with war now looming, O&W took the brave decision to invest in what was, for them, a radical departure from previous acquisitions. In 1939, they ordered a further new-build from Charles Hill's, to be built to their Yard No. 276.

The new ship was to be larger than anything they already had in service and furthermore, it was to be diesel powered. ***St. Vincent***, as the new ship was to be named, would be a genuine medium-sized coaster, with good accommodation and proper ballasting. The ship was to be an entirely different concept to the company's last new-build, ***Druid Stoke***, which owed so much to the earlier barges. With a raised foc'sle and quarter-deck, a well-deck forward and with full deep-bottom tank ballasting, the ship was clearly in a different category altogether and was to be the basis of all further vessels that the company had constructed.

St. Vincent was 160 feet long, with a beam of 27 feet and a grt of 484. She was fitted with steel roller hatches for the forward hold, and conventional beam and board hatches for the main hold.

Her main engine was a Ruston & Hornsby six-cylinder 6VEBXM fitted with a Napier turbo-blower, which drove a 7 foot diameter, four-bladed propeller through an MWD gearbox. She had a four-cylinder Ruston & Hornsby VRO auxiliary engine for the generation of electricity, compressed air pumping and ballast pumping. A further small R&H engine gave power for battery topping while the ship was in port for any length of time.

Incidentally, the main engine is the earliest example of the VEBXM recorded in the Ruston & Hornsby archive and it is believed to have been placed on display by the company at a large engineering exhibition held during 1939. Certainly, the engine was beautifully finished and lined above the normal standard for industrial plant. It was sold to Charles Hill by R&H on 12th February 1940.

The ship was completed during 1940 and delivered to O&W. With the war having begun, she was painted grey, and her wooden wheelhouse was given steel armoured protection.

Having worked through the difficult war years without mishap, ***St. Vincent*** achieved fame for the wrong reasons on 17th February 1949. Returning in thick fog from Penarth Ely Harbour and loaded with coal for the power station, she went aground on Black Nore Point, Portishead. Two

An official Ruston & Hornsby photograph of the VEBXM engine, as fitted in *St. Vincent* in 1940 and the first of its type. R&H are believed to have taken the engine to an engineering exhibition when it was first built, hence its showroom finish. *Courtesy Ruston & Hornsby archive*

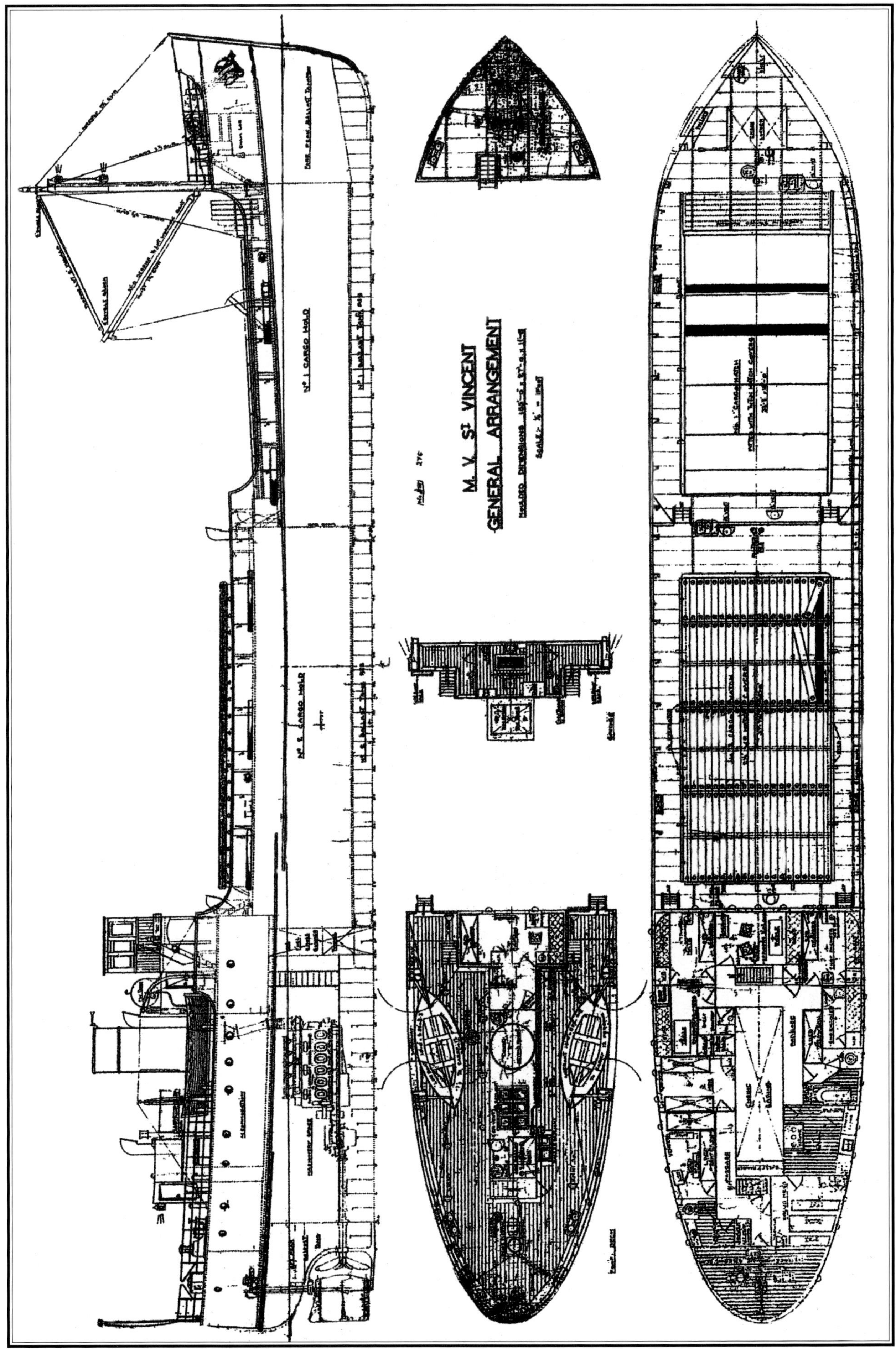
M. V. St VINCENT
GENERAL ARRANGEMENT
No 1 CARGO HOLD
No 2 CARGO HOLD

The recently completed *St. Vincent* alongside the discharging berth for Portishead Power Station in 1940. Her wartime grey livery will be noted and also the armour plated wheelhouse, just forward of the funnel. *Courtesy Ruston & Hornsby archive*

Bristol tugs, ***Kingsgarth*** and ***Plumgarth***, tried to pull her free but failed to do so and the decision was made to jettison much of her cargo to lighten her. There was insufficient depth of water to get even a small craft alongside to save the coal and it was simply shovelled over the side by hand. The ship became a local spectacle and her plight received much press coverage.

Much of the dumped cargo was spirited away but was doubtless a huge disappointment to its salvors, since it was low-grade coal which would only burn slowly in normal circumstances and produced a thick green smoke. It was incapable of burning properly without the forced draught conditions in the power station furnaces.

After four days aground, at the fourth attempt ***St. Vincent*** was successfully towed into deeper water and she then proceeded to Portishead, to complete the discharge of the remainder of her cargo. Fortunately, she was not damaged at all, having run aground on what was mainly a mud bank. Just a few yards further would have had her sitting on very uneven rocks which, given her loaded condition, could have

St. Vincent circa 1946-47, now wearing the standard O&W colours and with the wheelhouse armour removed. Note the resemblance of her wheelhouse and bridge to that of *Druid Stoke* – still a lingering echo from the past. Note too that the wheelhouse is the only passageway from one side of the bridge to the other. The steel hatch covers to the forward hold can be seen in their stowed position under the mast and derrick. The lack of freeboard at the after end of the welldeck can be clearly seen when assessed against the Load line, something which was addressed when O&W's next ship, *Hotwells* (nominally *St. Vincent*'s sister ship) was built in 1949-50. *Capt. C. Reynolds*

O&W's motor coaster *St. Vincent* aground off Black Nore Point in February 1949, with a relic of an earlier coasting age, believed to be the schooner *Kathleen & May*, sailing serenely past (albeit under power from her auxiliary engine) in the background. *St. Vincent* sustained no damage and, after partial unloading of her cargo, was eventually floated free. *Author*

been a serious situation for the ship. Dense fogs, often lasting for several days, were the biggest peril to small ships working the upper Bristol Channel at that time.

During 1950, new maritime legislation was brought in which decreed that any ship over 150 feet in length must carry two masthead lights and ***St. Vincent*** was modified accordingly. She remained as a useful part of the fleet right up until the end of O&W's ship-owning commitment in 1969 when, along with the other remaining ships, she was sold to new owners for future trading elsewhere.

A post-1950 view of *St. Vincent* in the River Usk, after fitting of the new mainmast and masthead light. Newport transporter bridge is visible in the background. *Chris Witts*

Opposite page: An aerial view of Portishead Power Station taken during 1948, with expansion of the Turbine Hall and Boiler House under way. The base for the second chimney can be seen just above the roof. Note the existing buildings and the chimney are still in wartime camouflage paint. Also of interest in this view are Dock Mill, operated by E. Baily & Sons Ltd, and the Granaries on the extreme right, with Portishead railway station and the Burlington Café (at the end of the footbridge) bottom left. All of this was to be swept away when the second even larger power station was built in the 1950s. Much of the O&W fleet can be seen in the photograph; *St. Vincent* is in the New Berth, at the bottom of the picture, whilst astern of her, in the Dock Office berth, is *Downleaze*. Behind *Downleaze* is *Rockleaze*, still with her Carley Float Liferaft launcher in place, and alongside her is *Salcombe*. Astern of this pair, at an angle, is *Sneyd*. *Author's collection*

The major expansion of Portishead Power Station during 1948-49, was but a foretaste of the future. This was a time of enormous increase in the demand for electricity and the Nationalisation of the industry was in hand. The proposal to build a second even larger power station at Portishead was already on the table, and the studies and engineering preparations had been done by the Bristol Corporation Electricity Department. Although Portishead 'B' Power Station was eventually built under the newly nationalised industry, it was completed to the design and specification already drawn up by Bristol City Council.

Osborn & Wallis were, of course, aware of all of this and the resultant increase in coal requirement that would go with it and knew that they themselves would need considerably more shipping capacity in order to meet this demand. Accordingly, they had begun negotiations with Charles Hill for a further three ships.

SALCOMBE Official No. 166428

In July 1941, O&W had suffered a grievous loss when ***Lunan*** had been destroyed by a mine off Penarth. However, with able-bodied men being called up, undoubtedly a greater loss to the company at the time were the five crew members killed in the explosion. Although ***Lunan*** herself was by then not a major unit within the fleet, her demise nevertheless left a gap in the scheduling of the ships in the vital task of fuelling the power station, now itself under great pressure due to the demands of war production. Although the company had bought the two steamers ***Downleaze*** and ***Rockleaze*** only two or three years previously, whilst just a year had passed since taking delivery of the new ***St. Vincent***, there was still a gap in the running programme caused by ***Lunan***'s loss and this needed to be filled. Accordingly, representations were made to the appropriate Government Ministry seeking assistance with this problem. A response was to come under somewhat unusual circumstances.

The Newcastle Coal Shipping Company had a fleet of ships carrying out a similar task to that of O&W but on the East Coast, running coal from the northern coalfields to the power stations located on the Thames. All of their ships bore the name ***Camroux***, along with a Roman numeral suffix denoting their number in the fleet and they were heavily built to withstand the rigours of the North Sea. The ships were of very low profile, with lowerable masts to enable them to pass under the Thames bridges. In 1938, the Newcastle Coal Shipping Co had taken delivery from T. van Duivendijk's Scheepswerf N.V. at Lekkerkerk, Holland of a brand new ship, the biggest in their fleet at 590 grt, with a length of 162 feet and a beam of 28 feet. This was ***Camroux IV***.

The ship was fitted with a normally aspirated, eight-cylinder diesel engine of German (Deutz) manufacture. Cooling was by direct seawater circulation. It was coupled directly to the propeller shaft without a gearbox and sternway was accomplished by means of stopping the engine, sliding the camshaft along by means of a large lever to a different set of cams, which altered the valve events and injection timing, and then re-starting the engine which would now run backwards.

Early during 1941, while going about her business, ***Camroux IV*** was unfortunate enough to be near a mine which exploded but which was not sufficiently close to do any actual apparent damage. However, two days later the engine's crankshaft broke, and this was attributed to shock and concussion damage from the explosion. Investigations showed that the crankshaft had broken at the front of the engine (away from the driving flywheel end). It broke in such a way that the No. 2 main bearing remained intact and was thus supporting the No. 2 cylinder's big end but No. 1 cylinder and its big end bearing was detached and isolated from the length of the crankshaft.

This being wartime, spare parts for the German-built engine were of course unobtainable, so the decision was made to remove the piston and connecting rod from No. 1 cylinder and to leave the engine running as a seven-cylinder unit. This of course created vibration and also reduced the

A rather poor quality view of *Camroux IV* when newly built and lettered on the hull with the name of her original owner. *Author's collection*

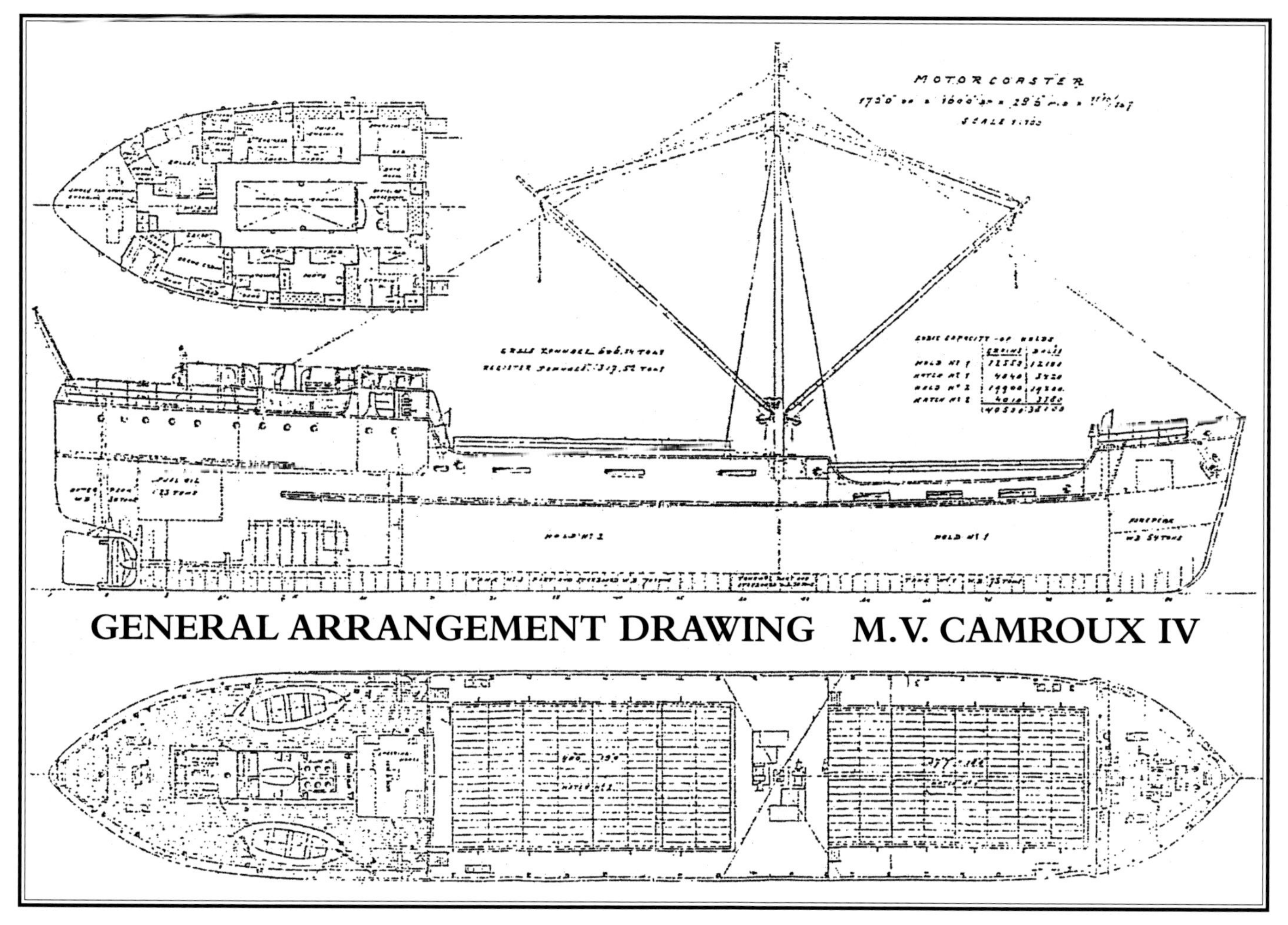

GENERAL ARRANGEMENT DRAWING M.V. CAMROUX IV

ship's speed but it was seen as the best compromise available at the time. The fact she was virtually brand new and, at 730 tons cargo capacity, relatively large and valuable, obviously influenced this thinking. However, bearing in mind her reduced speed, there were concerns at her vulnerability to aircraft and E-Boat attack in the North Sea.

With Osborn & Wallis making requests for an additional ship to help maintain supplies of coal for Portishead Power Station, it was decided to send ***Camroux IV*** round to the Bristol Channel, where the shorter journeys and greater distance from enemy aircraft and surface raiders would make for a safer environment for her. However, the circumstances under which she was needed, following the loss of ***Lunan***, indicated that nowhere was totally safe during the war.

Camroux IV was therefore purchased by O&W during 1942. The first need was to demount the central large and cumbersome mast, with its two derricks. This was replaced with a much shorter mast mounted on the after end of the forecastle, to carry the derrick for the working boat and the single masthead navigation light required at the time. She retained the anti-aircraft machine gun mounting fitted aft of the funnel. She also kept her DEMS Gunner, whose responsibility the guns were. The original large mast and derricks were left lying on the ground in O&W's yard at Hotwells and were still there during the 1950s.

The ship was still only four years old when she was bought by O&W and of particularly stout construction. Following her purchase, she was renamed ***Salcombe***. Her peculiar appearance, arising from the special needs of her original owners, meant that she was always something of an oddity within the fleet and, as the years passed, she came to stand out from the other ships even more by virtue of her engine and machinery. As well as her German-built main engine, she was fitted with two Paxman Ricardo two-cylinder

Below: This photograph of *Salcombe* was taken very early in her career with Osborn & Wallis. Note the machine gun mounting on the Engine Room casing. *Author's collection*

auxiliaries but when these expired much later in her life, they were replaced with Ruston & Hornsby three-cylinder units. Indeed, all of the machinery in Osborn & Wallis motorships, other than in ***Salcombe***, was of Ruston & Hornsby manufacture. She was also the largest ship engaged in O&W's coal carrying business, which was later to become more important with the impending enlargement of the power station.

In keeping with her original need to pass under the River Thames bridges, she had been built with a very squat funnel, which was no higher than the top of the wheelhouse. This created uncomfortable conditions both in the wheelhouse itself and in the accommodation, the entrances to which were common with that of the engine room and located at deck level on the after end of the deckhouse.

In 1946, O&W ordered a new crankshaft to be made by a South Wales engineering firm but the restrictions on work and materials in the post-war climate, and the fact that it had to be made to metric measurements, meant that it was not delivered to Hill's dockyard until late in 1947. The Chief Engineer had been 'bought' with the ship and he took the first opportunity to inspect his new crankshaft, immediately declaring it to be "*No good*". He pointed out, quite rightly, that two of the crank throws had been transposed during the design and manufacturing process. Having waited so long for their expensive crankshaft, there was great concern until the Chief Engineer, having quietly pondered the problem for a few minutes, announced that the quickest and cheapest way out of this dreadful position was to have a new camshaft made, which would re-time the valve events and the fuel injection sequence to match the out-of-step crankshaft. This was done quickly by the engineering firm, anxious to close the door on this unfortunate episode and the crankshaft and camshaft were duly fitted.

The engine ran in this condition for the rest of its life, with no ill-effects from the out of sequence firing order other than, if allowed to get low on bunkers, the ship would hop and bounce at the after end, a situation easily remedied by always keeping sufficient bunkers on board to ensure that the stern was down in the water. Indeed, a threepenny bit could be stood on the engine while it was started up and run right up to its 230 rpm maximum. The weight of this extra ballast of fuel was not sufficient to affect her loading capacity, as it was not sufficient to replace a further railway wagon-load of coal.

While this work was going on, the opportunity was taken to remove the primitive Radio Direction Finding gear and to extend the funnel top by about two feet. This worked remarkably well in keeping the fumes from the wheelhouse and the accommodation, as well as providing a convenient site for the traditional O&W black top to the funnel!

With the 1950 legislation requiring ships of over 150 feet in length to carry a second masthead light, one of her original derricks was used and planted immediately forward of the wheelhouse, whilst her other original derrick served in the capacity of mainmast on the ***St. Vincent***. Apart from the visual obstruction, the mast was so close to the after end of the main hatch that it was a complete nuisance to the chutes on the tips when loading and again to the cranes while discharging and, in both situations, the stays supporting the mast had to be let go. It was an untidy and ill thought out solution, which led to so many incidents that, in 1962, the mast was removed and relocated on the after end of the deckhouse, with two supporting legs.

Above: This side profile of *Salcombe*, heading in to Portishead on 27th June 1947, gives a good indication of how different in appearance she was to the rest of the O&W fleet, with her cut down funnel and superstructure. *Author's collection*

Opposite page top: Riding high in the water, *Salcombe* is seen in the River Usk approaching the entrance lock to Newport Docks to collect another load of coal in April 1959. The remasting, carried out to accommodate the new navigation lights, created numerous problems as outlined in the text. The funnel had also been heightened by a couple of feet. *Courtesy John Clarkson*

Opposite page bottom: *Salcombe* in the lock at Newport, with a glimpse of the *St. Vincent* on the left. Note the workboat still connected to the derrick which had been used to lift it onto the coal in the forward hold following completion of loading and note also that the rear mast has been moved to a more amenable position. *Chris Collard*

SALCOMBE

SALCOMBE

EMPIRE RUNNER Official No. 169093
EMPIRE TOWNSMAN Official No. 169088

In 1943, O&W were charged with the management and operation of two small ships, newly-built, which belonged to the Ministry of War Transport (MoWT). They were two of a class of six ships, four of which had been built by Richard Dunstan Ltd and the other two by John Harker Ltd, both based in Yorkshire. All were registered at Goole.

Appropriately named the 'Severn Collier' Class, they were 148 feet long, with a 22 feet beam and could carry 350 tons of cargo. Fitted with a diesel engine, they were capable of 8 knots. The two which came to O&W were ***Empire Runner*** and ***Empire Townsman***, both Richard Dunstan-built ships. According to an old ex-O&W sailor, they were not crewed by O&W men (the company was short of men in any case).

They were not used exclusively for supplying Portishead Power Station but also helped with the supply of coal for that at Gloucester as well. There were problems of access to Gloucester Power Station, however, and extra dredging was required. It was also necessary to manoeuvre the ships into the Gloucester Docks stern first. It was the arrival of these two craft which allowed the release of ***Downleaze*** and ***Rockleaze*** for other war duties for just over a year, including their participation in the landing of supplies on the Normandy beaches following D-Day.

Empire Runner and ***Empire Townsman*** were returned to the MoWT during 1946 and both were disposed of to private buyers for further trading in 1947.

This then was the situation with O&W up until the end of the war. They entered the post-war years with a mixed fleet of ships, ranging from the small and old, as represented by ***Ocean***, ***Orb***, ***Ferric*** and ***Morvah***, through the larger but still elderly ***Sneyd***, ***Druid Stoke***, ***Rockleaze*** and ***Downleaze*** (the last two recently returned from war service), onto the largest and more modern of their vessels, ***St. Vincent*** and ***Salcombe***, the latter with her damaged engine. Additionally, they were also managing the two MoWT owned vessels.

They had also suffered the loss of men, when ***Lunan*** had met her end but, despite the unbalanced and motley collection of ships and the difficulties that this created, they had unfailingly maintained coal deliveries to Portishead Power Station and also, through the war years, contributed greatly to the fuelling of Gloucester Power Station. Maintenance of the ships had been difficult under wartime conditions, with little availability of dockyard time and this, too, had put the ships' crews under further pressure.

The company, the men and the ships had all made their contribution to the war effort and had done it well.

Below: No contemporary photographs of O&W's two Empire ships have been discovered but this view shows identical class member *Empire Rancher*, new from John Harker Ltd in January 1943, delivering the first boatload of coal to the newly opened Castle Meads Power Station, Gloucester, later that year. *Mike Taylor collection*

HOTWELLS Official No. 183679

During 1948, the extension of Portishead Power Station, doubling its capacity, was put in hand. Clearly, this was going to greatly increase the pressure on O&W in their task of delivering the fuel. In addition, their fleet of ships was mixed, unbalanced and largely elderly. There were two large modern motor ships, two smaller middle-aged steam ships, one other newer but smaller steamer, plus a very elderly and still smaller steam ship, along with the remnants of the barge fleet. Plans had also been drawn up at this time for the construction of an even larger power station at Portishead on an adjacent site. It was time for the company to take stock and to start rationalising their ships.

Accordingly, Osborn & Wallis approached Charles Hill & Sons with an order for a sister ship to their 1940 purchase, *St. Vincent*. This was to be Hill's Yard No 358 and the new vessel would be named ***Hotwells***. The company had by now established the principle of naming the ships after districts of Bristol, a policy which had begun with ***Druid Stoke***, although it will be noticed that the use of the name ***Salcombe*** for the ex-*Camroux IV* did not follow this pattern. As if to confirm her different origins, she was renamed after the Devon resort at which the Osborn family had a residence.

No. 358's keel was laid on 2nd May 1949 and she was launched on 12th December of the same year. On 14th March 1950 the completed ship was delivered to O&W. She was 163 feet in length, with a beam of 27 feet and her grt was 499. Although nominally a sister to *St. Vincent*, she was in fact 3 feet longer and had a slightly different hull form, designed to increase the freeboard and to give a slightly greater grt figure. Despite this, she was certainly based upon *St. Vincent* and only the different lifeboat davits and the bridge across the front of the wheelhouse made them visibly dissimilar.

Like *St. Vincent*, she was powered by a Ruston & Hornsby 6VEBXM six-cylinder main engine but fitted with a Brown Boveri turbo blower instead of the Napier unit of the earlier ship. The engine was fresh water cooled by means of a seawater-cooled heat exchanger. This drove a 7 foot diameter cast iron propeller via an MWD gearbox. She was fitted with a Ruston & Hornsby 4-cylinder auxiliary engine for electricity generation, ballast pumping and compressed air supply, coupled with a small single-cylinder R&H battery charging unit.

Top and right: Always a day for a little celebration, even though weeks of fitting out still remained to be done, these two photographs record the launch of *Hotwells* from Charles Hill's Yard on 12th December 1949. In the top view she is seen just entering the water, whilst a rowing boat is used for an inspection of the hull after she had been moored alongside a short while later. *Jim Crissup*

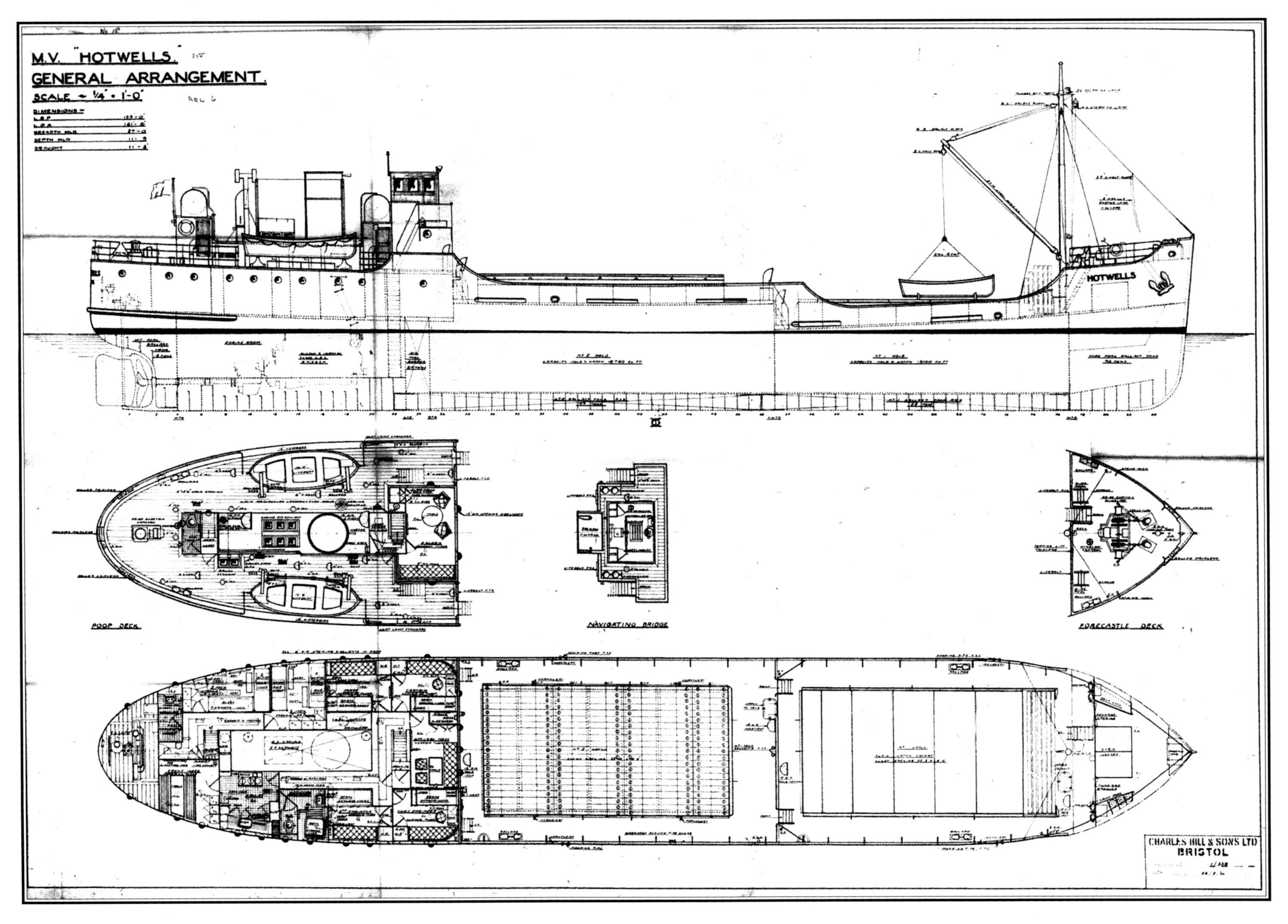
M.V. "HOTWELLS"
GENERAL ARRANGEMENT
SCALE ¼" = 1'-0"
DIMENSIONS
HOTWELLS
POOP DECK
NAVIGATING BRIDGE
FORECASTLE DECK
CHARLES HILL & SONS LTD
BRISTOL

An early view of *Hotwells*, showing the ship as built, with a single mast forward.
Capt. C. Reynolds

On deck, she also had steel roller hatches for the forward hold, with conventional beams and boards for the main hatch. Surprisingly, she was built and delivered with only the single foremast and derrick, despite the imminent introduction of the second masthead light legislation with which she would have to comply. An arrangement similar to that of ***St. Vincent*** was fitted within a few weeks of her delivery to O&W.

In appearance, she was absolutely conventional and straight laced. With her superstructure and bridge being built of absolutely flat steel plate with everything at right angles, as well as having a cylindrical funnel with a horizontal top, she demonstrated the reluctance of O&W to countenance any concessions to modernity in the appearance of their ships. Despite this, the ship was well built and fitted out to a high standard, whilst the choice of Ruston & Hornsby machinery showed a willingness to pay for quality in the essential aspects of the ship's construction.

The additional mast fitted soon after her building was to a similar arrangement as on ***St. Vincent*** but it was placed slightly further away from the funnel. The requirement for a second masthead light was to lead to a great pre-occupation with masts in the company. None of the improvised arrangements ever looked anything other than makeshift, until the final version of ***Salcombe***'s mainmast, which at last looked like part of the ship!

A prominent feature of ***Hotwell***'s appearance and, indeed, something which had been and was to remain a Charles Hill trade mark for many years, were the cylindrical water tanks with which she was fitted, the after one being her freshwater supply, while the one immediately behind the bridge contained salt water for toilet flushing, etc.

Her accommodation layout meant that all members of her crew, officers and men, had cabins, washrooms and mess rooms down below, as well as the galley, which resulted in somewhat compact arrangements. However, the whole interior of the bridge structure at deck level was given over to a large and rather unnecessary saloon.

The ship traded only to Newport for the first seven years of her life, so that she might be spared the rigours of being loaded while aground at Ely Harbour.

Hotwells was always to be the fastest of the company's diesel-engined vessels. The two later ships were able to carry over 100 tons more cargo but with only the same engine. ***Rockleaze*** and ***Downleaze*** could equal her speed, but only at the expense of great exertions by the fireman.

Hotwells making her way across Barry No. 1 Dock to head out via the Lady Windsor Lock in April 1965. She had by now been fitted with her second mast aft and is also sporting a red lead boot topping band. This came into view when she was unladen and improved her lines considerably, making her look longer and eliminating the rather sinister appearance she had hitherto. *John Clarkson*

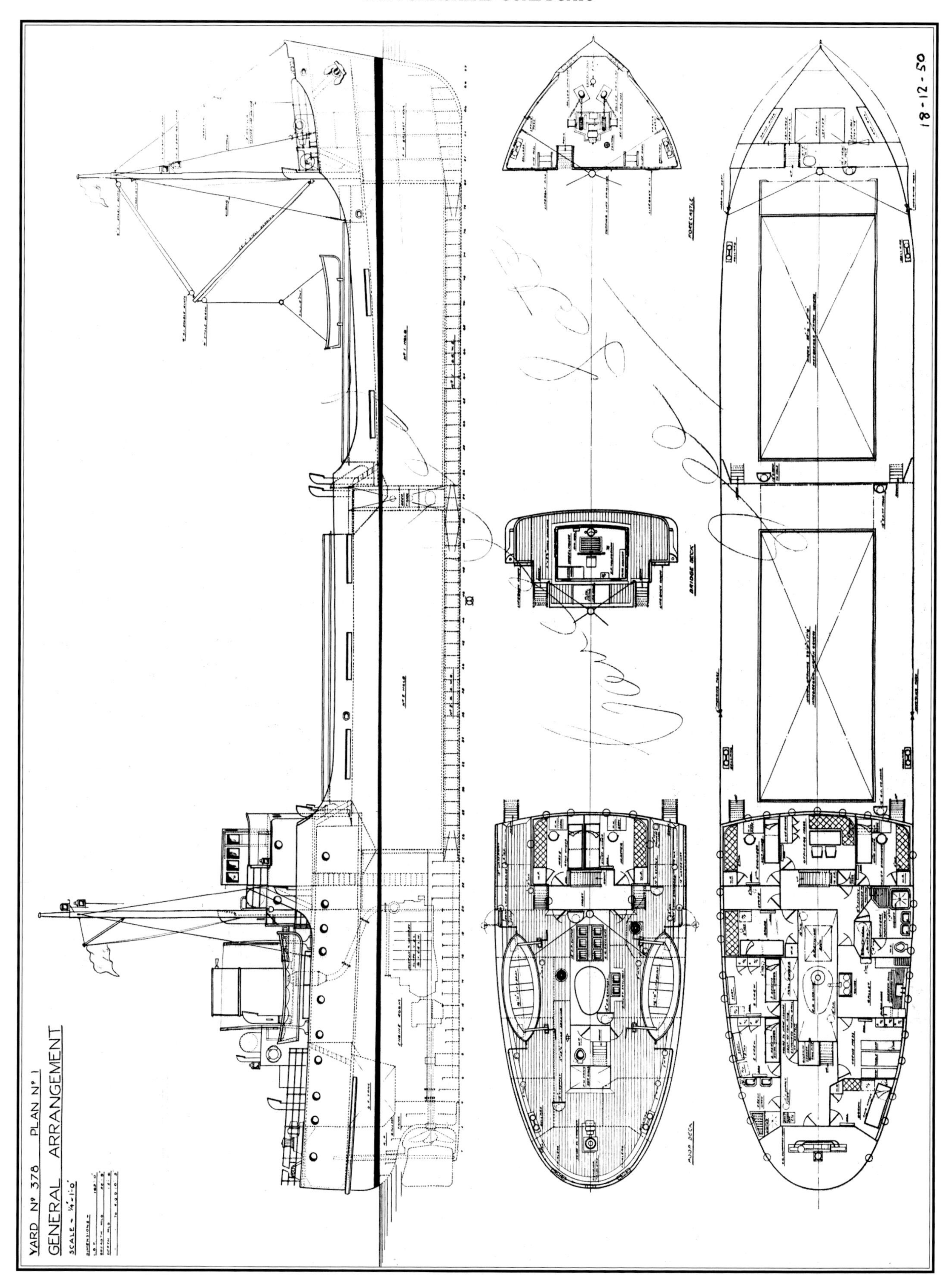
YARD Nº 378 PLAN Nº 1
GENERAL ARRANGEMENT
SCALE - 1/4" = 1'-0"
18-12-50
FORECASTLE
BRIDGE DECK
POOP DECK

COLSTON Official No. 186541

In 1950, within just a few months of the delivery of ***Hotwells*** and with construction of the new power station now confirmed, Osborn & Wallis were in initial consultations with Charles Hill for a further ship, with the strong possibility of another one after that.

The new ship was to be over 100 tons greater in cargo capacity than ***Hotwells***, in order to make best use of the length of time available between tides, both to load and to discharge the cargo. She was to be 169 feet long, with a beam of 29 feet, giving a grt of 586. She would be built to Yard No. 378 and would be named ***Colston***.

Hill's produced their first proposals for the new ship on a drawing labelled 'Plan No. 1' and dated 18th December 1950 (see illustration, page left). Although fundamentally little more than a bigger ***Hotwells***, the most significant change was that the hatches for both holds were to be of the steel roller type (Macgregor Patent Hatches).

The main engine would again be a Ruston & Hornsby six-cylinder 6VEBXM, but this time with a Napier turbo blower and freshwater cooling, via a seawater cooled heat-exchanger. This would drive a 6 feet 9 inch diameter cast iron propeller (three inches less than ***Hotwells***) through an MWD gearbox. She was equipped with two auxiliary engines, one a four-cylinder unit and the other one a three-cylinder. Both could fulfil all the auxiliary functions required. She also had a small single-cylinder battery charging unit. As with all the other motor ships, the new vessel had low-geared hand steering for use at sea and power steering to give rapid response when manoeuvring. She was equipped with ship-to-shore radio.

Although the construction of the second power station was well in hand by April 1953, no firm contract had been agreed for the building of the new ship, despite the initial negotiations haven taken place during 1950. However, the time had not been wasted and several important changes were made to the design (note that the first plan has '*Cancelled see later*' pencilled across it). Whilst remaining basically as originally planned in terms of size and layout, the decision was made to abandon the patent hatches completely and revert to beam and boards for both holds. The line of the break in the bulwarks from the main deck down to the well deck was softened and curved. Having managed (with some difficulty as was later learnt), to persuade O&W to permit a hint of modernity in the ship's appearance by giving it a curved front to the deckhouse and wheelhouse assembly, the builders pushed this theme a little harder by giving a raked top to the oval funnel and, most dramatically, by moving the mainmast further aft, thereby pushing the funnel itself forward. This allowed a much shorter exhaust trunking within the engine room. The after deckhouse was given a raked top and the mainmast was to be complete with crosstree and gaff. These small changes greatly improved the ship's appearance.

The cramping of the accommodation that had been a feature of ***Hotwells*** was resolved by giving the Captain a cabin at deck level on the starboard side of the deckhouse and matching it with a chart room on the port side. In all,

Above: *Colston*'s keel was laid on 15th February 1954 and she was launched on 28th October. Here, at the launch ceremony at Charles Hill's Yard, the traditional breaking of a bottle of champagne on the ship's bows is about to take place. Just behind and to the left of the platform, wearing a dark suit and spectacles, is Mr D. Osborn.

Right: Having successfully negotiated the slipway, *Colston* hits the water for the first time. After final fitting out, she was accepted into the company on 6th January 1955. *Both Jim Crissup*

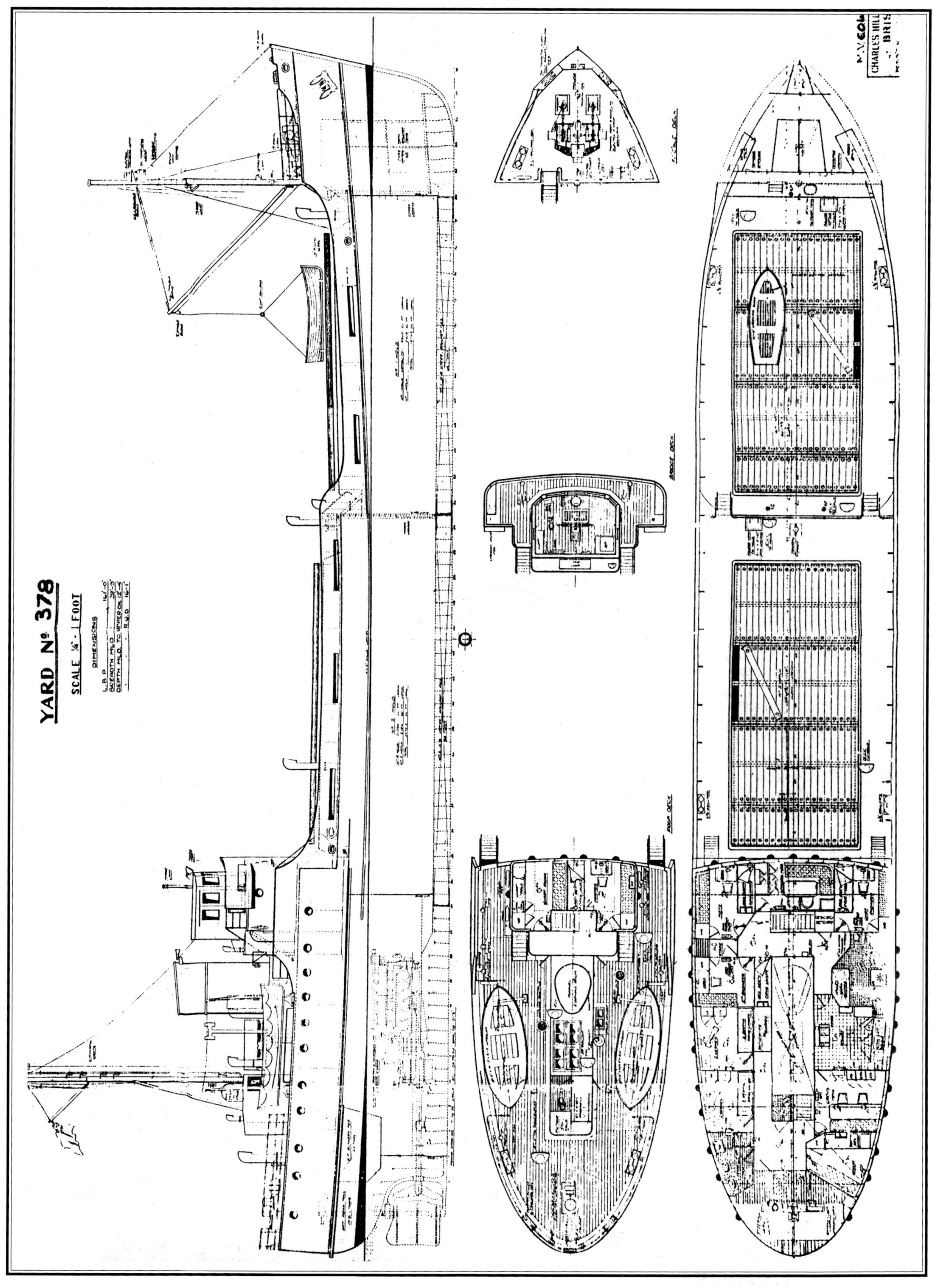
YARD No 378
SCALE ¼" - 1 FOOT
DIMENSIONS
L.B.P. 161'-0"
BREADTH MLD.
DEPTH MLD. TO UPPER DK 12'-4"
R.Q.D. 16'-1"

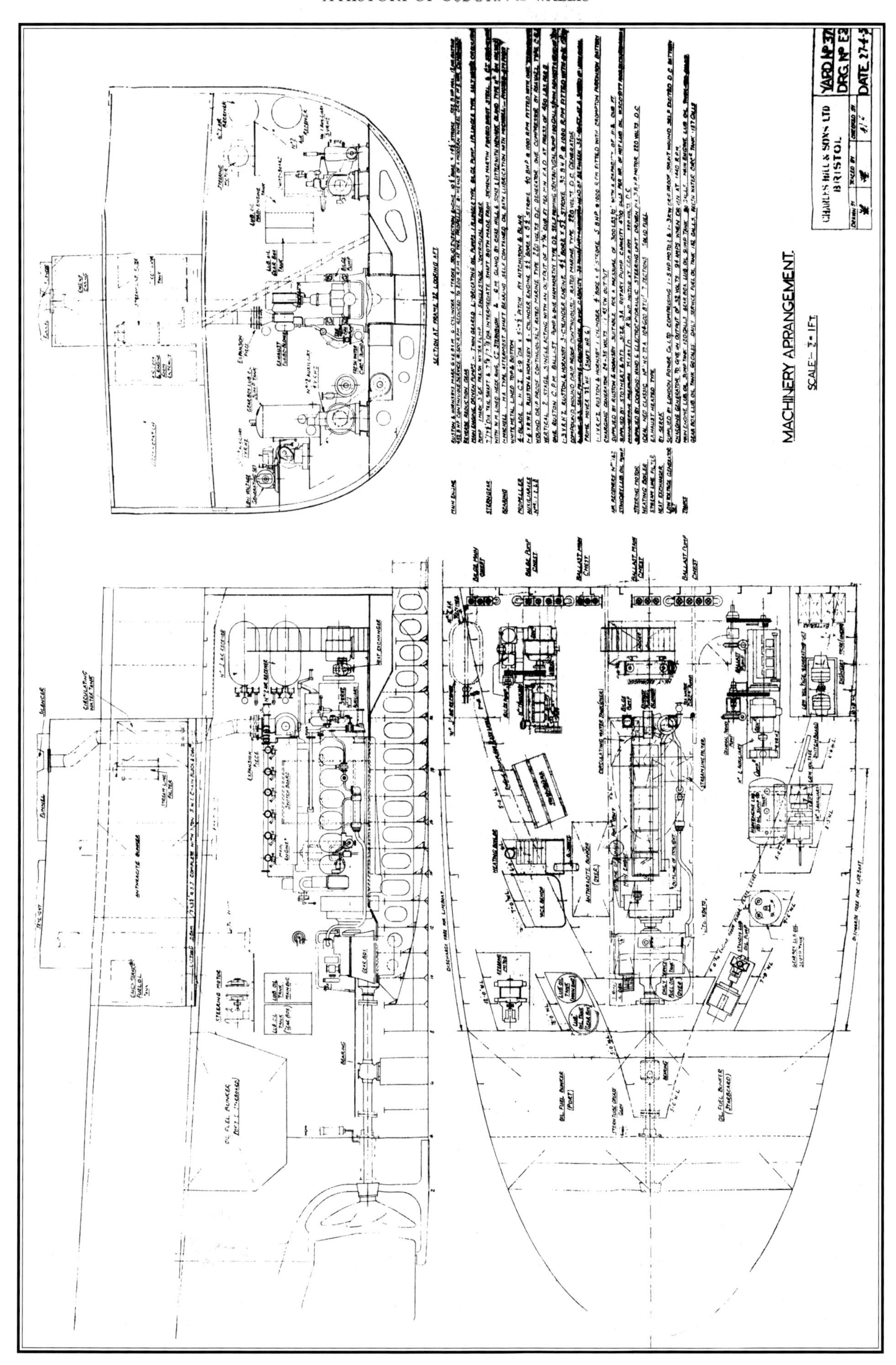
MACHINERY ARRANGEMENT.
CHARLES HILL & SONS LTD
BRISTOL.

Left: This view of *Colston*'s Engine Room was taken when the ship was still virtually new. *Courtesy Ruston & Hornsby archive*

Below: Several years after these photographs were taken, I spent some time on *Colston* as relief Second Engineer. At this time, the pipework for the main engine cooler (fresh and salt water) was revised and I took the opportunity to keep the identity disc from one of the redundant valves as a souvenir. *Author*

Another Ruston & Hornsby photograph of *Colston*'s Engine Room; note the 'RH' logo on the metal covering in the centre of the picture. With the vessel only a few weeks old, the copper pipes are not yet shiny from constant polishing. *Courtesy Ruston & Hornsby archive*

she was a very competent design of vessel, marred only perhaps by the choice of engine. More power would have been useful, especially in her later life.

On 6th January 1955, ***Colston*** underwent her acceptance trials and was duly handed over to Osborn & Wallis. With a cargo carrying capacity of 760 tons, she immediately became the biggest unit in the fleet, exceeding ***Salcombe***'s capacity by some 30 tons.

She very quickly settled into her work and no problems of any sort were encountered. Like ***Hotwells***, she was confined to running to Newport for the same reason – that of not wishing her to be loaded whilst aground. Although large for Ely Harbour, she would have been capable of going there and, indeed, the similar sized ***Salcombe*** was already loading there.

Fitted with radio from new, she was, at the end of 1959, also equipped with a Decca navigation system. This relied on radio beams from shore installations all around the coast of Britain and, by triangulating three beams simultaneously on the special gridded charts, the vessel's position was guaranteed to be given accurately to within sixty feet. However, this meant that allowance had to be made (where appropriate) for the fact that the receiving aerials were located on the mainmast, with approximately 140 feet of the ship still ahead of the position shown.

By 1961, the work of coaling the old Portishead 'A' Station was reduced as its viability declined and bigger ships from other companies were beginning to bring coal into the 'B' Power Station. As a consequence, O&W's decision to have a similar ship to ***Colston*** built in 1956 was beginning to look questionable.

Late in 1961, ***Colston*** and her newer sister ship (***Brandon***) were sent further afield, becoming engaged in the work of fuelling the power station at East Yelland on the River Taw, near Barnstaple in north Devon. Later, they went even further down the Channel to Hayle Power Station on the north Cornish coast. To bring her up to standard for this work and to help navigate these treacherous coastlines, ***Colston*** was equipped with radar very soon after taking on her new role. Her galley was also given gas-fired cooking facilities, operated by a full time cook employed to feed the crew, with the food allowance being made by the company.

In this work, ***Colston*** might run from any of the South Wales ports, including Cardiff, Barry and Swansea, and she shared the task with her sister ship ***Brandon*** and with two larger vessels belonging to the London & Rochester Shipping Company.

Colston always returned to Bristol for any maintenance and repairs required, and in so doing sometimes called into Portishead to renew her acquaintance with the other ships of the now diminishing fleet.

The two sisters were reported to be excellent sea boats in the bad weather often encountered below the Holmes Islands. Indeed, it was not unknown for them to leave port together with one of their bigger consorts and be left trailing as the larger ship thundered away, only to find further down the Channel that the bigger and heavier vessel had been forced to reduce speed because of the weather as they battered their way through the waves. Meanwhile, ***Colston*** and her sister would bob along riding over the waves and would thus overhaul the larger craft. An experienced hand and veteran of ***Downleaze***, very fond of his old ship, who had been transferred – much against the grain! – to ***Brandon*** as the steamers were withdrawn, once remarked: "*I thought **Downleaze** was a good seaboat but this 'un would drown her!*"

To ***Colston*** and her sister fell the dubious honour of being the last ships to leave the company's ownership, when they were handed over to W.E. Dowds Ltd of Newport, South Wales, in August 1970.

A new and smart looking *Colston* in Portishead Docks, with the 'B' power station under construction in the left background. *Courtesy Ruston & Hornsby archive*

Here, *Colston* has just left the Lady Windsor Lock and is bound for loading at the coal hoists in Barry No. 1 Dock. The angle shows off her lines nicely. The view was taken in April 1962, shortly after the photograph which appears on page 83 showing her approaching the lock.
John Clarkson

BRANDON Official No. 186554

In late 1955, having been completely satisfied in every respect with *Colston*, Osborn & Wallis ordered a further ship from Charles Hill, to exactly the same design and specification. The new ship was to be identical in every respect and, in fact, the same drawings that had been produced for *Colston* were to be used to build the new vessel.

She was to be built to Hill's Yard No. 407 and would be named *Brandon*. In the event, she was to be the last ship built for O&W. Details of her size, grt and her machinery are exactly the same as that given for *Colston*.

Brandon's keel was laid on 2nd May 1956 and she was launched on 28th February 1957. She underwent acceptance trials and was delivered to O&W on 12th June 1957.

There were a number of small detail differences between *Brandon* and *Colston* but these were not design changes, they were simply matters of convenience at the time the ship was being built and had no effect whatsoever upon her technical characteristics. It was impossible to tell them apart unless one was very familiar with them and could recognise these tiny differences, some of which are noted here:

The crosstrees on the mainmasts and the stays on the gaff on the mainmasts were positioned differently; the curve of the line from foc'sle to well deck was different; *Colston*'s funnel was truly elliptical, *Brandon*'s had straight sides; the handrails on the ladders from main to well deck were different; the builders' plaques on the front of the bridge were positioned differently; the morse light on the top of the wheelhouse was located differently; *Colston* had a deeper plate above the wheelhouse windows and floodlights which

A rather spectacular view of *Brandon* on the slipway at Charles Hill's Yard, with final preparations underway for her launch. It is likely that this view was taken early on the actual day, 28th February 1957, with a string of flags slung between her forward mast and wheelhouse, ropes hung over her sides at the ready and the raised platform, in the foreground, from which the launch ceremony would be performed awaiting only a top sheet. Across the river, the terraces of Hotwells made for a suitably dramatic backdrop to Hill's premises. The site of the yard is now occupied by up-market flats and housing, as is much of Bristol's waterfront following the closure of the City Docks but Charles Hill's long history in shipbuilding and repairing is well documented in the book *Shipshape and Bristol Fashion*. *Jim Crissup*

Following her launch, *Brandon* remained alongside Hill's Yard for fitting out. This deck view, looking over the open hatches, shows work in progress. One of Campbell's steamers can just be made out astern, no doubt in for a winter refit.
Jim Crissup

were a crew addition – ***Brandon*** had a fitted floodlight; there was a drain pipe under the bridge wing on ***Brandon*** and the lifebuoy there was located differently; the mainmast navigation light was slightly higher on ***Colston*** and the signal lamps on her mainmast were more widely spaced; ***Brandon*** had an extra draught mark on her bow, as can be noted from the photograph of her on the slip before launch.

Like her sister, ***Brandon*** was fitted with radio from new and she also had the additional Decca navigation equipment fitted at the same time as it was fitted to ***Colston***. She, too, was restricted to Newport loading only, although her arrival in the fleet meant that ***Hotwells*** would now begin to run to Ely Harbour. With her delivery in 1957, the firm was now operating five diesel-engined ships and three steamers, the fleet consisting of, in ascending order of age, ***Brandon***, ***Colston***, ***Hotwells***, ***St. Vincent***, ***Salcombe***, ***Rockleaze***, ***Downleaze*** and ***Druid Stoke***.

In her first year of operation, a loaded *Brandon* prepares to depart from Newport Docks. Note the height of the coal tip behind; these were used by the large deep sea colliers. *Chris Witts*

However, with the beginning of the decline in generating capacity of the two Portishead power stations, brought about by the reduction of loading on the older 'A' Station, the task of supplying them could now be adequately covered by the five motorships and, as a consequence, the demise of the steamers in the fleet was looming.

Brandon worked to Portishead for the next four years, until the work became so thinly spread that the company had to find employment elsewhere for at least part of the fleet. Clearly the best ships to take on this role were the two largest and newest ones, and so it was that ***Brandon*** and ***Colston*** were sent on to the Yelland run. This left such work as remained at Portishead in the hands of the older and smaller ships. ***Brandon*** was also given a modest upgrade with the fitting of radar and the modifications that were given to her sister. Both ships were also fitted with a large capacity fridge and freezer for longer storage of food and, like ***Colston***, she too carried a cook.

Brandon remained with the Company until 1970, when she and ***Colston*** were sold, as a pair, to W.E. Dowds Ltd of Newport. Both ships underwent some minor alterations at Hill's dockyard to prepare them for their new roles.

Opposite page: Spot the difference! These two similar poses of *Colston* and *Brandon* should be studied to pick out the various detail differences between the pair, most of which are noted in the text. In addition, the raised part of the foc'sle bulwark (right from the stem) was longer on *Brandon*, whilst although not discernible from these views, *Colston*'s draught marks went only to 13 feet whereas *Brandon*'s went to 14 feet. Both vessels are unladen and show off the band of red lead on their lower hulls which disappeared beneath the water when they were loaded. Both vessels were photographed approaching Lady Windsor Lock, Barry, *Colston* in April 1962 and *Brandon* in August 1963, with Bendrick Rock visible in the background. *Both John Clarkson*

COLSTON

BRANDON

CHRONOLOGY OF ACQUISITIONS AND DISPOSALS

The exact year of ship acquisitions is not known precisely in all cases. The small vessels owned by William Osborn are not included, although at the time of amalgamation he brought to the venture the following: *Thomas & Maria*, *Eclipse*, *Charlotte*, *Edith*, *Wye* and *Sunshine*. Of these, *Thomas & Maria* is thought to have been the last still in service with Osborn & Wallis, in 1916.

1878 William Osborn acquires ***Enterprize***.
1879 No movements.
1880 Osborn and Wallis form partnership. ***Alverton*** joins fleet.
1881 ***Alverton*** lost. ***Yan Yean*** joins fleet.
1882 ***Dolcoath*** joins fleet. ***Eureka*** joins fleet. ***Yan Yean*** sold.
1883 ***Euterpe*** joins fleet.
1884 No movements.
1885 No movements.
1886 No movements.
1887 No movements.
1888 ***Sneyd*** (1) joins fleet.
1889 ***Netham*** joins fleet. ***Thomas & Maria*** joins fleet.
1890 ***Wye*** joins fleet.
1891 ***Stakesby*** joins fleet. ***Blanche*** joins fleet. ***Eclipse*** joins fleet. ***Governor Albuquerque*** joins fleet.
1892 ***Eclipse*** damaged, probably broken up. ***Governor Albuquerque*** damaged, sold.
1893 ***Saltwick*** joins fleet. ***Ocean*** joins fleet.
1894 No movements.
1895 ***Charlotte*** joins fleet. ***Marion*** joins fleet. ***Enterprize*** lost.
1896 No movements.
1897 No movements.
1898 ***Herschel*** joins fleet. ***Sunshine*** joins fleet. ***Charlotte*** lost. ***Netham*** lost.
1899 No movements.
1900 ***St. Vincent*** (1) joins fleet.
1901 ***Blanche*** lost. ***Herschel*** lost. ***Wye*** lost.
1902 No movements.
1903 ***Clifton*** joins fleet.
1904 ***Thomas & Maria*** hulked.
1905 No movements.
1906 No movements.
1907 ***New Zealand*** joins fleet. ***Sunshine*** sold.
1908 ***Eureka*** sold.
1909 No movements.
1910 ***Stakesby*** sold.
1911 ***Orb*** joins fleet. ***Ferric*** joins fleet. ***New Zealand*** sold. ***Saltwick*** sold.
1912 No movements.
1913 ***Dolcoath*** sold.
1914 No movements.
1915 No movements.
1916 ***Euterpe*** mined and lost.
1917 No movements.
1918 No movements.
1919 No movements.
1920 ***Clifton*** broken up.
1921 ***A1*** joins fleet.
1922 No movements.
1923 No movements.
1924 No movements.
1925 No movements.
1926 ***Morvah*** joins fleet
1927 ***A1*** to dumb barge. ***Sneyd*** (1) wrecked, broken up.
1928 No movements.
1929 ***Druid Stoke*** joins fleet.
1930 No movements.
1931 ***Lunan*** joins fleet.
1932 ***Marion*** broken up.
1933 No movements. Hotwells Yard and premises occupied.
1934 No movements.
1935 No movements.
1936 ***Sneyd*** (2) joins fleet. ***St. Vincent*** (1) broken up.
1937 No movements.
1938 ***Downleaze*** joins fleet.
1939 ***Rockleaze*** joins fleet.
1940 ***St. Vincent*** (2) joins fleet.
1941 ***Lunan*** mined and lost.
1942 ***Salcombe*** joins fleet.
1943 ***Empire Runner*** joins fleet (management only for MoWT). ***Empire Townsman*** joins fleet (management only for MoWT).
1944 No movements.
1945 No movements.
1946 ***Empire Runner*** leaves fleet. ***Empire Townsman*** leaves fleet.
1947 No movements.
1948 No movements.
1949 No movements.
1950 ***Hotwells*** joins fleet.
1951 ***Ocean*** broken up. ***Orb*** broken up.
1952 No movements.
1953 No movements.
1954 No movements.
1955 ***Colston*** joins fleet. ***Ferric*** broken up. ***Morvah*** broken up.
1956 No movements.
1957 ***Brandon*** joins fleet. ***Sneyd*** (2) broken up.
1958 ***Rockleaze*** broken up.
1959 No movements.
1960 ***Downleaze*** broken up.
1961 No movements.
1962 No movements.
1963 No movements.
1964 No movements.
1965 ***Druid Stoke*** broken up.
1966 No movements.
1967 No movements.
1968 No movements.
1969 ***Salcombe*** sold. ***St. Vincent*** (2) sold. Company ceased trading.
1970 ***Hotwells*** sold. ***Colston*** sold. ***Brandon*** sold. The yard and all assets disposed of.

In the Floating Harbour circa 1910, with O&W's steam barge *Clifton* on the left. *Neil Parkhouse collection*

SUMMARY OF O&W HISTORY FOR EACH SHIP

Ship	Type	Build Year	Bought	Left	Years	Conclusion
A1	Stm barge	1895	1921	1927	6	Conv. to dumb barge
ALVERTON	Scr stmr	1880	1880	1881	1	Wrecked
BLANCHE	Scr stmr	1863	1891	1901	10	Wrecked
BRANDON	Motorship	1957	1957	1970	13	Sold
CHARLOTTE	Sloop	1848	1895	1898	3	Lost
CLIFTON	Scr stmr	1857	1903	1920	17	Broken up
COLSTON	Motorship	1955	1955	1970	15	Sold
DOLCOATH	Scr stmr	1882	1882	1913	31	Sold
DOWNLEAZE	Scr stmr	1924	1938	1960	22	Broken up
DRUID STOKE	Scr stmr	1929	1929	1965	36	Broken up
ECLIPSE	Sloop	?	1891	1892	1	Damaged. Broken up?
EMPIRE RUNNER	Motorship	1943	1943	1946	3	Returned to MoWT
EMPIRE TOWNSMAN	Motorship	1943	1943	1946	3	Returned to MoWT
ENTERPRIZE	Scr stmr	1860	1878	1895	17	Lost
EUREKA	Scr stmr	1882	1882	1908	26	Sold
EUTERPE	Scr stmr	1883	1883	1916	33	Lost
FERRIC	Stm barge	1911	1911	1955	44	Broken up
GOVERNOR ALBUQUERQUE	Scr stmr	1876	1891	1892	1	Damaged. Sold
HERSCHEL	Scr stmr	1884	1898	1901	3	Lost
HOTWELLS	Motorship	1950	1950	1970	20	Sold
LUNAN	Scr stmr	1909	1931	1941	10	Mined. Lost
MARION	Stm barge	1879	1895	1932	37	Broken up
MORVAH	Stm barge	1926	1926	1955	29	Broken up
NETHAM	Stm barge	1878	1889	1898	9	Lost
NEW ZEALAND	Scr stmr	1886	1907	1911	4	Sold
OCEAN	Stm barge	1893	1893	1951	58	Broken up
ORB	Scr stmr	1911	1911	1951	40	Broken up
ROCKLEAZE	Scr stmr	1924	1939	1958	19	Broken up
SALCOMBE	Motorship	1938	1942	1969	27	Sold
SALTWICK	Scr stmr	1882	1893	1911	18	Sold
SNEYD (1)	Stm barge	1872	1888	1927	39	Wrecked. Broken up
SNEYD (2)	Scr stmr	1910	1936	1957	21	Broken up
STAKESBY	Scr stmr	1880	1891	1910	19	Sold
ST.VINCENT (1)	Stm barge	1866	1900	1936	36	Broken up
ST.VINCENT (2)	Motorship	1940	1940	1969	29	Sold
SUNSHINE	Ketch	1862	1898	1907	9	Sold
THOMAS & MARIA	Trow	1841	1889	1904	15	Hulked
WYE	Trow	1860	1890	1901	11	Wrecked
YAN YEAN	Scr stmr	1880	1881	1882	1	Sold

Ocean, O&W's longest serving vessel, left, in the yard at Hotwells and, right, in the Floating Harbour. *Courtesy Bristol Museums & Art Gallery*

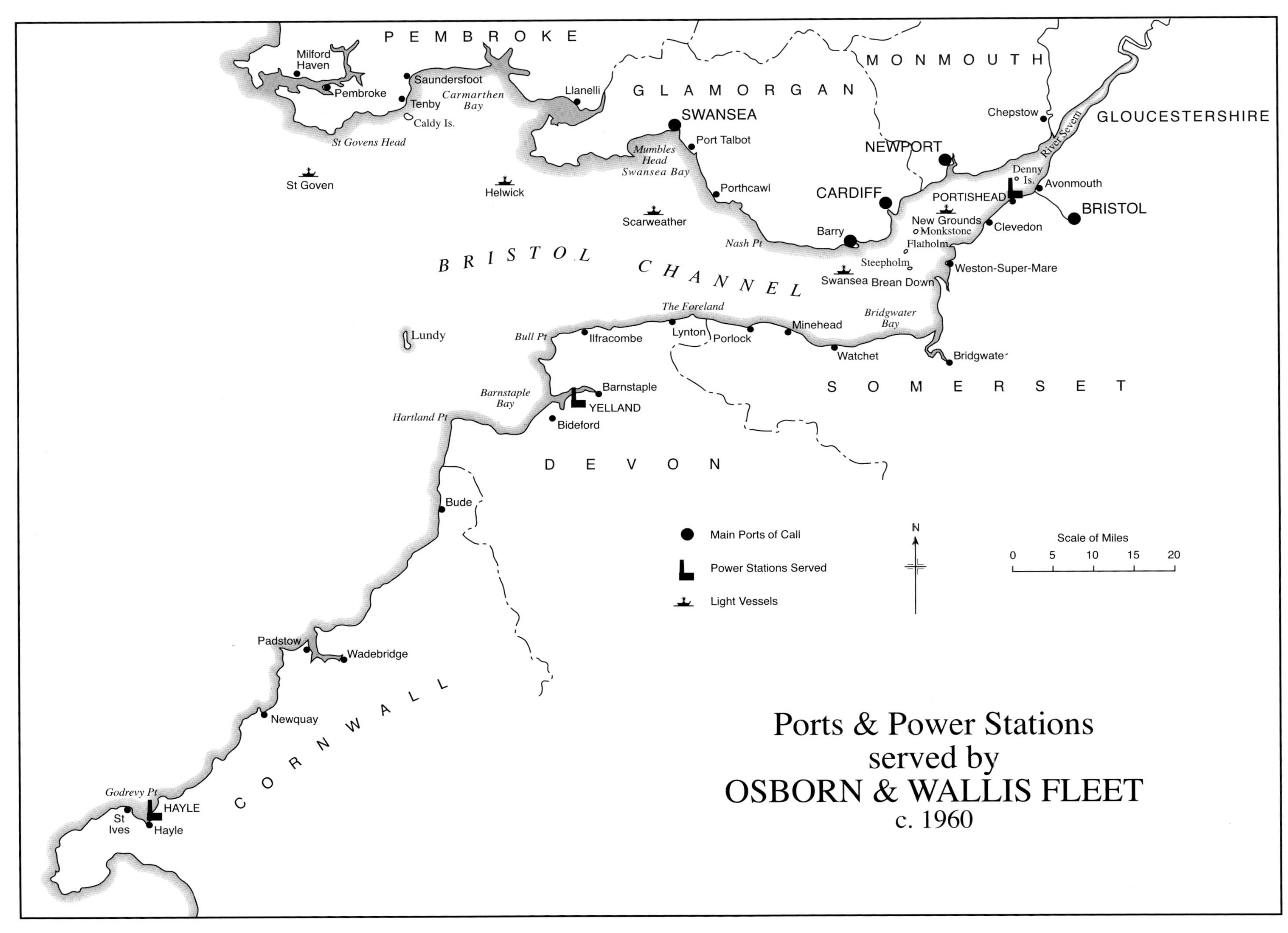
PEMBROKE
Milford Haven
Pembroke
Saundersfoot
Tenby
Carmarthen Bay
Caldy Is.
St Govens Head
St Goven
Helwick
Llanelli
GLAMORGAN
SWANSEA
Port Talbot
Mumbles Head
Swansea Bay
Porthcawl
Scarweather
MONMOUTH
Chepstow
GLOUCESTERSHIRE
River Severn
NEWPORT
CARDIFF
Barry
Nash Pt
Denny Is.
Avonmouth
PORTISHEAD
BRISTOL
New Grounds
Monkstone
Clevedon
Flatholm
Steepholm
Weston-Super-Mare
Swansea
Brean Down
BRISTOL CHANNEL
Lundy
The Foreland
Bull Pt
Ilfracombe
Lynton
Porlock
Minehead
Bridgwater Bay
Watchet
Bridgwater
SOMERSET
Barnstaple Bay
Barnstaple
YELLAND
Hartland Pt
Bideford
DEVON
Bude
Main Ports of Call
Power Stations Served
Light Vessels
N
Scale of Miles
0
5
10
15
20
Padstow
Wadebridge
Newquay
CORNWALL
Godrevy Pt
HAYLE
St Ives
Hayle
Ports & Power Stations
served by
OSBORN & WALLIS FLEET
c. 1960

Part Two THE JOB

During early 1955, at the age of 15, I joined the company. I had long had a fascination for ships but it had been drummed into my head at school that, without competence in mathematics, there was no worthwhile career to be had and I was certainly incompetent at maths! Accepting this as being the case, I had to find myself gainful employment. Following my two trips on the coal boats a few years previously, I had kept in touch with the gentleman who had been the Mate on *St. Vincent* at the time of my trips and who lived nearby. My father was away overseas with the army at this time and I kept my contact with the ex-*St Vincent*'s Mate very discreet, asking him to let me know if ever a vacancy arose for a Deck Boy on any of the ships.

In due course he told me that a vacancy had arisen for Deck Boy on the brand new *Colston*, of which he was now the Mate and that, if I was interested, I should go to the ship in the morning next day, a Saturday. I was to ask to see the Skipper, and see if and how things worked out. I duly presented myself as instructed and after ten minutes was given the job on probation. That was the easy bit!

I returned home and anxiously explained to my mother what had occurred, that I had a job, so would she please write the necessary letter to secure my release from school. Mother, realising that she was confronted with a done deal and knowing of my unhappiness at school, eventually and reluctantly agreed. So on the Monday morning, I set off for school to work out my days of notice.

In fairness, I have to explain that three people in this chicanery were innocent. The Mate on *Colston* assumed that I had parental permission, my dad was on the other side of the world in Japan and would therefore not know about the event until it was too late to intervene, and my mother did what seemed to be right to her under the circumstances – although only after lengthy attempts at persuading me to think again, which I stubbornly argued against. The responsibility was entirely my own. I accepted that there would be terrible retribution when my father finally came home in about a years time but, for now, I would be free of school and, moreover, earning some real pocket money.

My pay was to be £3 a week basic, with a further ten shillings for each trip that the ship made in the week after the first one, which was deemed 'the company's trip'. With the ships then averaging three trips per week each across to South Wales to fetch the coal for the two power stations at Portishead, I could look forward to the prospect of having £2 a week for myself after paying my tax and my thirty shillings a week to my mother for keep.

I duly reported to the ship and was told that we would be sailing that night, so I would need to bring some food (none was supplied), changes of clothes and wet weather clothing. I was shown the crews mess room, used by the two Sailors and the Boy and where we each had a locker, and I was told the sort of things that I should stock it up with for everyday use and for emergencies. Every member of the crew had his own cabin, with the two Sailors and the Boy living at the after end of the accommodation, while the Mate, Chief Engineer and Second Engineer had more comfortable cabins at the forward end of the accommodation. The Skipper had his own cabin on deck level under the bridge.

The facilities aboard this brand new ship, still smelling of new paint and varnish, were excellent, with a well-equipped galley, central heating to all the accommodation and comfortable separate mess rooms for the officers and crew. The officers also had their own washing and bathroom.

The Mate told me to put my belongings in my cabin and then to report to him. He gave me my very first job on the ship, showing me where the Brasso was kept and sending me along to the fo'csle to polish the bell.

The galley was to become the focal point of my life as, among my other duties, I had to learn how to prepare and cook the meals. It was also the place that every visitor to the ship immediately headed for in the expectation of a mug of tea. After the morning's work and finding my way about, I was allowed to go home for the afternoon but was told to be back on board that night ready to sail. For a fifteen-year-old, it was all very new and exciting.

I joined *Colston* as her Deck Boy on 8th February 1955. The ship had been in service for just four weeks, having been accepted into the company from her builders, Charles Hill & Sons Ltd of Bristol, on 5th January 1955.

After a couple of weeks, and several trips on probation, I was confirmed in the job and the position formalised by a visit to the Merchant Navy Office in Prince Street, Bristol, accompanied by the Skipper, on 1st March 1955. Here I signed on the Ship's Articles as one of her crew. The process included being photographed and finger-printed, after which I was issued with my Merchant Seaman's Identity Card and my Discharge Book. Re-signing onto the Articles was an annual occurrence thereafter and on each occasion the Discharge Book was stamped to indicate how satisfied, or otherwise, the Skipper had been with the past year's performance. On transfer to another ship, it was a requirement that a seaman would sign off from the Articles of the ship that he was leaving and sign on to the Articles of the one

2 Particulars
(1) Surname.... WINTER (BLOCK CAPITALS)
(2) Christian or First Names.... Michael Jim
(3) Date of Birth 27. 3. 1939
(4) Place of Birth Portishead
(5) Colour of (a) eyes Blue (b) hair Brn
(6) Complexion Fresh
(7) Height 5 ft. 10¾ ins.
(8) Distinguishing Marks none
(9) Nationality—see Panel 7.
LEFT-HAND FINGERPRINTS (Plain Impressions of four fingers)

3 Photograph of Holder
C.R.S.53
M.M.O. Embossing Stamp
R642885
Signature of Holder M.J. Winter
THUMBS—PLAIN IMPRESSIONS
LEFT RIGHT

4 Particulars—continued
(10) Dis. A. No. R642885 (To be entered in all cases.)
(11) Certificates held— Grade.......... No.......... (including E.D.H., Ship's Cook, Lifeboat, etc.)
(12) Rank or Rating if not a certificated Officer (if A.B. Supt. to verify and initial). Deck Boy
National Service Registration No.

5
(15) N.H.I. Appd. Soc. Membership No.
(16) U.I. Local Office.......... Serial No..........
(17) Whether subject to Essential Work (Merchant Navy) Order..........
(18) Union or Society— Name.......... No..........
(19) Pension Fund and Regd. No.
(20) Former N.R. Identity Card No. (to be copied from N.R. 110 or Civilian Identity Card)
(21) Name, relationship and address of next-of-kin or nearest friend—
Name Michael Winter
Relationship Father
Address "St. Kilda" South Road Portishead
(22) Address of holder (if different from above)—

C.R.S. 53
BRITISH SEAMAN'S IDENTITY CARD
Issued by the Ministry of Transport and Civil Aviation, London.
MN
Surname and Initials of Seaman (BLOCK CAPITALS) M.J. Winter
Any person finding this card should drop it into any Posting Box for transmission to the Registrar-General of Shipping and Seamen, CARDIFF.

that he was to join. However, a local arrangement allowed for temporary, short-term transfers between ships for the purposes of holiday reliefs, cover for sickness, etc, without having to go through this formality on every occasion.

Having completed this requirement, I accompanied the Skipper back to the company yard at Hotwells, where he had some matters to attend to and I was told to wait outside for about half an hour. I took the opportunity to have a look round the yard. The old steamship ***Sneyd*** was tied up in the basin awaiting a decision as to her fate. By now 45 years old, she was still capable of being returned to service but it was unlikely that she would ever sail again. Her 'laid up' condition was clearly intended to be permanent, other than in an extreme emergency.

At the far end of the yard and tied up one behind the other in the main harbour waterway were the last two remaining Osborn & Wallis barges from an earlier era. These were ***Ferric*** and ***Morvah*** and, having heard about 'the barges' from *Colston*'s crew during my short time with the ship, I had a good look at them. Three weeks later, on 20th March, they left the yard under tow, bound for Cashmore's at Newport for scrapping.

At the time I joined the company, there were seven working ships in the fleet, with ***Sneyd*** held in reserve. Four were motorships – ***Colston***, ***Hotwells***, ***St. Vincent*** and ***Salcombe*** – and three were steamships – ***Rockleaze***, ***Downleaze*** and ***Druid Stoke***. There was also a further new vessel on order

Colston's crew, 1955.
Back: Jimmy Wong (Sailor); Ronnie Pring (relieving Second Engineer); centre left: Arthur Anderson (normally *Colston*'s Second Engineer but at this time acting Chief); right: Gordon Richards, (the Mate); sat on deck: Fred Knight (Senior Sailor); left, seated on the rope: myself (Deck Boy, aged 15). The Skipper, Captain 'Sammy' Taylor, took the photograph.

Sneyd tied up in the Yard. *Jim Crissup*

from Charles Hill's yard; this was to be an exact duplicate of ***Colston*** and would be named ***Brandon***.

Colston and ***Brandon*** had been ordered in anticipation of the demand for more coal carrying capacity when the new Portishead 'B' Power Station, then in the early stages of construction, came on stream. However, it was to be many months before it would begin generating and, for the meantime, the seven ships had only the task of fuelling the original 'A' Station, which was well within their capacity.

Even by the standards of the 1950s, the firm was somewhat old-fashioned and conservative in its management style and can perhaps best be summed up by making the observation that everything about it would have been quite familiar thirty years previously. The stone-built office block looked old and rather forbidding, both inside and out. Everything about the company was sober and restrained but it seemed to work.

At this period, the company was run by Mr Dennis Osborn, who had followed his father, Mr Ivor Osborn. There was an unconscious but very clear dividing line within the company employees, between the 'old hands' and the 'newcomers'. The old hands still had the habit of calling him "*Mr. Dennis*" from the days when both he and his father were in the office and they needed to be able to explain which one of the two Mr. Osborn's they wished to see. The rest of us spoke of him as "*Mr. Osborn*" and called him "*Sir*" if speaking to him. Somewhat daunting in appearance and manner at first, I was to find later that, behind this front, there was a considerate nature and a kindly disposition toward all the employees, each of whom he knew by name. A little indicator of his respect for the employees was that he always addressed the Skippers as "*Captain*" and the rest of us as "*Mr*", never simply by surname alone.

The day-to-day management of the office and the ships was given over to a gentleman employed as the Company Manager but who, having served as an officer in one of the Armed Forces, had not yet adjusted to the handling of

Colston moored alongside Albright & Wilson's wharf at Portishead, with the new 'B' power station rising in the background. This is another view taken in early 1955, when the vessel was only a few weeks old. *Courtesy Ruston & Hornsby archive*

civilians – especially when dealing with the old hands, who could be somewhat blunt in their responses when put out!

The technical supervision of the ships was in the process of being handed over when I joined O&W and the outgoing Superintendent, Mr R.G. Paynter was a man with a fearsome reputation. Capable of being quite as blunt and forceful as any seaman when his instructions were questioned, he was held in considerable respect and awe by everyone in the Company. Even after he had officially retired, he would still appear occasionally and the word would quickly go round that HE was about!

The incoming Superintendent, Mr M. Goodacre, gradually took over the job and, whilst he too would not be trifled with, he was of a more mellow disposition and would at least listen to suggestions on any matters concerning the working and the care of the ships, from any member of the crew, even the Boy, as I was to find out. He respected the crews and provided the ships were being looked after, and were available when needed, he left the running of them entirely to the Skippers and their men. When an opportunity occurred for members of the crew to have a day off, he accepted this and did not question it, as long as there were sufficient crew left aboard to look after the ship and to move her if necessary when discharging. Other than that, the crew were left to make their own arrangements for time off but a ship always had either the Skipper or Mate and the Chief or Second Engineer aboard them during the day or while discharging.

The office was run by the Head Clerk, with two assistant Clerks and a Secretary. The company had a thriving domestic coal round, employing six lorries with a driver and a mate to each. There were five employees working in the yard, including the Yard Foreman, and there were the seven ships, each with seven crew members. The paperwork involved in running all of this, plus the technical and insurance arrangements for the ships, the surveys and necessary repairs in Hill's dockyard, ordering of coal and arranging schedules for the transportation of it to Portishead, ordering stores for the ships, coal for the domestic round, the wages and much more, was all dealt with by a tiny group of administrators in the office, with the only modern office aids being telephones and manual typewriters.

There was a corner of one of the buildings in the Yard, which was a small separate and very independent kingdom. This was the lair and workshop of George Henry. George had been a fitter with Charles Hill but he had been lured away to work for O&W. George was short and thick-set but one of those men who could do anything with metal. He could mend, repair, improvise and generally keep anything mechanical going.

From Charles Hill's 1951 staff Christmas card.

George's lair was full of valves, pistons, pipes, tools, and other unknown bits and pieces, and not a few domestic odds-and-ends that had been sneaked in for his attention. He would always be on hand whenever there was anything out of the ordinary to be done on any of the ships – a general 'Mr. Fixit' and a great asset to the company.

The yard was served by a telfer crane which had its own driver and this was kept busy, not as much by O&W's own ships but by vessels belonging to other owners, which would visit the yard for discharging.

The London-registered coaster *Herb* discharging at O&W's wharf, circa 1960. She is seen here when in the illustrious ownership of a reknowned Bristol Channel 'seadog', Captain Peter Herbert. Her lowered profile enabled her to pass beneath the bridges on the River Thames, although she was actually built in Holland in 1928 for Dutch owners, probably for trading up some of the larger European rivers. She was sold and renamed *Rhone* in 1935 and was bought in 1960 by Peter Herbert in conjunction with his wife Gwendoline, who renamed her *Herb*. She was only with them for a short while, being sold the following year and then again in 1962, to R. Lapthorn & Co of Hoo, who renamed her *Hoocreek*. She was finally scrapped in 1976. *Jim Crissup*

THE BOY'S JOB

The Boy's job on each of the ships was to keep the accommodation clean, shop for the crew between trips, help with the ship's maintenance as instructed by the Mate and generally to be available to do anything that was required. Additionally, on most of the ships, cooking came into the job and it certainly did on *Colston*!

The ships were not provided with anything in the way of food. Although every facility was provided to prepare and cook food, it was left to the crew to feed themselves. The only meal which was communal in content was the main meal of the day. The Boy was expected to provide the basic vegetable content of the meal, to which each man would add his own choice of meat, such as chops, liver, or sausages, etc. This could create some problems of timing. It was sometimes difficult, due to the loading schedule, to decide exactly when the meal should be ready. Getting each of the different items of meat ready at the right time, often with sittings staggered if the meal was to be taken while making the crossing, could be – and often was – a bit hit and miss. Until I became used to this, there were many cuts of meat rapidly seared on the outside to look cooked but which were still pink on the inside. Having never had to cook anything before, I had to learn quickly before the crew went down with food poisoning. Gravy without 'doughboys' (lumps) was another trick I had to try to master.

Most of the shopping for the crew was done in Portishead and the boys from the coal boats were regular apparitions in the High Street, riding their bikes with bags of assorted loaves, vegetables, newspapers, bacon, etc, swinging from the handlebars. We usually got priority in the shops due to having to catch the tide, as it was explained to other waiting customers and we never disabused the kindly shop staff of this notion. There were occasions when a quick turn round would catch us out and an out-of-schedule replenishment of food was required. There were many times that I went to the back of the bakers shop in the village at 4 o'clock in the morning to buy bread straight from the oven, so hot that it couldn't be handled!

Being a very small town with few shops, each of the Boys had establishments that they favoured, usually influenced by the attractiveness of the young lady shop assistants. I regularly used one particular greengrocers shop for no other reason than it was the nearest one and the less distance on the bike with fourteen pounds of spuds swinging from the handlebars, the better. Many were the occasions that I bought vegetables very early in the morning from the lady who owned the shop, who was still clad in her dressing gown. Having to wait until after our arrival in Newport to go for the shopping would cramp my after hours activity (which will be explained later), so I tried as far as possible to get fixed up before we sailed. We sometimes had to shop at Newport but it was some distance from the docks to the town, so to avoid having to make this journey just for a couple of packets of cigarettes, I invested some of my own money and kept a small stock. This consisted of the various brands of cigarettes and tobacco, plus a couple of spare tins of Nestlé's condensed milk in my cabin. Although technically under age to buy tobacco, I never experienced any difficulty in this regard.

The vegetables, etc, were bought by myself and each Friday I would tot up what I had spent and then, having divided it up, I would collect the money from each member of the crew. There were never any complaints.

Colston had a well laid out galley, easy to use, with plenty of utensils and crockery. The large, black, coal-fired range was fed with coal taken from the bunker. This was filled from the deck above with good domestic coal and there was an outlet hatch in the galley alongside the stove. Firewood for the stove was chopped on a steel plate, about a foot square and let into the tiled deck.

The Mate was a good cook and, every now and again, he would take on the task of organising something a bit special for the main meal (perhaps he was anxious to quell mutinous rumblings from the crew but, whatever the reason, it was a godsend to me). Curries were his favourite and they were powerful!

During the autumn and winter time, when the fogs were about and there were going to be many hours spent on deck in the clammy cold, we would make up a huge pot of stew in the galley cauldron. Boiled meat marrow bones would be the basis of it, with all manner of vegetables chopped and tossed in, along with lumps of stewing steak, all bought as a communal project. There would be literally two or three gallons of this brew on the galley stove, all the time just bubbling gently. A pint mug of this broth would be taken along the deck to the men on the foc'sle on fog lookout, or on anchor watch standing in the cold, clammy

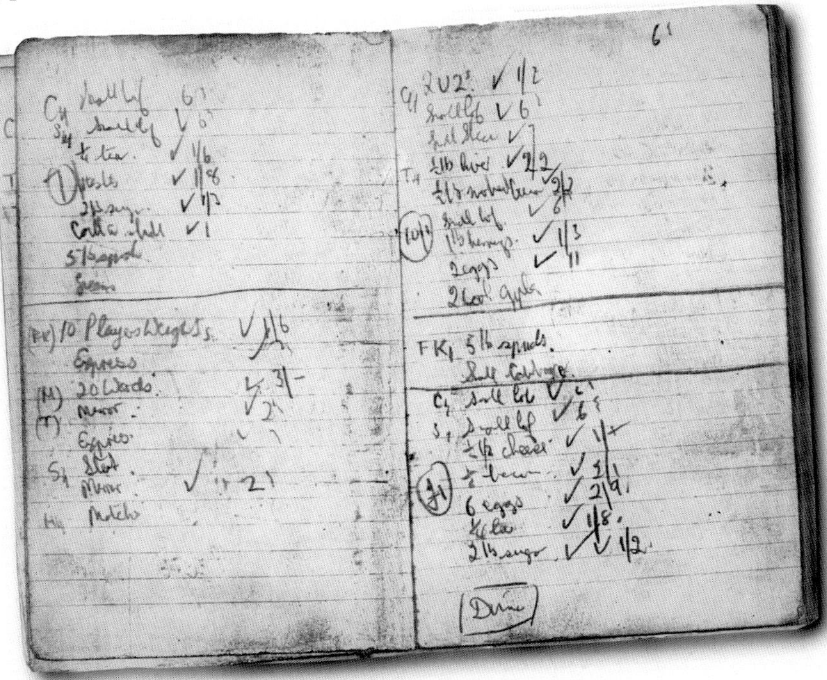

A typical shopping list from one of my notebooks.

air peering into the gloom with condensation from the mast stays dripping on them. It was welcome indeed!

Tea was a staple, served in pint mugs and the teapot was NEVER cold. Every visitor to the ship would make straight for the galley in the expectation of a mug of tea. The difference with our tea was that it was always made with Nestlé's condensed milk, as that would keep and cows milk wouldn't. So if you didn't ordinarily like sweetened tea, you soon learnt to!

As explained, *Colston* was only four weeks old when I joined her and still had that new ship smell about her. This was particularly noticeable in her accommodation and consisted of a mixture of paint, varnish and new upholstery but, as yet, without the all-pervasive smell of diesel fuel and cooking which becomes part of a small motorship's character later in her life. All her accommodation was below deck, except the Skipper's cabin which was on deck level (as was the chartroom), under the wheelhouse and bridge.

My cabin was at the after end of the ship and was very comfortable, with a proper bunk bed complete with reading lamp and a large upholstered settee, a central heating radiator for warmth, two portholes (with curtains) to give ample daylight, a wardrobe, a locker, and a folding table. All of the accommodation was painted a light cream colour, except the two washrooms and the galley which were painted white.

The crew's bathroom had a white tiled deck and was fitted with two hand-wash basins, a shower and a large square sink for washing clothes, all with hot and cold running water. The officers' washroom was similarly equipped. The fresh water on board had to be used economically. It was held in tanks built into the aft end of the superstructure and was replenished each trip with the softer South Wales water. In times of fog, water had to be used as sparingly as possible, in case we were forced to anchor for several tides as sometimes was the case.

The crew's mess room had a long table, with an upholstered bench seat along one side and two chairs on the other side. A locker for each crew member was fitted to the bulkhead for food storage. The mess room adjoined the galley, which was the focal point of the ship's social activity.

The alleyway from the galley led past the officer's washroom and the entrance to the engine room, to the officer's accommodation, where the Mate, the Chief Engineer and Second Engineer each had cabins. The officers' mess room was also located here, and this was spacious and well furnished. Completely panelled out in dark wood, with two portholes looking forward, it contained a large sideboard and glass cabinet, with a polished wood table flanked by two large chairs on one side and a brocade upholstered settee on the other.

It was going to be my job to keep the ship clean and tidy as far as the accommodation was concerned. The Skipper and crew were conscious of the very acceptable living facilities the ship offered and did what they could to keep her tidy. Inevitably, though, especially bearing in mind that the ship was transporting coal, it was going to take regular efforts to keep it all up together and, to this end, I worked out a programme by which I thoroughly cleaned a different part of the ship's accommodation one day each week, giving the other parts just a light spruce up on those days. In this way all the accommodation was thoroughly cleaned each week and it was quite presentable all of the time. The two Sailors looked after their own cabins, the crew's washroom and the crew's two toilets (one at deck level, and the other in the accommodation), and the central lobby around which the aft end accommodation was arranged. At the extreme after end of this was the steering flat, housing the hydraulic steering gear and the Chief Engineer's jealously guarded bag of cleaning rags. The steering flat was kept locked and the Chief had the key! The rest of the ship's accommodation and her wheelhouse was mine to look after.

Small though she was, the Skipper quite properly took the care of his ship very seriously and woebetide the crane driver at Portishead if he heard the grab clattering heavily against her side when she was discharging. After each loading, she was completely washed down and the wooden deck aft was scrubbed.

Whenever new coils of rope were delivered to the ship, they always had an eye spliced in each end before they were stowed in the foc'sle and, like the Skipper, the Mate too was very careful of the ship and its day-to-day management.

Thus I settled into the routine of the job and learnt, for the first time in my life, to think and plan for myself and that, unlike the years before, I now had responsibilities. I quickly found out that forgetting things that needed doing and promising to do things tomorrow was just not good enough. I soon worked out that it was best to make an early start each day on whatever cleaning was to be done and to leave the shopping (when we were in port) until later that morning. This way I avoided having to go to the shops again to buy something which someone had forgotten. It gave the crew time to decide what they wanted. Returning from the shopping, I would prepare the mid-day meal (again when we were in port and for whoever was going to be aboard) and would also have bought the food for the next trip if in the immediate future. So I learnt that a degree of planning and forethought made life much easier.

It had its advantages too. Providing that everything was done and finished, I was allowed off early during most afternoons when we were in Portishead, to return to the ship when we sailed, or earlier if I was needed to help move the ship when the discharging was completed.

Early on, I used to find matchsticks in corners and other unlikely places while cleaning. I didn't think too much about it until the Chief Engineer, a kindly man, confided in me that this was a ploy of the Skipper's to see how thoroughly, or otherwise, the cleaning was being done.

Wednesday was the day on which I cleaned the wheelhouse. This included cleaning the windows, polishing the fittings and furniture, scrubbing the duckboards and the deck, and polishing the brass. Having completed this one day while we were at Portishead and having done the rest of my tasks, I was anticipating an early departure and was in the galley when, sure enough, the Skipper entered and enquired if everything was done. On being informed that it was, he then said "*Come with me*". We went up on deck and then on up to the wheelhouse. He unlocked it and, stepping inside, told me to follow. No comment was made about the cleanliness but he went to the binnacle and, pointing to a small streak on the wooden base, asked "*What's this?*" Looking at it, I recognised it as a tiny smear of Brasso remaining from the mornings clean up and, licking my finger, I wiped it away. He looked at me and told me that I had better clean it again. I asked, somewhat bemused, if he meant that I should clean the whole binnacle again, to which he replied that he wanted me to clean the whole wheelhouse again. So that was my early afternoon shot to pieces!

Such episodes were few and far between but they taught me never to relax my guard and that, in the long run, it was better to get it right first time than risk being caught out.

At the age of 15, I was very proud of the ship. I did my first growing up aboard her and will always be grateful to the ship, the Skipper and the crew for teaching me that there are responsibilities in life as well as rights.

THE WORKBOAT

Having learnt the rudiments of sculling, a benefit which I greatly enjoyed was that of being allowed to use the workboat at Newport when the loading was finished. I used to try to ensure that my jobs were up-to-date, so that I could have some free time once the loading and washing down was completed. This could be as much as three hours.

While most of the crew would settle down to a game of crib in the mess room or try to catch up on some sleep, I would get permission to use the workboat. I tried to avoid being sent into the town on my bike for shopping during this period after loading. At first, this would happen frequently, when one of the card players ran out of cigarettes or tobacco. This is when my little hoard of cigarettes, matches and tobacco came into its own.

The Mate had realised that sculling was something that I enjoyed, so instead of lifting the boat aboard and stowing it in the forward hold as soon as the loading was completed, he would leave it over the side for me to use. I became quite proficient (or so I thought at the time) at sculling the boat and could even scull it backwards. In this manner, I spent many happy hours simply dawdling about all over the busy docks looking at the big ships.

However, I was to learn the hard way that it was one thing to be able to simply scull the boat about on a quiet sunny evening and to play with it but to actually use it was another thing altogether.

I was not the only one to make use of the workboat other than in its official role of providing a means of painting the sides of the ship. One day, in the dark of a winter evening, the Mate and one of the sailors set off in the workboat, giving me instructions to be on deck in half an hour to help them with the boat on their return. I duly waited and soon, out of the darkness, came the sound of the boat being sculled with some vigour, accompanied by the clinking of glass and the slopping of water...

They had visited a Swedish ship moored at the buoys and had returned with some souvenirs in the form of a few bottles and some cartons of cigarettes. Somehow, they had managed between them to kick the bung out of the bottom of the boat and the water was coming in fast, leaving the cigarette cartons afloat. The boat's lifting strop was hastily attached to the derrick and it was later lifted aboard slowly to drain it out as it rose.

My own wish to learn how to use the boat was in response to the horror stories I had heard about mooring up at Ely Harbour, where use of the boat was central to the whole operation and I knew that I couldn't count on us never having to go there.

On the few occasions when there might be a lull in the work, mainly during the summer, the two Sailors would come to the ship each day to undertake maintenance and painting. If the ship was empty, this would usually mean it was over-the-side painting, using the workboat. If the potential was for a few days without a trip, the Skipper would arrange for the engine room not to have pumped in the ballast, so that the ship was as high as possible out of the water. These days were known as 'a day's docking', for which the Sailors were paid extra in the absence of trip and discharge payments. Unfortunately, the Boy didn't get this benefit – he was on flat money!

THE SHIP'S PLAQUE

After 1953, every ship built by Charles Hill carried a bronze plaque, almost eleven inches in diameter, which was fitted prominently on the vessel. Those of ***Colston*** and ***Brandon*** were fitted to the front of the bridge structure.

Colston's bell was kept polished, as was the builder's plaque. The plaque could only be polished when there was coal in the hold, on which to stand the ladder. The bell was easily accessible and it was a job that I never minded doing.

Prior to 1953, ships built by Charles Hill & Sons Ltd carried the usual plate giving the name of the builder, their Yard No. and year of build. After 1953, Hills fitted instead a circular cast bronze plaque, almost eleven inches in diameter. Cast in high relief, it was dark in colour but the lettering, the star and the rims of the scroll were polished, as were the high points of the central picture.

Above: A mock-up of *Colston*'s plaque, Yard No. 378 of 1955. After cleaning the genuine article, I would coat it with Linseed Oil to protect it from the salt air and spray.

Left: This replica plaque was cast using the original mould.

LOTS OF LESSONS

There were many little lessons to be learnt. During only my second or third week aboard, while we were on our way back from Newport, I decided to chop some fire wood for the galley range. I set too splitting the particularly knotty wood, using the little plate in the galley deck put there expressly for this purpose.

I had only been at it for a couple of minutes when the engine stopped. I hadn't heard the telegraph ring so, wondering what the problem was, I went up on deck to see what was happening. I could see no obvious reason for the stop and after a few minutes it started again. Thinking perhaps this was something that was done every now and again to test something or other, I went back to my job of splitting firewood. Suddenly, the engine stopped again.

This time I carried on splitting wood, until the Chief Engineer came up from the engine room, to where he could see directly into the galley and what I was doing. Stalking in, he told me in no uncertain terms that when I wanted to chop firewood, to take it up on deck at the forward end of the ship and positively never – EVER – do it again in the galley, directly over the engine room! The irregular thudding had put an almighty fear into him that something was coming adrift inside his brand new engine.

Lessons such as learning to make sure that the cork fender (the Skipper wouldn't have the hard cane ones) was actually on the belting under the bridge whenever we came alongside in the locks and NOT on the plating – and being reminded by a voice from above if it wasn't (he didn't miss much).

Portishead Dock had no natural inflow of water, so when the water became low, two large diesel pumps located alongside the lock gates would be started, to feed water into the dock via a small canal. This was an expensive business and the Dock Master tried to avoid the process by minimising the use of the locks as far as possible. With its extensive range of tides, however, the situation would often occur when, approaching the top of the big tides, the level outside, in the Bristol Channel, would reach and even become higher than the level of water in the dock. Naturally, in these circumstances, both sets of lock gates would have to be opened, leaving a common level straight through.

Arrival at these times was welcomed, especially if there was a chance of catching the last bus home that evening, as the time normally taken to lock in would be saved. The ship would just sail straight through on receiving permission to proceed and would be taken close to the wall of the lock as she passed through. The Sailor and the Boy, landing to take the ropes, would then clamber onto the narrow rail on the top of the bulwarks and leap ashore across the gap without the ship stopping. Luckily, no one ever fell in, as they would have been unlikely to have survived if they had done so, almost certainly being crushed between the moving ship and the wall. This was a particularly risky part of the job especially if it was a damp and dark night, and the ship's rail and the wall were wet and slippery.

The Dock Master got his free top-up by closing the lock as soon as the tide had receded level with the tops of the gates, the maximum level that the dock could retain.

One afternoon, we loaded in the top dock at Newport, which was a fairly unusual occurrence. Here, because the coal tips in the top dock were on the quay wall, instead of built on a jetty as were the tips in main dock, the ship had to be kept clear of the wall throughout the loading, so that the chute dropped the coal into the hold instead of over the (outboard) side. This necessitated a stern rope being taken out to one of the buoys in the middle of the dock, about fifty yards away and the workboat was used for this. With the eye of the rope in the boat, it was sculled out to the buoy, towing the rope behind.

Letting go the rope when the ship was sailing involved using the boat to go out to the buoy, detaching the rope from the mooring ring and keeping the eye of the rope in the boat while it was pulled in by the capstan on the stern of the ship. This ensured that the rope was not free to sink into the water, where it might well become entangled with the ship's propeller.

On this particular day we were due to sail from Newport at about 10pm. It was a dark, wet and windy winter evening. Fred, the senior of the two Sailors, usually sculled the boat on occasions such as this but, this particular night, anxious to prove my competence with the boat, I badgered him into letting me go to bring the rope in when letting go. He hesitated but eventually agreed and, as it was dark when the time came to let go, no one noticed what happened.

Unlike the flat-topped buoys in the main dock, the ones in the top dock were shaped exactly like oversized fishing floats, having a domed conical top with the mooring ring at the apex.

On reaching the buoy, it was necessary to climb onto it to let the rope go to bring the eye back into the boat. I started to climb aboard but it was very slippery with the rain and the coating of seagull's droppings, and I made the almost inevitable mistake of having one foot on the buoy and the other in the boat. The latter began to move rapidly away from the buoy and I fell into the water. Luckily, despite the shock, I had the presence of mind to keep hold of the boat's bow rope. Dressed up in my oilskin and wellingtons, I was in no state to swim but I managed to pull myself to the boat, where I made my way to the stern and climbed back in. Having heard the splash, Fred alerted the Skipper, who took the powerful Aldis signal lamp and shone it over the water, just in time to see me getting back into the boat.

There was nothing anyone could do to help as, of course, I had the boat with me. I got back onto the buoy, let go the rope and was eventually pulled safely back to the ship. After a change of clothes, although the whole episode was a bit humiliating, I could see the funny side of it and didn't really realise how serious it could have been. However, once on our way back, the Skipper called myself and the Sailor into the officer's mess room and gave us both a severe dressing down, especially Fred. As he pointed out, he did not relish the prospect of having to attend an inquest to explain the loss of the ship's Boy, as could so easily have been the case.

Very often, on the return trip from Newport, I would steer the ship, never unsupervised of course but with no interference as long as things were going alright. This would include passing other ships and making the way from one navigation buoy to another. It was while doing this that I realised how much rudder had to be kept on when going across the tide, especially with the big tides, to counteract the sideways push and keep the ship in a straight line whilst making for where I wanted to go. The result was a distinctly crabwise progress across the Channel. The ship would be in hand steering mode out at sea, the power steering being used only for manoeuvring in dock.

Colston's Skipper would have been quite at home with a tug. He could handle the ship with a great deal of confidence and flair, as far as was possible given that she was no speedboat. The best example of this was mooring her up in O&W's yard at Bristol. This was positioned at more than ninety degrees back on itself relative to the main waterway of the dock and it was therefore, a greater than right-angled turn to take a ship into the yard when arriving from the locks and the Cumberland Basin.

The conventional way of taking a ship in was to approach slowly, to land a rope on the knuckle at the end of the basin and to slowly check the ship round on this spring using short and gentle 'Ahead' nudges with the engine, until she was lined up. The other ropes were then landed and the vessel was gently pulled into her berth.

Colston's Skipper used to do it differently...

He used to hang right back in the Cumberland Basin, in order to have the furthest possible distance to travel after other ships locking in had gone clear. Once ready to move, he would ring down for 'Full Ahead'. The ship would gradually pick up speed as she travelled the length of the basin, before dashing through the narrow swing bridge opening, still gathering way. With some distance still to go but at just the right time, judged to perfection as the yard entrance was approaching, the engine room telegraph would be put to 'Full Astern'.

Like all single-screw ships, she would 'quarter' when going astern and in ***Colston***'s case this was to starboard. With a lot of way on, she took a deal of sternway to stop her, especially when loaded. With the engine still bellowing away and the water in the dock now muddied and in turmoil, she would be gradually coming to a halt but the quartering effect would

Skipper Sammy Taylor on *Colston*'s bridge. *Author*

throw her stern out and around, as her bow slowly turned towards the yard entrance.

Having judged it perfectly, by the time the ship was completely stopped, she had made the turn and was now virtually pointing straight into the basin, at which point she was given a short squirt of headway, to slide gently and calmly into the berth. The first ropes to be landed would be her final moorings. No fuss, no bother. It was then just a question of mooring her exactly where the Yard Foreman wanted her relative to the crane.

It was a feature of a trip to the yard at Bristol that no ship could moor up there without there being a war of words between the Yard Foreman and the Skippers.

The Foreman during my time was a very likable chap but could not stop himself from shouting instructions to the sailors on the ship, such as "*Slack off*" or "*Heave in*" regarding the various ropes. However, these instructions were not always in accordance with what the Skipper wanted to happen. After a while, with the Foreman's instructions becoming ever more forceful with his frustration, a comment such as "*You run the yard, I'll run the bloody ship*" would emanate from the wheelhouse. Once the principle was established that the Yard Foreman had every right to have the ship positioned where he needed her to be for access by the crane but that it was the Skippers business as to how she was put there, peace would be restored. It was always a source of amusement to the crews but no lasting animosity ever arose.

Being a disused dry dock, the stepped sides of the basin did not make for easy access and a ladder from ship to shore, rather than a gangway, was used.

With Mr. Osborn's office window directly overlooking the basin, the opportunity was always taken to do a bit of over the side painting, particularly as the stepped sides of the dock also gave good access.

THE ROYAL VISIT TO BRISTOL

On 17th April 1956, HM the Queen and HRH the Duke of Edinburgh made a ceremonial visit to Bristol. This was to include a short trip in the Royal Barge along the length of the Floating Harbour. The Barge had arrived at Charles Hill's dockyard several days before and was kept under cover in conditions of tight security and safety.

Each Bristol-based shipping company agreed to send a vessel to line the harbour and to represent O&W, ***Colston*** was selected. Several days before the occasion, she arrived at the company yard, where she was partly discharged to give her a nice trim in the water. Her hatches and hatch cloths were put on, not only to give a tidy appearance but also because she was to play host to any of the company employees who wished to be aboard for the big day. ***Colston*** was well supplied with drinks and refreshments, with soft drinks for the children, and she was dressed overall. With so many youngsters aboard, having virtually free run of the ship, it quickly became necessary to lock the engine room telegraph and ships wheel.

Once the Royal visit was over, ***Colston*** returned to the yard the next morning, where the discharge was completed and she returned to normal duty.

ROYAL VISIT. 17. 4. 1956.

Please permit BEARER to have access to m.v. "COLSTON" to view the passing of Her Majesty the Queen and H.R.H. Duke of Edinburgh in the Royal barge.

Visitors must embark latest by 10.0.a.m. on 17th April 1956 and may be requested to be ashore by 11.45.a.m.

The Western Daily Press on the morning of Monday 16th April will give the position of the vessel.

Smoking on the quays is not permitted and car parking at or near vessels will not be possible.

for OSBORN & WALLIS, LIMITED.

Director.

BERTHING PLAN FOR HARBOUR

Ships on Royal route

THE Floating Harbour was busy over the weekend as big and little ships moved into the berths alotted to them by the Port of Bristol Authority for tomorrow's visit of the Queen. The Royal barge will pass along the waterway from Charles Hill's shipyard to the Bridgehead.

There is likely to be just as much activity today and up to 10 a.m. tomorrow when all shipping has to be settled and the water completely clear except for the craft of the River Police which will flank the Royal barge throughout the short voyage.

As far as is possible, and weather permitting, tomorrow will be a normal working day, and about two vessels are expected to arrive by 10 a.m., while about 11 ships will be working. Indeed, some of them may have left by the time the Royal party embark at Charles Hill's premises, for "time and tide wait for no man," and schedules must be observed.

Provision has been made in the berthing plan for the mooring of about 30 private yachts along the harbourside, of which 24 will tie up alongside Narrow Quay, and the rest alongside the harbour railway wharf.

NAVAL SHIPS

When the Royal barge leaves the embarkation point, the route will lead downriver for a short distance towards Mardyke ferry, passing H.M.S. Recruit. The barge will then turn about and head upriver, passing on the port side. H.M.S. Flying Fox, H.M.S. Locust, H.M.S. Venturer, and the Bristol Queen, as well as a collection of small craft moored in any available space against the quay at Hotwells Road.

Proceeding, the Royal party will pass the Stanleigh on the port side, and the Portway, while on the starboard side there will be a number of "arrivals" and ships being worked.

Having passed the Gas Works and with Sheds A, Y and Z on the port side, the Royal visitors will see the crowds on the Apollo, and any of the crews of ships working. Opposite Shed Z on the starboard side will be a few private yachts.

At this point, as the barge turns towards the Bridgehead, the vessels alongside both port and starboard sides of the harbour will be getting more numerous. The Colston, the Steepholm, and the Camerton will fill the port gap between Z Shed and Tb Shed, while on the other side of the water will be the Denby, the Cardiff Queen, and two working ships, the Juno and the Stalheim, loading and discharging from Sheds M and L.

NEAR THE BRIDGEHEAD

The Stalheim is the last big ship which will be moored on the starboard side except for the Peter Leigh at Narrow Quay. Otherwise most of the quay space will be taken by private yachts and other similarly-sized "grandstands." Last along the starboard quay will be the Sea Scouts and Rangers.

One of the expected arrivals will birth at Sheds Ta and Tb, on the port side, while the Laverock will be working at Shed V, and the Ystroom at Shed U.

The Cambell steamer, Glen Gower, and the Sea Queen, no doubt crowded with onlookers who will in that position be able to see the landing stage, will berth alongside Shed W, and the West Garth and the Cabot, with two of the best berths opposite the landing stage, will moor alongside Shed E.

The journey is likely to be exciting and colourful as the Queen passes along the historic waterway between lines of "dressed" ships crowded with cheering people.

THE ROYAL ROUTE THROUGH THE PORT OF BRISTOL

SHOWING THE LATEST FIXED POSITIONS OF THE VESSELS THE QUEEN WILL SEE

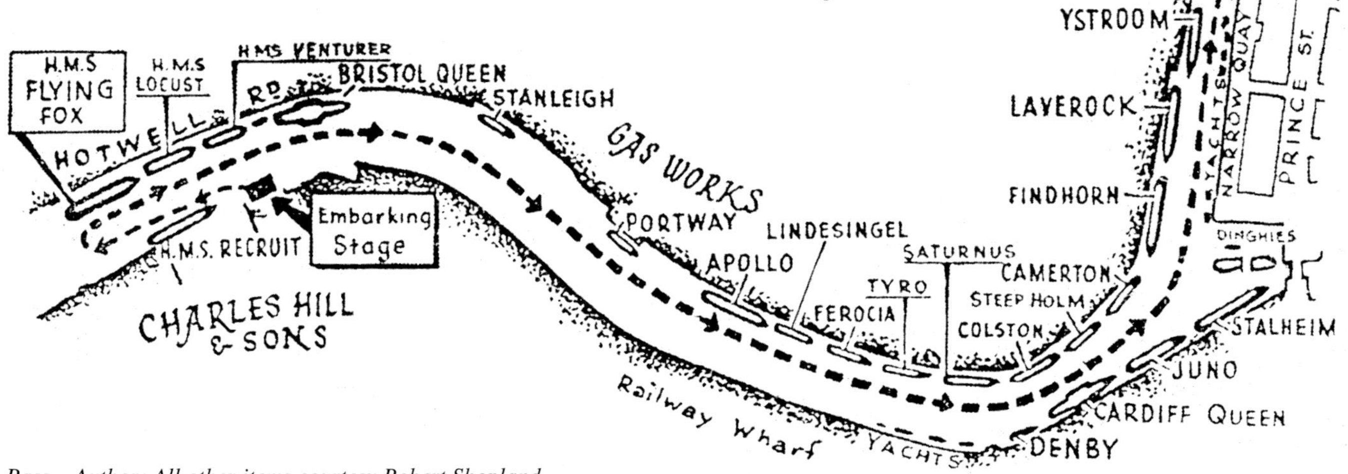

Pass – Author; All other items courtesy Robert Shopland

This page: Various views of *Colston* on the day of the Royal Visit to Bristol, 17th April 1956. She was dressed overall for the occasion and played host to a party of company officials, employees and invited guests. *All author*

Opposite page: The official invite, which was needed to be able to get on board *Colston* for the day, along with a selection of newspaper clippings recording the visit and a plan of the route, showing the various locally-owned ships especially moored for the Royal Barge to pass by.

HOLIDAY RELIEFS

During my second year with the company – and still Boy on *Colston* – I was asked if, during the holiday period, I would like to stand in and help the Chief Engineer in the engine room while the Second Engineer was away. I would not be completely absolved from all the Boy's duties because, whilst arrangements were made for all the crew to look after their own accommodation, I should still have to fit in the galley cleaning and the shopping. I would be paid my Boy's money plus £20, which seemed like a potential fortune at the time. It would undoubtedly be good experience for later and I was only too pleased to accept the opportunity.

Consequently, I spent as much time as I could in the engine room, where, with the Chief looking on, I learnt which to use of what seemed a multitude of valves to pump the ballast in and out and, of course, how to start the auxiliaries, to put power on the deck for the winch and capstan. For this, I made my own crib note book and, after the first week, I was able to do all of this unsupervised without doing any damage!

The Chief Engineer had a particular anxiety that whenever the main engine, or the auxiliaries were started (all by compressed air), the FIRST thing to do once they were running, before anything else at all was done, was to shut off the compressed air bottles. For some reason, he had an anxiety about the compressed air leaking away. Quite why this was I never understood, as the auxiliaries could be started by hand, after which the bottles could be pumped up. However, this was his Golden Rule and I was in no position to challenge it.

I was also able to handle the main engine in response to telegraph orders, again under supervision. That seemed to go well enough with no great dramas.

The firm could be flexible with its crew members and there was a considerable amount of movement between the ships during the holiday periods.

So it was that the Chief Engineer had gone away with *Hotwells* for a trip and it was up to me to look after *Colston* while she was discharging. This only required starting the generators and pumping ballast, with which I was by now quite competent. *Hotwells* was due back on the next tide, the one on which we were due to sail. The Chief would come straight on board from her and would sail again immediately with us. However, the Dock Master came to the ship and asked the Skipper to put her in the locks as soon as possible, which would then be levelled down so that *Hotwells* could come straight in on her return. This would save a precious lock full of water from the dock.

The Skipper came to me and asked if I was happy to use the main engine on my own to carry this out and I told him that I was. In due course, with the discharge completed, we got ready to move her into the lock. I was confident enough that everything would be alright but just in case I stalled her, I made the decision that having started the main engine, I would leave the compressed air on so that it could be started again immediately, without having to dash the length of the engine room and up the short ladder to the air bottles to open them up again. I was just sixteen years old and felt terribly responsible for this, the newest ship in the company, and the vision of her drifting powerless and maybe hitting the lock gates, unable to go astern while I wrestled with the compressed air supply, seemed too dreadful to contemplate. However, all went normally and having moored in the lock, the engine was shut down and the air turned off. When the Chief came on board and asked who had put her in the lock and was told that I had, he asked me if everything had been all right and, perhaps unwisely, I told him what I had done.

At first, he hit the roof and angrily informed me that what I had done was against all that he had been telling me. Ten minutes later, however, he came to me and actually apologised. He told me that if circumstances were such again and I was left in charge, I could make the same decision but would answer for it if things went wrong. When he was on board, however, the engine room was to be run his way. I accepted this and there were no repercussions for the rest of my time down below. It had been the first adult decision that I had ever made.

Later that same summer, I went as relieving Sailor on *Rockleaze* and this time I was paid the full rate. This meant helping with the discharging – known as a 'hobble', whilst those doing it were called 'hobblers' – which involved going down into the holds when the unloading was nearly complete and shovelling the difficult to reach coal so that it was accessible to the crane. There was extra pay for each hobble. Although it was summer-time and consequently the ships were not too busy, my wages still seemed to be a fortune. This also broke the ice for me regarding the living conditions on the steamers. With their 1920s accommodation and lack of facilities, it was quite a shock living in the foc'sle and sharing with the other Sailor after the luxury of *Colston*. At least *Rockleaze* had a half decent galley and an amiable crew, and was thus a happy ship to be on.

This also gave me my first sighting of Ely Harbour (other than my pleasure trip of several years before when I had not taken too much notice). Her permanent Sailor used the workboat to moor up every trip, since I was an unknown quantity and the boatman was crucial to the operation of mooring here. I watched and took note. It seemed to be an uncomfortable enough exercise in summer weather, with daylight and decent conditions, still less having to do it at night, in the winter, in the dark and with wind and tide to contend with. It did nothing to ease my apprehension of ever going on to one of the Ely Harbour trading ships permanently. The odds of staying on the two vessels that ran to Newport only were obviously pretty small. I didn't realise at the time that they were, in fact, non-existent, as it was the company's procedure to ensure that all the Sailors could work on any of the ships.

After my two weeks on *Rockleaze*, I realised that sculling and playing with the boat in Newport Dock, whilst better than nothing, was poor preparation for what might be coming! The other thing I had to master and practice until I could do it in the dark was the tying of a Bowline knot. At Ely Harbour, this knot had to be tied quickly and absolutely securely, often on a stiff and unyielding five-inch rope, with freezing hands, while standing in a rocking boat, which was being tugged by the wind and tide. My memories of Ely Harbour are always of cold, wind, rain, pitch dark and strong tides, and the difficulties of pulling the rope around the dank and slimy piles of the coal tip to tie the long eye in the rope... It was not always like this, of course. There must have been nice weather and good days sometimes but I don't seem to remember those!

I was glad to return to *Colston*, in due course, with her comfortable, civilised living and the ease of a Newport only running regime. Things were never quite the same again, however, for now I had the bogeyman of Ely Harbour always in the back of my mind. I felt sure that, sooner or later, I would be confronted with it.

Over the next year, I was called upon several times to go relieving in the other company ships and, like most of the other men, I could eventually say that I had been on all but one of them, if only for a couple of weeks. Only ***Salcombe*** was missing from my experiences. I enjoyed the Second Engineer stints most of all and, luckily, this was always in one of the motorships.

I was never called upon to act as Second Engineer, (Fireman) in one of the steamers and, though glad of it at the time – it was really hard, continuous and dirty work, in contrast to the wearing of clean overalls whilst monitoring the temperatures and pressures of the diesel engine – in some ways I regret never having had just a brief experience of it. I do not think that I would have liked it, though, even if I could have stood the pace.

THE LEVEL OF EQUIPMENT ON THE SHIPS

As I previously mentioned, at the time that I joined the Company, they were operating three steamships and four motorships.

The steamers were very basic in their level of equipment, there being no electricity at all on board. Lighting was by paraffin, in shared cabins with no separate washing facilities. ***Downleaze*** and ***Rockleaze*** at least had adequate cooking facilities but ***Druid Stoke*** was extremely basic and inadequate in her provision for all of her crew.

The motorships were better equipped, with proper washing and toilet facilities, and a civilised galley. All the accommodation was aft, below deck. The two smaller motorships, ***St. Vincent*** and ***Hotwells***, had separate cabins, washing facilities and messroom for the officers, while the Sailors and the Boy shared two cabins and their own messroom. ***Salcombe*** was similarly equipped but with sufficient cabin accommodation for each member of the crew, including the Boy, to have their own cabin. The last two ships, ***Colston*** and ***Brandon***, were very well fitted out in terms of domestic facilities. The officers and crew had separate mess rooms and separate bathrooms, with hot and cold running water, laundry facilities and showers.

Board of Trade regulations were introduced during 1950 requiring that all ships over 150 feet in length carry two masthead navigation lights. Consequently, ***St. Vincent***, ***Hotwells*** and ***Salcombe*** each had to be fitted with the second mast to comply with these new requirements. These second masts were basic poles simply there to carry the light and they were supported by wire stays. In fact the new masts fitted to ***Hotwells*** and ***St. Vincent*** were the redundant derricks from ***Salcombe***'s original centre mast. The two '***leaze***'s each had three masts already, whilst ***Druid Stoke*** was just under the length requiring the second light.

Colston and ***Brandon*** were built with second masts from new, which meant they at least looked like part of the ship and also served several purposes, carrying the docking lights, radio aerials and a gaff for the ensign as well. The main masts had a full-height access ladder and were supported by two fixed stays forming a tripod base. The foremast also had an access ladder.

Salcombe's mainmast was initially fitted directly in front of the wheelhouse but was found to be vulnerable to damage while loading and discharging. Its forward supporting stays had to be dismounted on each occasion, so it was later moved to the after end of the superstructure and supported with fixed legs, as in ***Colston*** and ***Brandon***.

Also to comply with Board of Trade regulations requiring every vessel of 700 grt or more to carry ship-to-shore radio and a qualified radio operator, ***Colston*** and ***Brandon*** were so equipped from new, with sets in the wheelhouse. ***Salcombe*** was also fitted with radio and this was situated in her officers messroom. The other motorships had nothing in the way of communication except a fitted Morse lamp, while the steamers carried nothing at all. The motorships carried docking lamps to indicate their intended destination. Each ship, including the steamers, carried a full set of international signal flags.

During 1958, ***Colston*** and ***Brandon*** were fitted with Decca Navigator equipment. This operated by taking triangulated bearings from shore-based radio beacons. The bearing of each signal was shown on the indicator dials and repeated on a master dial for confirmation, and the results were plotted on specially gridded charts. This was accurate to within sixty feet anywhere on the British coast, to the extent that allowance even had to be made for the position of the receiving aerials relative to the length of the ship – even such small ships as ours. When anchored at the turn of the tide, the ship's swing around her anchor chain could be clearly and accurately plotted. This enabled ***Colston*** and ***Brandon*** to leave the recognised navigation channels in fog, in order to take advantage of their Skippers' local knowledge and go over the sandbanks to avoid other shipping.

A Decca Navigator set, identical to those fitted to *Colston* and *Brandon*, showing the indicator dials on which each radio beacon signal was shown.
Author's collection

During 1960, ***Colston*** and ***Brandon*** were also fitted with radar for their work further down the Bristol Channel. With the fitment of a liferaft to supplement the lifeboats, they were thus equipped to the same standard as most other coasting vessels.

With the different conditions on their new tasks, these two ships had their galley cooking facilities changed to gas fuelling and each vessel was also fitted with a food freezer. Both now carried a permanent cook too. No changes or improvements were made to any of the other remaining ships in the fleet and thus they retained a 1950s level of equipment and facilities until their disposal by the company in 1969-70.

TIDES

With its huge tidal range, the upper Bristol Channel demanded its own specialised understanding and knowledge. In this and in common with other small ship Skippers trading in the region, as well as the Channel Pilots, the Captains of the O&W ships were very skilful and knowledgeable. The ships were small, just about adequately powered and required a good deal of experience to navigate safely. On the largest tides each year, the sea can run at up to six knots in places and navigation buoys can be seen lying at severe angles as they stream in the tidal run. With the ships having speeds of between 8 and 9 knots, progress was very slow when punching against such tidal runs. Conversely, the ships would fairly hurtle along (relative to the ground) when running with the tide. Small tides, with the least range between high and low water, would have runs of only 2 or 3 knots. A ship's speed over the ground still changed in relation to this and of course, there were almost infinite variations in ship-over-ground speeds for tides inbetween in size.

Straight into, or straight against the tide was difficult enough but on big tides, the approach to another ship dead ahead necessitated an early change of course, since one of the ships would be bowling along far more rapidly than would at first appear to be the case. Much of the time during a trip, though, would be spent running either directly or diagonally across the tidal run and a considerable degree of 'heading off' would thus be necessary. The ship's bow would be aimed at a point much further upstream or downstream than where it was actually desired to go, to allow for the fact that the vessel would be carried bodily up or down the Channel with the movement of the water.

It was this factor which called for the profound experience necessary to navigate the ships in fog, when nothing in the way of shore or navigation buoys and lights could be seen. There was, therefore, no visual reference to show exactly just how far upstream or downstream, the ship was being carried by the tide.

Thus the tides were of the utmost concern to the Skippers and they learnt to take advantage of big tides and the consequent increased depth of water by going over the sandbanks when conditions were right, thereby considerably shortening the trip. Sandbanks move, however, changing in response to the forces of the tides. It was only the most exact local knowledge and experience which enabled the Skippers of all of the little ships trading in the upper Bristol Channel to get their craft about with such apparent ease and relative lack of incident.

It is difficult to understand and compare the difference today, when even the smallest of private pleasure craft carries satellite navigation gear, echo sounders and often even radar, whilst drawing only a couple of feet and moving in a Channel virtually empty of other ships. In my day, as for many decades previously, there would be many ships, large and small, fast and slow, all making their way through the confined and congested navigation channels, very often, as with the O&W ships, groping their way blindly along in zero visibility, whilst coping with the second highest tidal range in the world. It required a very special skill and great experience to be able to do this.

WIND

The wind would create its own problems. Blowing against the tide, it could bring up some choppy conditions and although with short voyages such as between Newport and Portishead there were no big seas to contend with, the power stations were not at all happy with excessively wet and salty coal going into their boilers. The ships habitually ran without their hatches and cloths on, and with only a two or three hour trip from Newport or Ely Harbour, this was normally the case. Not a strictly seaworthy practice, of course, but battening down was a considerable chore, especially when it was all going to have to come off again a couple of hours later, whilst going over 'hatches on' when travelling light ship was unheard of. In later years, though, when trading below the Holms Islands down Channel to Yelland and Hayle, the ships were battened down completely whenever they were at sea, whether light or laden.

So our degree of preparation in the event of wind for a return trip to Portishead varied from just dragging a hatch cloth over the coal at the after end of the forehatch to keep the coal dry, through a partial battening down with boards and cloths for the forehatch (in which case the coal in the main hold needed to be kept dry by the hatchcloth), to a full battening down of both hatches if really bad conditions

Fred and Jim run the beams along the main hatch coamings. *Author*

Fred, Jim and Gordon. *Author*

were expected. In this event, the workboat was stowed down in the forward hold and the cargo had to be trimmed down sufficiently to allow the hatch beams to be travelled over the hold.

The wind did, however, create one problem when the ship was light. On arrival at Newport locks, the engine room would normally begin to drain the ballast tanks. Much of it could be jettisoned by gravity to save pumping. However, as the ship came higher out of the water and with her hatches open, she would, in gusty enough wind conditions, blow about on the surface like a balloon – most unhandy when trying to get alongside a tip. If this seemed likely to be a problem, the engine room would be told to keep the 225 tons of ballast in the tanks until the ship was completely moored up at the tip.

FOG

Our main weather problem in the winter months was fog. This could be extremely dense and at times, the length of the ship could not be seen and the bridge would be invisible from the foc'sle. In these conditions, of course, we would not sail. The Skippers would visit the Dock Master's office at Portishead and would phone Walton Bay Signal Station to ask what conditions were like down there. They would then make their individual decisions whether to sail or not, based on that information and their own experience.

However, that did not prevent us getting caught out in it. With no navigational aids whatsoever (until the Decca Navigator equipment was fitted later on), it really was a problem and it depended entirely on the knowledge and skill of the Skippers to work out the compass course between the navigation marks. These compass courses and the time between marks altered with the height of the tides and consequent speed of the tidal currents. Big tides could produce runs of water of up to five knots and small tides of about three. The state of cleanliness of the ship's bottom and whether she had not long been dry docked, or was due for docking, also had an influence and, of course, it was critical that the engine was ALWAYS run at the same revolutions to keep the times between marks relevant.

In good weather, the compass courses and times between marks would always be noted down as a reference for foggy conditions and this was what the ships were run on in conditions of poor visibility. It was not just the fog itself that had to be contended with. There was always other shipping on the move as well and, in the very confined navigable channels, this was another serious consideration. With a reluctance to reduce the speed, which would thereby introduce a variation in the times and the compass course, and to have to make the consequent allowances for this, navigation in fog became a matter of the greatest skill on the part of the Skippers. While the missing of one navigation mark was just about acceptable, missing another one meant that they were now really unsure as to where they were. In the upper Bristol Channel, it was unwise to stray unsighted even a modest distance from the navigation channels, so that would mean anchoring, after first taking the depth of water with a lead line. This latter was important if there was any doubt at all that there might not be sufficient water under the ship, to allow for the possibility that it might have to remain anchored there through the ebb and bottom of the tide. With the rise and fall in the Bristol Channel, especially during the Spring Tides, the ship could be anything up to thirty-six feet nearer the Channel bottom at low tide than she was at the top of the tide.

The fitting of the Decca Navigator later on, with its great positional accuracy, solved all these problems. The ship would quite often be deliberately taken out of the navigation channels and in over the sandbanks, in places where there was known to be sufficient depth of water, in order to get out of the way of other shipping staying strictly in the authorised navigation channels.

Fog meant that everyone was on deck except the Engineers. As the Boy, I was allowed to turn in at night when we had an early morning sailing and to stay there until 7 o'clock in the morning. Often during the winter, though, there would be a banging on the cabin door and the message that "*The Skipper wants you on deck*". This would mean fog. The two sailors were stationed on the foc'sle, the Skipper on the wheel, the Mate on the starboard bridge wing and myself on the port bridge wing. The Skipper would call out which mark to be looking for and approximately where and when he expected it to appear.

However, the difficulty with fog was that you had no idea how FAR you were seeing. It was just a grey featureless shroud and this effect was worse at night, when there was just a blanket of damp blackness to peer into, with only the fog swirling about in the loom of the navigation lights to give any idea of its density. In daytime, the visibility to the bow of the ship might give a slight indication but, other than that, you might be peering through the gloom and seeing a quarter of a mile, or you might be seeing only twenty yards or less. So you had no idea how large the buoy that you were expecting to see would appear to be. The whistle would be sounded at regular intervals when on the move and would be answered by any other ship in the vicinity and this would continue until the vessels had groped their way past one another.

A ship at anchor would ring its bell at intervals but, again, as with sight in fog, it was difficult to judge how far away the sound was and there were many instances of a ship suddenly materialising out of the gloom looking far bigger (nearer) than had been expected. This did at least give an indication of how far you were seeing at that point and at that time. However, the fog might be patchy and uneven, and could not be relied upon to be constant and uniform. It could sometimes be very dense but only very close to the water, whilst on occasion, the view from the mast top would show the tops of other ships masts poking up through the dense blanket of cotton wool-like fog.

Once anchored in fog, the foc'sle and the bridge would be manned at all times, the Sailor on the foc'sle having to ring the bell as required. There was also the added necessity of checking that she wasn't dragging her anchor. With the very strong tidal runs in the Bristol Channel, a lot of chain would have to be let out and it would be under considerable tension. By placing a hand on the length of chain from the hawse pipe to the windlass, you could feel it vibrating evenly with the water passing round it if the anchor was holding. If it was dragging, this could be distinctly felt as a series of irregular jolts through the anchor chain. It was an eerie situation to be stopped out in the Channel, with no engine sound and surrounded by this grey, clammy, impenetrable blanket. At night, the fog could be seen swirling around the anchor light and, looking aft from the foc'sle, the illuminated wheelhouse might appear as a faint yellow glow in the murk. The condensation would drip from the masts and stays, and everything would be cold, wet and still, the only sounds being the rippling noise of the water passing around the anchor chain, past the ship's bow and along her sides, accompanied by the lonely clanging of the ship's bell at regular intervals.

ICE

The power stations were under their heaviest loading during the winter period and the ships consequently experienced the greatest workload at this time, as they worked to maintain the supply of fuel. Courtesy of the winter weather, it was also precisely at this time that the greatest difficulties were encountered with loading the ships. The coal tips were hydraulically operated, not with oil but with water. As temperatures dropped, this would freeze and even when unfrozen, operation of the tip would be sluggish. The first problem.

The next problem was that the coal used was very low quality and would burn adequately only under the extreme forced draught conditions of the power station boilers. It was virtually waste. Much of it comprised of the washings from better grade coal. This wet coal would have been loaded into railway wagons several days before, so now, in freezing conditions, it was a solid block in the wagon. In this condition, it would not pour out of the wagon, despite the frantic shaking and crashing of the tipping platform by the tip operator. Under these circumstances, large fires comprised of old railway sleepers were set between the railway tracks and each wagon spent ten minutes or so over the flames as its predecessors were tipped, in the hope that the heat would begin to soften the frozen coal. In my day, the wagons were normally the steel-built variety but the occasional older wooden one still survived in use. These could not be taken out of the line, thus adding an air of anticipation in case they began to burn but usually the melting ice and the resultant water pouring through the wagon bottom would keep the floor cool. In the case of the steel wagons, the coal was even more sloppy than usual as the melted water poured into the ship's hold. The ships would load in about four hours in normal conditions but in severe cold, the loading could take three or four days. With every vessel being so delayed, the power stations began to rapidly consume their reserve stocks of fuel and the pressure for more coal to be delivered would mount to the extent that the ships would be told to sail on the next tide, as soon as most of the coal had been unloaded. In extreme situations, ships would sail from South Wales 'short-loaded' and would leave Portishead for another cargo with up to a hundred tons from the last one still on board.

During the winter of 1963, ***Salcombe*** was instructed to load at No. 6 Tip in Newport Top Dock but the dock was frozen over at the time. The ship was unable to get anywhere near the tip due to the thickness of the ice. A tug had to be sent to smash the ice up, so that ***Salcombe*** could be brought under the tip. It was at this time that there was ice in the Channel, even as far down as the English & Welsh Grounds Lightship. It was sufficiently thick that, as the ship pushed her way through the ice with the sound of cracking and grinding, lumps of broken ice skittered their way for great distances over the unbroken surface.

SUNSHINE

We also experienced nice weather! During these times, it was pleasant to be able to sit out on deck with a mug of tea and watch the Campbell's steamers churning past, loaded with passengers who had paid to enjoy seeing exactly the same sea and land as ourselves. While we had time to take it all in, though, these elegant greyhounds were whisking their passengers past it all in short order. Once moored up and with loading completed at Newport, there were a couple of hours to sit on deck, play cards or fish for eels – all with the bonus of being paid to do it.

NEWPORT DOCKS

The main docks at Newport were the Alexandra Docks and they were situated south of the town and to the west of the River Usk, close to its mouth. They were built by the Alexandra (Newport & South Wales) Docks & Railway Company, with successive docks in the complex opening progressively between 1875 and 1907 as trade expanded. Like the other large South Wales docks, the primary trade was for many years the export of Welsh coal to countries all over the world but there was also a wide range of general cargoes imported and exported. One side of the docks was dedicated entirely to coal handling and there were at one time twenty coal hoists in operation. The heyday of the docks had passed by the time I started calling there in ships of the O&W fleet, however.

NEWPORT DOCKS

A 1924 Great Western Railway plan of Newport Docks, which shows them at the greatest extent of their development. Note the East Lock into the South Dock from the River Usk is still in use at this date. the separate railway lines leading to and from each coal tip (or hoist as the railway termed them) are also clearly shown. *Neil Parkhouse collection*

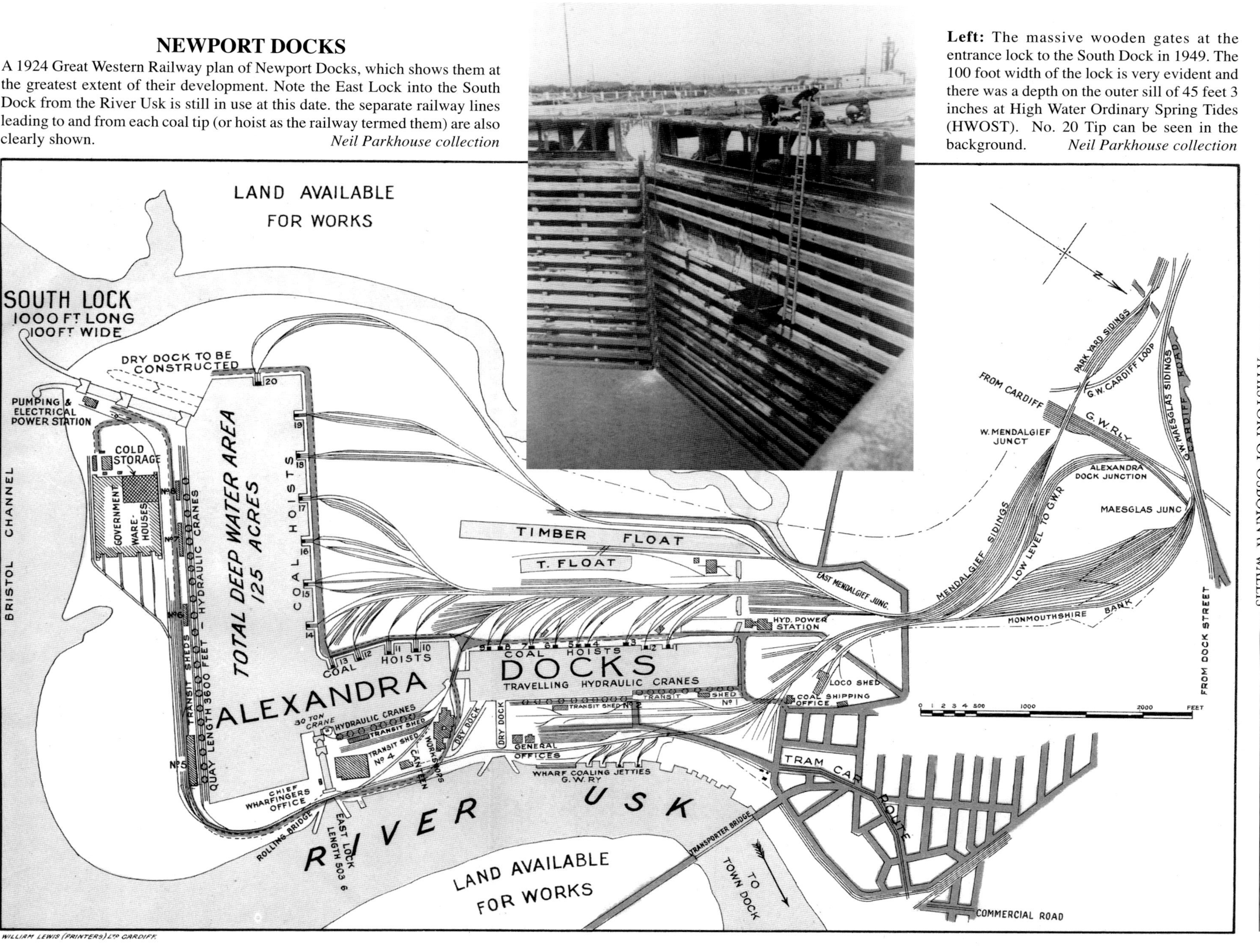

Left: The massive wooden gates at the entrance lock to the South Dock in 1949. The 100 foot width of the lock is very evident and there was a depth on the outer sill of 45 feet 3 inches at High Water Ordinary Spring Tides (HWOST). No. 20 Tip can be seen in the background. *Neil Parkhouse collection*

This aerial view of Newport Alexandra Docks dates from circa 1950. The Alexandra Docks comprised the Old or North Dock, seen here nearest the camera, and the later, larger South Dock beyond. There were at one time, twenty coal hoists (or tips) here but, by the date of this photograph, some of the older hoists at the top (nearest) end had been demolished. Tip Nos. 11 and 12 in the main dock had also gone, whilst No. 10 Tip still stands in this photograph but was gone before 1955. No. 13 Tip, one of the ones most regularly used by the O&W ships, can be seen right on the corner of the main dock.

The complexity of the railway tracks serving each tip is evident. Note that there are further coal tips on the bank of the River Usk, on the left of the view, although these also were closing by this date. At the bottom of the picture, just to the right of the housing estate, is Newport (Pill) locomotive shed, which was home to over fifty tank engines used for shunting the massive sidings complex serving the docks and which closed in 1963. Just to the right of that, on the corner of the North Dock, can be seen the chimney and buildings of the Central Power Station, opened in 1904 to provide power for the operation of the docks. There is as yet, no sign of the Uskmouth 'A' Power Station, with its two chimneys, which was built on the far bank, almost at the mouth of the river, from where it took its cooling water. This was later joined by Uskmouth 'B' Station, with its single chimney, located close to the 'A' Station but just slightly upstream. Uskmouth 'B' is still in periodic 'as required' operation today, although now renamed Fifoots Point Power Station.

The large entrance lock to the dock complex can be clearly seen. This lock is 1,000 feet long and 100 feet wide, and used to be split into two sections by a further pair of gates. The outer, seaward section was 400 feet long and the innermost section 600 feet in length. In this way, economy of water loss could be maximised by either using the locks singly, in 400- or 600-foot lengths, depending on the number of ships in any one locking, or in the full 1,000-foot length when necessary, such as when locking one (or more) large ships and their attendant tugs, in or out, at the same time. To compensate for the water loss involved, the dock was served by a large pump house, pumping extra water into the dock when required. This was originally steam driven but the pumps had been changed to electric operation by 1955. In this view, the large chimney for the steam boilers and the pump house complex can be seen alongside the 400 foot lock section, right by the entrance.

The pair of piers outside the lock was an attempt to reduce the effect of the fast flowing and complicated tidal streams caused by the junction at this point of the River Ebbw, seen on the extreme right of the photograph, with the larger River Usk. On the big tides, especially when the tidal streams were at their strongest, large and cumbersome ships were often seriously affected by these flows and currents. Despite the strenuous efforts of their attendant tugs and the great skill of the Pilots, the piers suffered almost constant damage and there was a full-time repair crew working on repairs.

The 29-acre North Dock was opened in 1875 by the Alexandra (Newport) Dock Company and the entrance to it was by means of a lock off the River Usk, which can still be seen at the bottom left or south eastern corner of the dock. In 1894, the first section of the South Dock was opened by the Alexandra (Newport & South Wales) Docks & Railway Company, the name change having taken place in 1882 as the company's railway interests expanded. This was the 21-acre area just below the lock entrance to the North Dock in this view. The South Dock had its own separate lock entrance into the river, just beyond the warehouses at the southern end of the dock. The massive 40-acre extension to the South Dock, running across the centre top of this view, was completed in 1907, although the huge new entrance lock into it from the mouth of the river was not opened until 14th July 1914. The two older lock entrances were closed shortly after and both were converted for use as dry docks and, indeed, both have ships in them in this picture. The original dry dock, at a slight angle to the old North Dock lock, can also be seen.

The two expanses of water on the right are the timber floats, where imported timber was seasoned after arrival and the premises of various timber importers can be seen alongside. Much of the timber brought in was for use as pit props. Finally, just to the right of the railway lines as they disappear off the bottom of the view is a wagon repair yard, where damaged or crippled wagons would receive attention to get them running again.

With the development of the steelworks at Llanwern, imported iron ore began arriving at the docks, with ore carriers up to 27,000 tons able to access the entrance lock. Today, the docks are still busy with a range of traffics both in and out, including timber, sand, clay, steel products, minerals and general goods. Coal exports have long since ceased but, ironically, some coal is now imported through the dock for use at Fifoots Point Power Station. Both docks are still in use, with the South Dock being the centre of commercial activities, whilst the North Dock is used mainly for maintenance purposes, the stabling of tugs and stevedoring. Having passed through the ownership of, successively, the A(N)D Co, the A(N&SW)D&R Co, the Great Western Railway and, after Nationalisation of the railways, the British Transport Commission, Newport Docks are now in the hands of Associated British Ports. *Courtesy National Museums & Galleries of Wales*

NEWPORT DOCK COAL HOISTS

The tip operator was stationed on the operating platform, located high in the structure with a view over the working area and equipped with all the controls for the hydraulic machinery. At the start of loading, he would set the height of the tip's chute according to the size of ship to be loaded, small ships low down, while larger ships needed to have the chute set much higher. Once set, the chute would be lowered from its raised position so that its mouth was aimed into the ship's hold. The loaded coal wagons would now be bought singly, by gravity, down the gently inclined track, which passed over the weighbridge and arrived at the base of the tip at ground level.

Having been weighed, the wagon was now pulled onto the tipping platform by a chain pulley mechanism, fitted expressly for this purpose. The wagons rear chain link coupling would be secured to an anchoring point on the platform and it would then be raised until it was level with the chute. Once there, another man, who rode the platform throughout the loading process, would knock the pins from the closures on the wagon's end door, allowing it to swing open. With this done, he signalled to the tip operator and the platform would be slowly raised at the back end to a steep angle, allowing the coal to pour from the wagon in a controlled flow, into the chute and thence into the ship.

The mouth of the chute was fitted with doors controlled by ropes from the deck of the ship, which could give a small measure of directional control to the flow of coal. Cargoes of wet coal needed to have the chute at a steeper angle to aid its flow. The operation of the tip, the railway wagons and the chute doors required a considerable amount of understanding between the personnel involved but, with years of experience amongst the operators and crews, the process, repeated many times during a loading, was carried out with the minimum of shouted instructions.

With the wagon discharged, the rear of the platform would be lowered first to the level position, for the wagon door to be secured. The platform was then lowered to the exit track level, which was higher than and directly above the incoming track. The exit track was also at a slight incline away from the tip, allowing the wagons to run by gravity. The empty railway wagon was now run off the platform and down the exit track, where it was met by another man who controlled its speed by means of the wagon brake. It then passed over another weighbridge and finally was linked to the end of a growing train of empty wagons.

The complete cycle – ingoing loaded wagon, weighbridge, tip, outgoing empty wagon, weighbridge – would be in the order of four minutes. The actual amount of coal loaded was established by the simple expedient of deducting the weight of the outgoing, empty wagons, from that of the loaded incoming ones.

On 3rd September 1955, there was a minor drama with *Colston* whilst loading at No. 13 Tip, Newport. Tipping had not long begun, with the after end of the main hatch being loaded first, which meant that the ship was very severely stern down and bows up. Without warning, the wagon which was being tipped came adrift from its fastenings at the back and somersaulted down into the chute. The weight of the heavy steel wagon, complete with its load of coal, landing in the chute placed a sudden and severe strain on the wires which raised and lowered it. These were the only support for the chute and they were now also holding the wagon in an almost vertical position. If the wires had failed, the chute would have fallen against the tip face and the wagon would have dropped into the hold, with who knows what consequences.

The tip operator decided at first that he would raise the chute to the horizontal but the Skipper was having none of it while the ship was still underneath! The wagon could have crashed back onto its wheels, the tip ropes could have chaffed through while lifting the chute – all in all, it was an uncomfortable situation and the Skipper decided, quite rightly, that nothing was going to happen until *Colston* was out from underneath it. However, she was going to be difficult to handle in her present trim, so he had the fore peak and No. 1 (forward) ballast tank filled. This corrected her bow up trim to some extent, by which time arrangements had been made for the ship to go to another tip to complete loading. It was not an easy move, however, for the ship was still very much bow up.

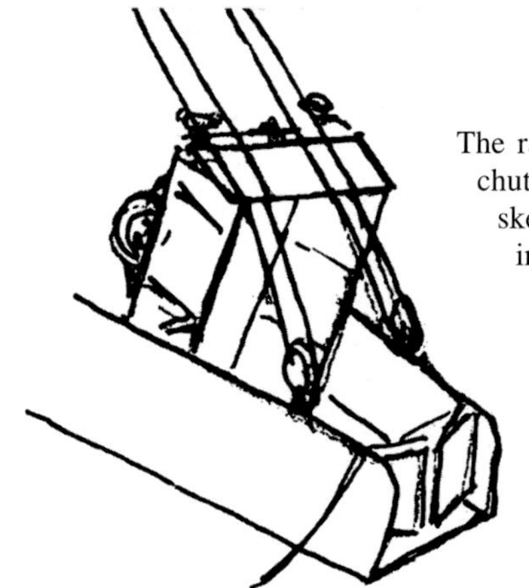

The railway wagon lodged in the chute at No. 13 Tip, from a quick sketch I made at the time of the incident. Note the doors on the end of the chute, which could, by means of ropes, be operated to roughly control the direction of flow.

DISCHARGING AT PORTISHEAD

The entire O&W working fleet in the mid to late 1950s ran only between Portishead and Newport Docks or Ely Harbour, Penarth, and none of them had ever traded anywhere else, except for ***Salcombe***, ***Rockleaze*** and ***Downleaze*** in pre- O&W ownership. Additionally, ***Colston*** and ***Brandon***, as the two newest ships, were limited to Newport only, where they would lay afloat whilst being loaded, as opposed to Ely Harbour where much of the loading occurred with the vessel aground, with the consequent risk of damage and strain to the hull.

Discharging at Portishead was at that time carried out at dedicated berths in the docks, equipped for the purpose of handling power station coal deliveries only. The two berths for the 'A' Station were located at the top end of the dock, nearest the town. They were known as the Old Berth and the New Berth, a still recognised throwback to the times when the facilities were extended to match the expansion of 'A' Station. Two standard luffing and slewing grab cranes were stationed in each of these berths.

No. 13 Tip at Newport. The loaded wagon weighbridge was operated from the small building at the centre of the photograph. The man standing outside is waiting for the next loaded railway wagon to arrive. The ship beneath the chute is O&W's *Salcombe*. The chap on the stern, in the light-coloured overalls and with his back to the camera, is Tom Scarrett, who was then her Second Engineer and who I later worked with when he became her Chief. *Courtesy National Railway Museum*

The two levels of railway lines serving No. 14 Tip. The lower ones, full of incoming loaded wagons, are bridged by the higher track, for empties, as it leaves the tip. Note the gentle incline on both lines, which allowed all wagon movements to be carried out by gravity. On the higher level, in the centre, is the empty wagon weighbridge. The vessel loading at No. 14 Tip, *Tewkesbury*, belonged to Houlder Bros Shipping Co Ltd, whose vessels were regular traders into Newport. *Courtesy National Museums & Galleries of Wales*

This view of *Brandon* loading at No. 13 Tip shows her in almost the same trim as *Colston* was at the time of the incident with the coal wagon. *Chris Collard*

The crew of No. 13 Tip photographed raising a toast. It is thought the occasion was the final shipment of coal from this, the last of the tips at Newport Docks. Coincidentally, the ship loaded was O&W's *Hotwells*. It really did need a crew of ten men to operate the tip and associated railway works; such intensification of labour was no longer cost effective. *Courtesy National Museums & Galleries of Wales*

Having grabbed the coal from the ship's hold, the coal was dropped into a hopper behind the berth, which was the start of a long conveyor belt system into the back of 'A' Station, where it was delivered directly into the station bunkers, or diverted to the coal storage yards for later use. The Old Berth cranes had grabs of one and a half tons capacity, while the slightly larger New Berth cranes had a capacity of two tons. The cranes were mounted on railway lines so they could travel along the quay wall and were thus able to operate to either side of the hopper. The ship and its cargo was placed so that it was within the crane's radius of action but whilst discharging the ship had to be moved so that the hopper was always within reach of the crane – travelling the crane was not part of the discharge operating pattern.

Once the crane had grabbed all of the cargo that it could reach without assistance, there was always a considerable quantity left around the edges of the holds and under the decks and to clear this, four men were required to work down in the hold. Two hobblers, who were employed by the Port Authority, worked the inboard side of the ship (against the quay wall), while the vessel's own two Sailors worked the outboard side. A power station employee, known as the 'hatchman', would stand on the ship's deck on the outboard side and he would signal to the crane driver where the next grab should be placed. Although the crane driver could see into the hold on the outboard side, the inboard side was hidden from him and he relied entirely on the hatchman as to where the next grab should be dropped.

There was a great variation in the skills of the crane drivers and while some of them could make the task of discharging comparatively easy, by being able to swing the grab and 'fly' it about, others would only be able to drop it vertically. In the latter case, almost all of the coal directly under the deck of the ship and in the ends of the holds, would have to be shovelled out into the open manually, which was far harder work for the men in the hold and meant a slow discharge. The more skilful crane drivers, however, depended on the hatchman for safety, whilst the hobblers working on the inboard side had to rely on him doing exactly as he was told, so that they could be sure of being well out of the way of the grab. It would come flying rapidly in as the driver used the momentum from a combination of luffing and slewing to fling the grab bodily into the under-deck reaches of the hold. A good driver turned these skills into an art form and it was a joy to watch.

The next berth down the dock was known as the Dock Office Berth and it was the usual waiting position for ships next in line with an 'A' Station cargo for discharge. It was here also that the huts for the crane drivers and hobblers were situated. Inside these two primitive amenities, the air was blue with tobacco smoke and the reek of burning toast!

The loaded ships would wait their turn for discharge and the crews became very adept at working out which ship would move into which berth, how long she would take to discharge (assuming no plant breakdowns) and so just when

An aerial view of Portishead Dock, showing the 'A' Station discharging plant. *Downleaze* is in the Old Berth, far left, with *St. Vincent* astern of her in the New Berth. *Rockleaze* is next, lying in the Dock Office Berth and *Druid Stoke*, testing her boiler safety valves, is on the right. The photograph was taken on 23rd October 1951, when the wharf in the foreground was in the process of being cleared prior to construction of the Albright & Wilson phosphorous manufacturing plant. *Author's collection*

their own ship would be needed. About half an hour before the ship they were to follow was completely discharged, they would get ready to move into her berth, unless it was night-time, when they would wait for the hatchman to give them a shout.

During 1955, the quay wall for 'B' Station was in a parlous state, with huge holes, only half of the mooring bollards yet installed and the whole area an obstacle course for crew members when ashore moving ropes.

By 1956, the construction of 'B' Power Station had advanced and the first of its two generators had been commissioned. The station was equipped with twelve boilers, eight of which were coal-fired, whilst the other four were oil-fired. With the old 'A' Station still carrying full load, the demand for coal gradually increased as 'B' Station's coal boilers came on stream. The quay wall towards the lock gate end of the dock had been completed and the coal handling gear for the new station had been installed.

The discharging facilities for the new power station were completely different from those for 'A' Station and were capable of handling much larger quantities of coal. The ships were to be discharged by means of two large Telfer-type cranes. These consisted of a large mobile structure, able to travel along the length of the quay wall on widely spaced railway track. At the top of each structure was a horizontal

Left: The 'B' Station discharging wharf, showing the two Telfer discharging cranes, the nearer one with its boom lowered. On the left is the long stockyard Telfer gantry, while the small travelling Throw-Off machine is in the middle foreground. This sent the coal on the inner of the two conveyors over the wall of the stockyard for storage. On the right, *St. Vincent*, still loaded, lies astern of *Colston*, while an empty *Druid Stoke* is further down the quay wall. *Author's collection*

Below: At the peak of their activity, one entire side of Portishead Dock was taken up with the discharging plant for the power stations, with the O&W fleet being the sole users. This superb composite panorama shows both stations, although not all of the discharging plant is in view, that for 'A' Station being further to the left. The ships at the quayside are, from left to right, *Colston*, *St. Vincent* and *Salcombe*, with *Brandon* in the lock – a very special picture for me, showing three of the ships on which I had permanent positions, as opposed to just relief postings. *Author's collection*

rail, continued on a gantry out over the dock, which could be raised or lowered. The control cab ran on this rail and from it was suspended a large, five-ton grab. The cab backed out over the ship being discharged and the grab was lowered, under power, into the hold. These were very cumbersome machines and no help whatsoever could be given to the men in the hold by 'flying' the grab as with the older cranes. It could only be lowered and raised vertically, and was far too heavy to be pushed about manually.

Having collected a grab full of coal and hoisted it from the bottom of the ship to about sixty feet above ground level, cab and grab would travel in over the quay wall and drop the coal into a hopper built into the structure. From there it fed onto a short conveyor belt, which dropped the coal onto a long conveyor belt running the length of the quay and heading towards the power station. However, alongside this belt was another, running away from the station. The coal on the first belt could either be sent directly to the station's bunkers or onto this second belt. Built into the second conveyor was a further machine, a type of elevator, capable of travelling the whole length of the belt and by means of which coal was deposited over the store wall. From here, it would be picked up by a further cab and grab, identical to the ones on the quayside machines but

This superb aerial photograph of Portishead 'B' Station, taken on 22nd April 1960, nicely illustrates the coal discharging arrangements and the coal store, with both Telfer cranes, the elevator and the travelling gantry in view, and part of 'A' Station on the left. Under the cranes are *Salcombe*, nearest, which has completed discharging, with *Hotwells* astern, facing the entrance lock. For local ship enthusiasts, the little vessel in the lock is T.R. Brown's *HRB*. Today, the whole site is completely unrecognisable from this view. *Author's collection*

running on its own long-span gantry over the coal store. This machine's job was to handle coal held as stock fuel for the station. Its traversing rail was identical in height from the ground to the quayside ones and, with the machines suitably positioned, it was possible to walk directly from cab to cab on each for maintenance purposes, though this was rarely done.

The long quayside belt running towards the station also took the feed from a further system of conveyor belts, originating at the railway wagon tippler house. This was actually located some distance from the station. Coal tipped here would take over eight minutes to reach the bunkers and when the tippler house was operating, there would be over 100 tons of coal in transit, on the belts, such was the distance covered.

DRYDOCKING AT HILL'S

The company's ships always went to Charles Hill's yard for any work that was needed and this included the two-yearly Board of Trade and Lloyd's surveys. Hill's yard was situated almost opposite the company's dock and head office at Hotwells. Here, the ship would be thoroughly inspected and all of its safety equipment checked. Lifeboats would be inspected and swung out, and the Schermuly Life Saving Rockets would be changed, the old ones being dumped. The radio would be inspected and tested, and life jackets and fire extinguishers inspected too. Everything was checked and, in the case of the older ships, the metal plates on the hull (above and especially below the water line), decks and structures would be examined for thickness by drilling holes in them, the holes being welded up afterwards of course. As the ship aged, the Surveyor had the authority to lower the ship's Plimsoll marks, so that she would carry less cargo.

The ship would be dry-docked and the bottom scraped and painted. New anti-corrosion anodes would be fitted near the propeller and early on in ***Colston*** and ***Brandon***'s life they were fitted with bronze propellers, such was the extent of the deterioration of the original cast iron ones. It was always a surprise to me to see how big the ship looked when walking underneath it in drydock. The engines and the steering gear would all be stripped and examined. Three of Ruston & Hornsby's engineers would come aboard to dismantle and examine the engine, and to make such repairs and adjustments as were needed.

In truth, there was little that the crew could do in the way of maintenance while the ship was in dockyard hands, so they busied themselves with domestic cleaning jobs, such as washing the paintwork in the accommodation, etc.

I used to wander off around the yard, looking over the half-built ships (there was little in the way of Health & Safety regulations then to interfere with this fascinating past-time). Everything was interesting. The shattering chatter of the riveting and caulking guns, the screech of the grinders and the clanging of plates being hammered into position. Everywhere oxy-acetylene pipes and electric cables were strewn about and cascades of hot sparks would come flying down. Heavy plates swung through the air overhead, suspended from the big fixed cranes, with smaller parts being carried by the steam cranes, whilst the stuttering and spitting fierce bright blue flashes from the welding reflected on everything. Enveloping this was the smell – of hot metal, paint, tar, oil and, above all, the sickly sweet scent of oxy-acetylene gas. And out of this cacophonous, chaotic, combination would emerge, almost miraculously, a new born ship, pristine and almost always on schedule. It remained a source of fascination to me, even in later years.

Not long after I had joined ***Colston***, she returned to the yard for some minor work, where the first of the two big Polish tugs, ***Jantar***, was almost finished. She was impressive. At the time, these two tugs were the most powerful ever built in Britain. ***Jantar*** had two 2,000 hp diesels and three engines each the size of ***Colston***'s main engine to provide her auxiliary equipment with power. At just fifteen years of age, I was able to roam all over this ship and thought it wonderful. They were outstandingly handsome vessels.

Charles Hill's could certainly build fine ships of all types and I revelled at the chance to be loose in their yard every now and again.

A fine view of *Colston* in Hill's dry dock for one of her BoT/Lloyd's surveys, sometime in the early 1960s. The timber baulks were a standard arrangement for keeping vessels upright when in dry dock. Her superstructure has already received a fresh coat of brown paint, and bottom scraping and painting of her hull was also in hand. Note also the radar scanner on the roof of the wheelhouse. *J. Hill*

This overall view of the dock shows the amount of water which would be lost during a scouring operation, always carried out on the biggest tides when the mud was exposed to the full force of released water and the dock could subsequently be replenished for free. Looking to the left of the picture, it can be seen that the water level is down by six or more feet and it would thus have been necessary to jump down when boarding any of the ships seen here. *Author*

Left: Clearing the sills of the outer lock gates. The chains connecting with the winches operating the outer gates can be seen, as well as the men clearing the sills – a dirty and difficult task carried out with one eye on the tides. Harold Buckland and John Bence were the two dock maintenance men engaged on the job in this 1961 photograph. *H. Hamer*

Below: Low tide outside Portishead Dock and what would have been ideal scouring conditions except for the bitter cold. The photograph was taken in the winter of 1961-62 and the mud here at times was reported to have frozen solid, with temperatures at times dropping well below freezing. *H. Hamer*

Left: The Portishead Dock Master's office, from where the dock was managed. There was also a mess room for the duty shift of lock gatemen. Just beyond is the signal mast, used to indicate to ships whether they could approach the locks to enter the dock. Two balls, as shown meant no entry. A single ball gave permission to approach. In bad weather, storm cones were flown from the mast. If the cone had its point upwards, it indicated a northerly gale, with the point down, a southerly gale. In the foreground is one of the gate winches. There were two of these for each of the four gates, one for closing the gate and the other to open it. *H. Hamer*

Below: Port of Bristol Tide Tables, Jan/Feb 1956. Monday 30th January produced the highest tide of the year. *Author's collection*

PORTISHEAD DOCK

Portishead was a small dock with, as previously mentioned, no natural inflow of water. Thus, one of the Dock Master's main responsibilities was to operate the dock as economically as possible as regards its water. Big tides would replenish the water level naturally but two large diesel driven pumps were available to top up the dock when necessary. However, this added considerably to the cost of its operation.

On large tides, the level of water in the Channel would equal that in the dock, at which point both sets of lock gates would be opened so that the rising tide would fill the dock – a great economy as it saved running the pumps. As our ship entered the lock in these circumstances, we would not have to stop, cruising straight through. This procedure was known as 'docking on the level' and was much favoured as it saved over half an hour in the process of mooring the ship up.

Because of the extreme muddiness of the water in the upper Bristol Channel, caused by the fast tidal streams keeping the particles in suspension, silting was a real problem. The dock itself was regularly dredged, as well as the lock, whilst the approach to it from outside was kept clear by making use of the very high tidal range. At low tide, there would be no water outside the dock, so the outer gates would be opened, along with the lock sluices on the inner gates. Water from the dock itself, under considerable pressure, would then wash or scour the lock bottom clear of mud. The outer gates were then closed, and the lock filled from the dock. With this done, the sluices on the inner gates would be closed to isolate the dock and the sluices on the outer gates opened wide. Again, the pressure from the discharging water would scour the approach from the Channel. The lock gatemen would climb down to the bottom of the lock to remove any obstacles from the sills, which the lock gates sat and ran on.

Scouring of the approaches was always carried out on the biggest tides, when the absence of water outside exposed the mud to the full force of the tidal wave released from the dock and the following high tide would then replenish the inner water level free of cost. Because of the temporary loss of depth, scouring could not be carried out if a large ship was in the dock, usually at the Albright & Wilson berth.

There was one other factor which affected docking at Portishead during my day and this concerned the four big (4,500 tons) 'Mosquito' Class tankers which the Esso Company ran into the dock.

42 **Port of Bristol Tide Table** **JANUARY**

			h. m.
Last Quarter	Wednesday	4 day	22 41
New Moon	Friday	13 day	3 01
First Quarter	Friday	20 day	22 58
Full Moon	Friday	27 day	14 40

Days.	MORNING Time.	Avonmouth R.E. Dock.	Portishead Portis-h'd Dk.	Bristol Cumberland Basin.	EVENING Time.	Avonmouth R.E. Dock.	Portishead. Portis-h'd Dk.	Bristol Cumberland Basin.
	h. m.	ft. in.	ft. in.	ft. in.	h. m.	ft. in.	ft. in.	ft. in.
S 1	9 22	47 10	35 10	35 4	21 49	46 10	34 10	34 4
M 2	10 07	46 10	34 10	34 4	22 33	45 3	33 3	32 10
Tu 3	10 49	45 2	33 2	32 9	23 18	42 11	30 11	30 6
W 4	11 30	42 6	30 6	30 2	23 58	40 4	28 4	27 11
Th 5	—	—	—	—	12 15	40 0	28 0	27 7
F 6	0 47	37 10	25 10	25 5	13 08	37 5	25 5	25 0
S 7	1 46	36 0	24 0	23 6	14 16	35 11	23 11	23 5
S 8	2 57	35 5	23 5	22 11	15 30	35 10	23 10	23 4
M 9	4 08	36 6	24 6	24 0	16 39	36 11	24 11	24 6
Tu 10	5 12	38 4	26 4	25 11	17 37	38 9	26 9	26 4
W 11	6 04	40 3	28 3	27 10	18 26	40 5	28 5	28 0
Th 12	6 48	41 11	29 11	29 7	19 06	41 10	29 10	29 6
F 13	7 26	43 2	31 2	30 9	19 42	42 9	30 9	30 4
S 14	8 0	43 10	31 10	31 5	20 15	43 0	31 0	30 7
S 15	8 30	44 0	32 0	31 7	20 44	43 3	31 3	30 10
M 16	9 01	43 10	31 10	31 5	21 14	43 0	31 0	30 7
Tu 17	9 30	43 3	31 3	30 10	21 46	42 6	30 6	30 2
W 18	10 01	42 5	30 5	30 1	22 18	41 8	29 8	29 4
Th 19	10 35	41 4	29 4	29 0	22 54	40 4	28 4	27 11
F 20	11 11	39 8	27 8	27 3	23 37	38 8	26 8	26 3
S 21	—	—	—	—	12 02	37 9	25 9	25 4
S 22	0 34	36 9	24 9	24 4	13 11	36 5	24 5	23 11
M 23	1 53	36 4	24 4	23 10	14 41	36 8	24 8	24 2
Tu 24	3 23	37 9	25 9	25 4	16 12	38 9	26 9	26 4
W 25	4 44	40 3	28 3	27 10	17 22	41 10	29 10	29 6
Th 26	5 50	43 5	31 5	31 0	18 23	44 8	32 8	32 3
F 27	6 45	45 11	33 11	33 5	19 15	46 10	34 10	34 4
S 28	7 36	47 10	35 10	35 4	20 03	48 0	36 0	35 6
S 29	8 21	48 10	36 10	36 2	20 46	48 5	36 5	35 10
M 30	9 04	48 11	36 11	36 3	21 28	47 11	35 11	35 5
Tu 31	9 44	48 0	36 0	35 6	22 08	46 9	34 9	34 3

For **AVONMOUTH (OLD) DOCK**, subtract 8 ft. from Royal Edward Dock Tides.

FEBRUARY **Port of Bristol Tide Table** 43

			h. m.
Last Quarter	Friday	3 day	16 08
New Moon	Saturday	11 day	21 38
First Quarter	Sunday	19 day	09 21
Full Moon	Sunday	26 day	01 41

Days.	MORNING Time.	Avonmouth R.E. Dock.	Portishead. Portis-h'd Dk.	Bristol Cumberland Basin	EVENING. Time.	Avonmouth R.E. Dock.	Portishead. Portis-h'd Dk.	Bristol Cumberland Basin.
	h. m.	ft. in.	ft. in.	ft. in.	h. m.	ft. in.	ft. in.	ft. in.
W 1	10 22	46 4	34 4	33 10	22 44	44 4	32 4	31 11
Th 2	10 55	43 9	31 9	31 4	23 16	41 4	29 4	29 0
F 3	11 29	40 3	28 3	27 10	23 52	38 2	26 2	25 9
S 4	—	—	—	—	12 10	36 11	24 11	24 6
S 5	0 40	35 4	23 4	22 10	13 06	34 6	22 6	22 0
M 6	1 46	33 8	21 8	21 1	14 26	33 2	21 2	20 7
Tu 7	3 15	33 8	21 8	21 1	15 54	34 0	22 0	21 6
W 8	4 37	35 10	23 10	23 4	17 10	36 6	24 6	24 0
Th 9	5 40	38 8	26 8	26 3	18 05	39 4	27 4	26 11
F 10	6 29	41 3	29 3	28 11	18 47	41 8	29 8	29 4
S 11	7 07	43 2	31 2	30 9	19 23	43 3	31 3	30 10
S 12	7 39	44 6	32 6	32 1	19 56	44 4	32 4	31 11
M 13	8 11	45 3	33 3	32 10	20 27	44 10	32 10	32 5
Tu 14	8 43	45 5	33 5	33 0	20 58	45 3	33 3	32 10
W 15	9 14	45 4	33 4	32 11	21 29	44 9	32 9	32 4
Th 16	9 45	44 6	32 6	32 1	21 58	43 9	31 9	31 4
F 17	10 16	42 11	30 11	30 6	22 30	41 11	29 11	29 7
S 18	10 48	40 8	28 8	28 4	23 07	39 5	27 5	27 0
S 19	11 31	38 0	26 0	25 7	23 58	37 0	25 0	24 7
M 20	—	—	—	—	12 38	35 11	23 11	23 5
Tu 21	1 17	35 6	23 6	23 0	14 16	35 6	23 6	23 0
W 22	3 02	36 5	24 5	23 11	15 58	37 11	25 11	25 6
Th 23	4 31	39 9	27 9	27 4	17 14	41 8	29 8	29 4
F 24	5 40	43 4	31 4	30 11	18 10	44 10	32 10	32 5
S 25	6 33	46 2	34 2	33 8	18 59	46 11	34 11	34 5
S 26	7 20	47 11	35 11	35 5	19 44	48 0	36 0	35 6
M 27	8 02	48 9	36 9	36 1	20 24	48 5	36 5	35 10
Tu 28	8 42	48 10	36 10	36 2	21 01	47 11	35 11	35 5
W 29	9 18	47 11	35 11	35 5	21 37	46 9	34 9	34 3

For **AVONMOUTH (OLD) DOCK**, subtract 8 ft. from Royal Edward Dock Tides.

They brought in the fuel for the four oil-fired boilers in 'B' Station. They made no difference to the coal imports by Osborn & Wallis but were hugely inconvenient to the crews of the O&W ships. They were extremely slow and ponderous vessels, and were given absolute priority on the locking in and out of the dock. Even if they were still a long way down Channel, we would be forced to anchor in King Road to await their arrival, pick up their tugs, enter the lock (a very tight fit!) and then to lock in. The concern was that there was so little margin of room for them in the lock but, additionally, as they were such bulky craft, they needed slack water at the top of the tide (or as close to it as they could get) to make the handling of them as straightforward as possible. Their names are indelibly burned into my mind; they were ***Esso Chelsea***, ***Esso Wandsworth***, ***Esso Lambeth*** and ***Esso Fulham***, and they lost our crews many a chance of a night at home!

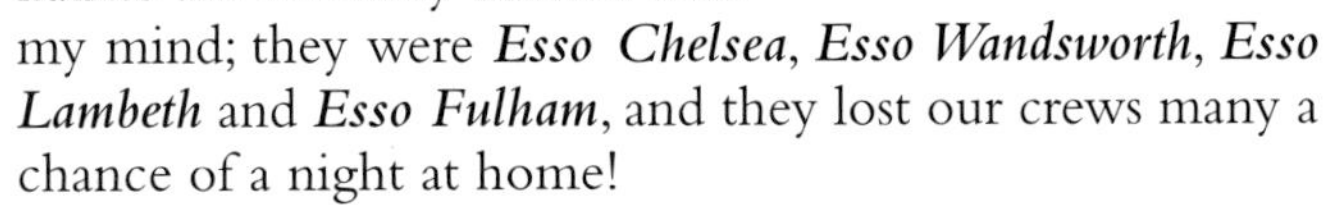

The massive bulk of *Esso Fulham* being carefully locked into the dock in 1965. She was delivering fuel oil for Portishead 'B' Power Station, on the right. The extremely limited clearance these vessels had to the lock sides is graphically demonstrated in this view. *Author*

MOVE TO BRANDON

On 2nd May 1956, the keel was laid at Charles Hill's for a sister ship to ***Colston***, which was to be named ***Brandon***. Identical to the earlier vessel in all but a few insignificant details, the new ship was launched on 28th February 1957.

During May 1957, ***Colston***'s Skipper was told that he would be moving to the new ship when she was completed and, with his approval, his present crew would be going with him. As a result, we were told to prepare to hand ***Colston*** over in about a month's time as we would all be transferring to the new ship.

So it was that, late in May, with the hand over of ***Colston*** completed, we went to Charles Hill's yard to go aboard the new ship. She was indeed virtually identical and there was nothing new to get used to. Everything looked familiar, although she still had some way to go to be completed. The accommodation was unfinished, the galley was not yet equipped, some of the smaller items of machinery still had to be installed and there were no deck plates in the engine room. Also, the radio was not yet installed and, all in all, there was the seeming chaos of a ship being fitted out – pipes, carpentry, electric cables, hand lead lights and paint, and a host of shipyard workers all over the place – on deck, in the accommodation, in the engine room, everywhere. The ship as yet did not belong to Osborn & Wallis, so there was nothing that we could do or contribute to the work of getting her finished and ready. The Skipper and Mate, and the Chief and Second Engineers, stayed around to be on hand if any comments or advice were needed but there was nothing for the Sailors or the Boy to do.

So we lost ourselves in the uproar. I spent most of the days mooching around the yard, returning to the ship every now and again, and occasionally doing a bit of shopping for the crew as needed.

The work progressed though and it seemed that, quite suddenly, everything came together. Dockyard equipment was cleared away, cabins were finished, the galley was up together and all its pots and pans delivered and, eventually, there was the sound of first the auxiliary engines being started and run up, and then the main engine. We gradually became involved in the process of final checks, including doubling the moorings so that the engine and gearbox could be run for a couple of hours, while tests were made with the engine driving the propeller for the first time. By now, it was mainly senior staff and engineers that were aboard, including Ruston's engineers along with a number of dockyard hands, to make any alterations that were deemed necessary and, item by item, the ship was declared ready in all respects. The crew now had the task of carrying and stowing all the stores on board, and generally setting the ship up domestically.

On 11th June, although ***Brandon*** still did not yet belong to the Company, the crew took charge of her for the first time as she was moved to O&W's Yard to be made ready for acceptance trials the next day. There were going to be many people aboard for her trials and, if these were satisfactory, the ship would proceed to Newport for her first loading, where her load lines and insurance requirements would be confirmed. In readiness for this invasion of officials, a great deal of food was put aboard by Hill's, along with a cook who would be coming with us to prepare it. For one trip at

Following her launch on the last day of February 1957, *Brandon* is seen here being fitted out alongside Charles Hill's yard in the spring of that year. Note the walkway connecting to the vessel from the corner of the dock on the right.
Jim Crissup

least, I was going to be surplus to requirements in the galley.

The crew were going to run the ship entirely but to the instructions of Hill's engineers and the Lloyd's and Board of Trade officials, who were all aboard. Even for such a small ship, the whole procedure was going to be rigorously carried out before she would be given the necessary certificates to allow her to trade.

BRANDON'S TRIALS

On 12th June, **Brandon** set off down the River Avon to make for King Road, between Avonmouth and Portishead, where she would have her trials. Her speed was checked to confirm that she met the projections. The time taken to stop her from full speed was taken, her anchors were dropped and recovered, and the time taken for this was checked, fire fighting equipment was checked and her compass was swung and appropriate compensations made. Her turning circle and the times were checked. In all respects, she duplicated the performance of her earlier sister.

With all of this completed and found to be satisfactory, and still flying Charles Hill's houseflag, we set off for Newport. On arrival, the time was taken for de-ballasting the ship and we started loading, watched closely by the Board of Trade and Lloyd's officials.

These gentlemen made copious notes as the loading progressed, keeping a tight record of the ship's draught marks at the bow and the stern throughout the loading, and recording these together with the actual tonnage of coal that had been loaded at every stage throughout the process.

When she was eventually loaded down to the appropriate mark on her Plimsoll line array, she was found to have the projected weight of cargo on board as designed for, with room to spare in the forward hold, again, as had been allowed for in her design.

So far so good. Now the BoT men wanted to see her battened down completely, including the locking bars, double hatch cloths and every wedge. Every ventilator was sealed, the main hatches down to the hold secured, the foc'sle secured and weather-proofed (even to checking the deadlights over the portholes in the accommodation) and chain stoppers were fitted to the anchor chains – in short, everything relating to the safety of the ship was checked and approved.

None of this was normal during a trip for the crew and we were conscious that once these officials had departed, we would have the task of getting the ship all cleared down again ready for discharging.

With everything found to be in order, all the engineers and officials from Hill's, Lloyd's and the Board of Trade, along with Mr Osborn and the Skipper, trooped down below to the officers messroom, where the appropriate certificates were signed permitting the ship to operate. After this – and certainly not before – Mr Osborn signed to accept the ship and to pay Hill's for her. At that point, the Charles Hill houseflag was taken down and rolled up, and replaced with the Osborn & Wallis houseflag.

It had been quite a hectic day and a surprising amount of officialdom had been involved in passing even such a small ship as fit for duty.

After the process was completed, all of the officials, the few dockyard workers and the cook left the ship to go their separate ways by train, so at last we were on our own – and grateful for it!

Incidentally, the galley acquired a souvenir of the day – an enormous frying pan about two feet in diameter which the cook had been using for bulk production of food throughout the trip. He didn't wish to carry it back to Hill's yard, so 'forgot' about it. I didn't know what to do with it either but it stayed in the galley.

NEW TIDE BOOKS

Each year, the company produced a tide book for the Bristol Channel and each member of each ship's crew was given one (so you wouldn't be late next year!) at Christmas, along with fifty cigarettes. The same format and photographs for the tide book had been used for years, which was by now looking very dated, as well as including an out-of-date list of the fleet. There were photographs of ***St. Vincent*** and plant in the yard. The tide books were also handed out to firms with whom O&W had dealings and the lock gateman at Portishead, so by now they were doing nothing for the company's image. It was time for a re-vamp!

With the arrival of ***Brandon*** and ***Colston*** on the scene, Mr Osborn decided that a whole series of new photographs were required to show off the company's updated assets. Accordingly, the three largest ships, ***Brandon***, ***Colston*** and ***Salcombe***, were instructed to sail from Portishead on one particular day in the summer, with all hatches battened down and with hatch cloths on to give a seamanlike appearance, an instruction received with less than enthusiasm by the crews. Bad enough when returning loaded in the winter and the cold but to do a full batten down for the light ship trip over to South Wales on a hot, balmy, summer's day, only to have to strip it all off again immediately, was a bit much! The arrangements were that, on leaving Portishead, the little flotilla would be joined immediately by an aeroplane which would take photographs of them heading purposefully past Battery Point, the local landmark, with ***Brandon*** in the lead.

Came the day and the ships, all prepared as instructed but accompanied by mutinous mutterings from the crews, left Portishead. Slowing down to keep station, they were hailed from Battery Point by someone from the photography firm using a loud hailer, to advise that the aircraft had been delayed and could we wait there until it arrived. The currents off the Point are particularly tricky and waiting there was easier said than done. Eventually, the loud hailer informed the crews that the aircraft would not be coming after all and the exercise was off.

The news was greeted with typical seafarer's comments such as "*Oh dear, what a shame, I am disappointed!*" and we set off to carry out a normal cross-Channel trip, except for the additional task of stripping all the hatches off again.

A few days later, the Skipper returned to the ship having been to the office in Bristol, bearing the news that tomorrow when we sailed in company with ***Salcombe*** and ***St. Vincent***, the aircraft had been arranged and we were to do the whole thing again. However, the novelty had worn off by now and it was decided that we would put the hatchboards on but not bother with the cloths. This time the aeroplane arrived, circled a few times, got its pictures and then departed. (The resultant flotilla picture is the background to the title pages 2 and 3.)

We heard no more until several weeks later, when Mr Osborn visited each of the three ships involved and gave the Skippers a large print of their particular ship to hang in the officers messroom. Handing the picture of ***Brandon*** to the Skipper, he made the pointed comment "*Please notice Captain that I instructed the photographer to paint your hatchcloths on.*" Next door in his cabin, the Mate was heard to mutter "*Next time it's blowing up, he can come and paint the buggers on again!*"

Having missed out on the flotilla photograph, ***Colston*** had her own pictures taken when proceeding up the Avon Gorge later that year and one of those turned out to be the best picture of them all.

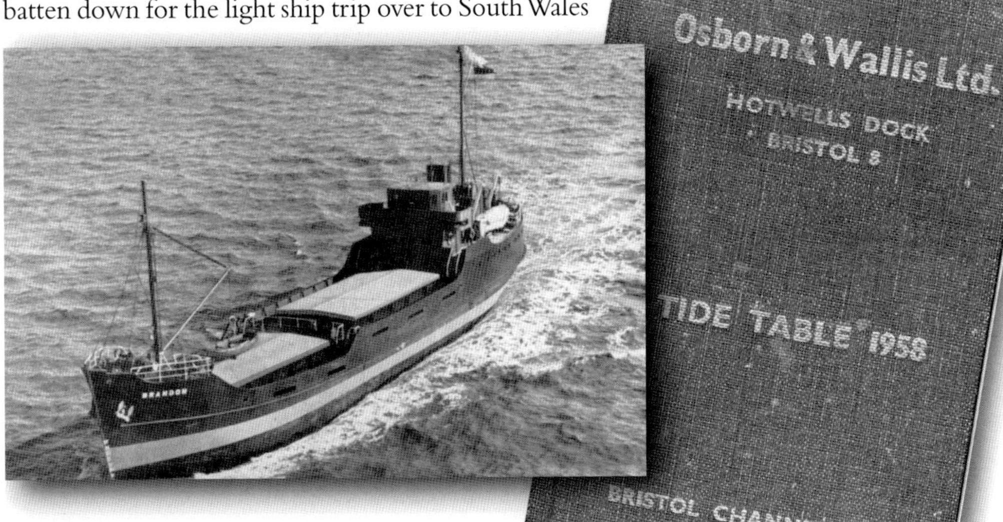

This is another of the aerial views taken for the Tide Book, showing the three ships departing Portishead. *Colston* can be seen discharging at the far end of the dock in the New Berth, whilst *Salcombe* and *St. Vincent* follow *Brandon* out and round the pier. Fred Knight, senior Sailor, and myself are standing on *Brandon*'s stern. This was one of the few occasions when the ships flew the O&W houseflag and note also the absence of the hatchcloths! 'B' Station is half-constructed and, again, the wartime camouflage paint is still visible on 'A' Station's original chimney, the second one being built immediately after the war. On the far right, on the skyline, can just be seen the four masts of Portishead Radio Station, a key element in the global maritime radio network. Although the station was moved elsewhere many years ago, the call sign "Portishead Radio" is still used to identify it. The kink in the pier was caused by a large ship bringing phosphorous ore to the Albright & Wilson factory, seen on the left, getting out of control in the currents around the pier, and hitting it almost straight on despite the best efforts of the tugs handling her. The pier was replaced many years later by a steel structure. *Author's collection*

I stayed with the ***Brandon*** for about a year by which time I was just 18. She was a nice ship in every respect but she never quite had the welcoming and cosy feel that ***Colston*** had. The other crew members felt this too and even when the two ships went on the Yelland run, crew members somehow preferred ***Colston*** for no real reason that they could identify. Many years later, I spoke to crew members who had been on both of them while with later owners and without any prompting from myself, they expressed exactly the same feelings. ***Brandon*** was a nice ship, a GOOD ship in every respect and there was nothing at all wrong with her but ***Colston*** somehow had an unexplainable feeling of home, safety and welcome. Who says that ships do not have souls?

Then came the news that I had anticipated with some apprehension. Very few people ever left the firm but retirements came along and, consequently, reshuffles among the personnel could be anticipated.

I was to be promoted to Sailor on ***Downleaze***. Goodbye to the comforts of the latest ships. Now I was going to have to get used to living in the foc'sle of a ship built during the 1920s. No electricity, minimal facilities but, most worrying, it meant that Ely Harbour was looming!

MOVE TO DOWNLEAZE

By this time, the steamers were taking it in turns to be laid up during the summer months. With the power stations on their reduced loading as the plant was shut down for maintenance, there was much less demand for day-to-day

Slightly before my time on her, this view of *Downleaze* loading at Ely Harbour, Penarth, was taken on 20th June 1956. The forward hold is being filled first, in order to raise her stern in the water and keep her afloat as long as possible on the ebbing tide. *Rick Cox collection*

fuel and the ships were mostly engaged in restocking the coal stores ready for the winter.

My move to ***Downleaze*** coincided with her wake up call for the winter running, hence she had some changes to her crew. She was to have a new Skipper and a new Sailor. ***Brandon***'s Mate was to become her Skipper, while I was to be her new Sailor.

I was called to the office to confirm my promotion and to complete the necessary paperwork, and I also had to see Mr Osborn. Although it might seem strange in these times, the purpose of seeing him was so that I could be advised and asked as to whether or not I was prepared, at the age of 18, to deal with the sudden huge increase in my pay which would result from the promotion and whether I could handle it wisely. And it WAS a big increase. I had remained on Boy's money ever since joining the firm, other than the times when I did relieving duties as Sailor or Second Engineer. This was now in the order of £4 per week, plus ten shillings for each trip over and above the first one each week, which still earned no extra. As a Sailor, however, my basic pay was quadrupled, plus £3 for every trip (still excepting the first one) and, in addition, I would be paid £4 for each hobble or discharge, which was part of the Sailor's job. So on a three-trip week, my wage would soar from £5 to about £34 – a big weekly wage for those times.

I took no offence at this paternal interest in my affairs by Mr Osborn; it was done tactfully and not in a patronising manner, and I knew that it was kindly meant.

I returned to ***Brandon***, packed up my gear, cleared the cabin ready for the new occupant and, not without a degree of apprehension, made my way to ***Downleaze***. Luckily, having done a couple of stints as relieving Sailor on her sister ***Rockleaze***, I knew what things were like on the steamers but this was going to be permanent, without any return to civilisation to look forward to shortly. It also involved much more physically demanding work and it meant that I would soon be using the workboat for mooring up at Ely Harbour, the ultimate challenge to an O&W deckhand.

Downleaze had a large foc'sle, divided along the ship's centreline into port and starboard cabins. Paint, ropes, fenders and other ships paraphernalia was stored in the port cabin, while the two Sailors shared the starboard side. The Skipper and Mate each had a cabin under the bridge structure amidships, while the two Engineers and the Boy had cabins aft. The Skipper and Mate's accommodation, midships, under the bridge structure, was reasonably civilised, with an adequately large and separate messroom. The Engineers cabins aft, were not so lavish but still reasonable, while the foc'sle was very basic. The Skipper's and Mate's cabins each had a washbasin fitted but nowhere else on the ship was there this degree of luxury and decadence.

The foc'sle contained two bunk beds, one over the other, three blankets for each man and two lockers attached to the bulkhead, some clothes hooks on the bulkhead and that was it. Apart from one small paraffin lamp, there was a slow combustion stove (known as a Bogey Stove) just inside the door. This stood in a large metal tray about ten inches from the bulkhead dividing the port and starboard foc'sle cabins. There was also a very large vertical pipe, about eighteen inches in diameter, from the deck to the deck head, through which the anchor chain ran from the chain locker below to the windlass above. There was a matching angled pipe at the forward end of the cabin, which contained the anchor stock when the anchor was stowed. Two small portholes let in a tiny amount of daylight. The deck was heavily angled upwards to match the sheer of the hull. There was a primitive toilet contained in its own small cubicle outside on the port side of the ship. Right outside the door of our side was the paraffin locker. Each man had one bucket and this had to serve for everything in our daily lives – washing clothes, washing up and washing ourselves.

She did at least, however, have a half decent galley – back aft! Any food cooked back there would be cold by the time it was carried along the deck, under the bridge, down into the welldeck and into the foc'sle – if it had not been blown off the plate or drenched with spray on the way!

As always and as on every ship, the galley was the focal point for all the crew. It was large enough to have several people sat on the long bench and the big black range kept it nice and warm in the winter. She was also fitted with a hot water boiler heated by steam from the main boiler. In theory this would supply constant boiling water to the galley but it was temperamental. There was no running water anywhere on the ship except for a gravity feed from the fresh-water tank to the galley. In the foc'sle, we used to obtain hot water for washing by cracking open the drain cocks on the two steam winches (one on the foc'sle for mooring and anchoring, and the other just outside the cabin for working the forward derrick) and admitting steam to the winch very gently. In this way, the incoming steam would push the condensed steam still lying in the pipes and cylinders, out through the drain cocks and into the waiting bucket. It sounds dreadful but that gave us the softest water imaginable!

So, living in ***Downleaze***'s foc'sle and, indeed, on each of the three steamers, was pretty basic and it was very much as comfortable or uncomfortable as we chose to make it. A bit of time and effort to make it clean (especially the bucket!) paid dividends and before long on a cold, wet and windy night, after hours of hard work loading the ship and trimming her cargo down, that foc'sle, with its smell of paraffin from the little light giving its yellow glow and the warmth from the Bogey Stove, seemed very inviting indeed. After a good wash down with the hot water from the winch, the couple of hours in the bunk before we sailed were precious.

For the Sailors sleep was at a premium. There were no regular hours, we slept when we could and we ate when we could, at whatever time, day or night, we could fit it in. The Sailors were involved with the loading and the unloading of the ship and the best – and often the only – opportunity for a couple of hours of uninterrupted sleep was during the trip from South Wales to Portishead. As soon as was possible after sailing, the chores would be done, the Bogey banked up to keep the foc'sle warm and it would be heads down for a couple of hours. The regular and muffled thump of the engine from so far back, and the irregular thud and gentle jolt as the bow hit a small wave, accompanied by the side to side rocking movement, soon induced sleep, despite the occasional clang from the anchor chain in its cast iron pipe running through the centre of the foc'sle.

One of the chores on ***Downleaze***, and the other two steamers, was the dumping of ashes. The ships boiler would consume a considerable quantity of coal each trip and it follows that this produced a great deal of ash and clinker, all of which accumulated in the stokehold as the fires were tended to and raked out by the Fireman. Each trip, this was dumped over the side after leaving Portishead. Officially, it was not supposed to be dumped until we were below Clevedon, as the Port of Bristol Authority (PBA) did not want to have to do any more dredging than was necessary. In practice, large though it was, the quantity that each ship produced was miniscule in comparison to the natural silting which occurred and, as waiting until we were below Clevedon would mean losing half of our sleep time, the sailors would begin to dump the ashes as soon as we were out of sight of the Dock Master and round the pier off Portishead! A set of big buckets made from twenty-gallon oil drums was used and, down in the stokehold, the Fireman would shovel the ashes into them. They were then hooked onto a cable dangling down one of the stokehold ventilators, from a drum with a handle on it built into the ventilator. An openable door in the side of the ventilator tube at deck level gave access to the buckets. At a shout from the Fireman, the handle would be turned by one of the Sailors and the bucket hoisted up the twenty feet inside the vent tube. Coming level to the access door, it would be unhooked and, although of considerable weight, would be manhandled out of the tube and passed to the other Sailor, who would tip the contents over the side – being enveloped in a cloud of dust if the wind was in the wrong direction and earning howls of protest from anyone in the galley next door cooking their breakfast as the dust would blow everywhere (gritty

Rockleaze, unladen and bound for South Wales. She is also seen in the process of dumping her ashes. *Author's collection*

food was par for the course on the steamers!).

The bucket would then be lowered back down, by which time another would have been filled and so the process would be repeated maybe twenty times, until all the ash was gone. It sounds simple enough but was not so easy if the Channel was choppy. The bucket was only slightly smaller in diameter than the vent tube, so the Sailor on the handle had to look carefully down through the stokehold grating and, watching the swing of the bucket, judge exactly when to give a quick turn on the handle to get the bucket into the tube. Conversely, lowering the empty bucket down the tube was sometimes awkward as it would be clanging against the tube on its way down. It was quite common for it to get hitched up momentarily and the hook would come off. This would be followed by a quick shout of "*Below!*" from the Sailor on the handle, at which the Fireman would step quickly to one side shouting such advice as "*Please do take a little more care*" – or something like that! There was no requirement to wear safety helmets in places of work in those days, you were simply that much more alert to possible dangers. No bad thing really.

The engine rooms and stokeholds of the steamers were dark echoing places and even during daylight, it was gloomy down there. At night, they became places of guttering light and large dark pools of shadow, with the hiss of steam from the glands and the regular thump of the engines adding its own rhythm and sound backdrop to the scene.

The Engineer would be seen moving about from light to shadow tending the engine, while the piston rods, bearings and eccentrics twinkled as they caught the light. The smell of steam and oil completed the unique atmosphere of a small ship's machinery.

The stokehold created its own vision of hell. Darker even than the engine room, there was no white paint to reflect the dim flame of the two paraffin lamps. But when the time came to put a charge of coal onto one of the three fires in the boiler and the firehole door was opened, the whole area would be bathed in red light, which flickered and glared angrily. The figure of the fireman could be seen sliding the big firing shovel under the coal at the bunker outlet and, judging his swing precisely with the movement of the ship, he would shoot the coal to the back of the fire, eight feet or so into the boiler. Maybe twelve or more charges would be shot into the fire, before the door was slammed shut again. With three such fires to be kept fed, as well as raking them out to keep them clean and free of choking ash, the Fireman had by far the most physically demanding task on the ship. The job was very much affected by the quality of the coal, and the skill and knowledge of the Fireman, who had to judge when to let the fires die down so as to prevent the safety valve lifting and when to keep the boiler right up to maximum working pressure. There was little, if any, let up for the Fireman during a trip.

While I was in ***Downleaze***, her Chief Engineer, Jack, was a short nuggety man, a Canadian. He used to feel the big end bearings while the engine was running. As the big ends came sweeping around with each revolution, he would slowly move his hand, with fingers outstretched, until he was touching the inner surfaces at the sides of each bearing momentarily, as it swept past his fingers. The gap was just wide enough to get his fingers in! Any misjudgement and he would have lost his hand or arm and, furthermore, this was done with the ship moving and swaying at sea.

Another incident involving Jack occurred just before one Christmas. We were due to sail and it worked out that we would be back perfectly set to give us a long Christmas off. However, as we walked down the quay wall, the tell-tale wisps of steam coming from her funnel meant, that once again, she had a boiler tube leaking, an increasingly common occurrence with her, by now, unreliable boiler.

The boiler was not serviceable in this condition and the leaking tube needed to be located and a tube stopper fitted to blank it off. The stopper consisted of a long metal bar, threaded at both ends, which was slightly longer than the boiler tubes themselves. A cap, made especially to fit the tubes, could then be screwed onto one end of the bar, after which it would be inserted into the tube, pushed through and a similar cap fitted to the other end. The outer, accessible, cap would then be tightened up, which pulled the cap on the other end tight against the tube end to seal it. However, it was no small task and it meant a long stoppage while the boiler was depressurised and the fires drawn, so that someone could enter the nearest firehole to the leaking tube, to locate and fit the cap on the inside end of the bar.

Knowing that our Christmas arrangements were going to be wrecked, even possibly having to spend the whole Christmas period in Newport Dock, the Chief Engineer asked if we were all prepared to help in the crisis in an effort to retrieve the situation. Luckily, by opening the front doors on the boiler's smoke box, the offending tube could be seen to be weeping at the front end, so its location was known. Jack told the Fireman to pull the fire out of the centre firehole (the nearest one) and to prepare the tube stopper bar. With the front cap already on the bar, it was slid down the offending tube. The rest of us were to go and find some substantial lengths of heavy timber. With all of this done and with every bucket in the ship to hand and filled with water, he supervised the job of putting the timber into the firehole onto the still hot fire bars and, wrapping himself in sacking, he then instructed that he be doused with water. Thoroughly soaked, he climbed into the firehole and clutching the other cap, he crawled his way as quickly as possible to the back of the boiler. In the space at the far end of the boiler he was able to stand up, then he swiftly screwed the cap partially onto the bar, which was just protruding from the offending boiler tube, centred it and then scrambled out again, with his clothes and the sacking, steaming.

He had gone into the boiler firehole which shortly before had contained a large fire (admittedly banked down) but flanked on each side by other grates still with their fires in and had fitted the stopper cap.

The fire, which had been shovelled out onto the stokehold floor, was then thrown back into the firehole and later that night, we sailed as arranged. No one in the firm, other than the crew, ever knew about that episode, which gave us all our long Christmas break.

LIVING IN DOWNLEAZE

Working the steamers was a whole different world to working the motorships. Dirty, dusty and primitive in their facilities, they were nevertheless kept as clean and tidy as could be by their crew and it was a strange thing but most of the crews who had been with them for a long time had a dread of being sent to the motorships.

All the lighting on board was paraffin, from the binnacle light, to the accommodation lights and navigation lights. One Sailor was responsible for the two masthead lights and the stern light, their cleanliness and refilling, while the other Sailor looked after the port and starboard lights and the binnacle lamp. Accommodation lighting was the province of the Boy. On one return trip from Ely Harbour, we had turned in when we were wakened by a series of short blasts on the whistle, the customary way of attracting our attention. ***Downleaze***'s Mate was a very droll and unflappable character, who never became excited whatever the crisis and when I looked out of the door at the wheelhouse (which was not very far away on ***Downleaze*** with her midships bridge) the Mate, who was on the wheel at the time, suggested that I rouse my 'oppo' and get him to "*have a look at the foremast light*", since it was his responsibility. Craning my head round and looking directly up and above me, I could see that at the top of the mast was a ball of flame, with the navigation light well and truly on fire!

While for ninety-nine per cent of the time, nothing went wrong and there were no incidents, another which did occur on ***Downleaze*** took place at about 4am in the morning, as we were leaving Portishead. Having got aboard at about 10.30pm the previous evening, the two of us had banked the Bogey Stove up to keep the foc'sle warm while we slept until sailing time. We must have found a bit of decent coal, because during the night we both woke up sweating with the heat. The sides of the Bogey were glowing and it was going really well. Eventually it burnt back, the temperature became more acceptable and we slept again until sailing time. Originally built with both sides of the foc'sle as accommodation, the port side was a mirror image of our side but its lockers, bunks, Bogey Stove, etc, had all been taken out when it became used as the paint locker and for ship's storage. However, the short length of chimney passing through the foc'sle deck for its stove had been left in place and as the ship went slowly down the dock and into the lock, our unflappable Mate on the foc'sle was seen to keep wandering over to the port side and peering at the deck.

Once moored up in the lock, he asked us if we had been in the port foc'sle cabin for any reason, because there were wisps of smoke coming out of the funnel stump. On being told that we had not, he fetched the key, opened up the port cabin door and found that it was full of smoke. The heat from our Bogey had gone right through the asbestos sheet fitted behind the stove on our side, with the result that the wooden partition between the cabins was smouldering nicely! A few buckets of water from over the side soon put it out but it was a good job that the paint and ropes, etc, had not been stacked close to the bulkhead.

So life on ***Downleaze*** became the norm for me but I still looked a bit wistfully at ***Colston*** and ***Brandon*** picking their dainty way to Newport only, with their crews all dressed in their 'tidy' ready to dash home as soon as they docked.

I was not asked to do the boat work for mooring up at Ely Harbour for the first couple of weeks but was told instead to watch and pay attention at what the boat was doing, while I worked in cooperation with it on the stern of the ship. Close understanding between the chap in the boat and the chap on the stern was vital. Failure to work together would, at best, make hard work for the boatman and at worst, could create a nasty predicament for the ship.

The Skipper had to be able to rely absolutely on the boatman to get the stern rope in and secured as quickly as possible. Until that was done, there was almost no control over the ship. She could find herself going sideways down the river on the outgoing tide, with no room for manoeuvre at all and, with other ships moored at the tips below her, there was a danger of collision, or even of getting the ship stranded across the river, with her bows fast on the mud on one side and her stern aground on the other. With the water receding from underneath her with the outgoing tide, there would be a strong possibility that the ship could suffer major structural damage and break her back. Hence, the crucial importance attached to the work of the boatman at Ely Harbour, something I had appreciated but had lived in dread of for a long time.

ELY HARBOUR

The coal tips at Ely Harbour were located on a bend in the river about a mile from the sea. At the bottom of the tide, the river was virtually dry except for a small amount of water still coming down but ships were left completely high and dry on the mud banks alongside the tips.

Because of this, loading at Ely was always done as quickly as possible, so that the ship could be moved while still afloat to load the last part of the cargo. However, it was never possible to complete loading while afloat and this meant that the remainder of the cargo had to be tipped where the ship lay aground. With no trimmers aboard, it was up to the two Sailors to trim the resulting considerable heap of coal down. This also meant that the ship could not be loaded to the Plimsoll line marks and the quantity of coal still to be put aboard had to be calculated from the weights given by the tip weighbridge. If there was the potential for bad weather and, therefore, the need to put the hatches on, the coal would have to be trimmed down below the hatch beams to enable them to be travelled along the coamings – a lot of shovelling to be done! It was often difficult to judge how the ship would sit in the water when she floated again and sometimes a slight list would result.

With the ship being naturally of a deeper draught at the stern, the forward hold was always loaded first to raise the stern, so that she stayed afloat for as long as possible. It also meant that she was going to be going with the tide when it came to moving her for loading into the after (main) hold. The ships with midship superstructure – ***Downleaze*** and ***Rockleaze*** – necessitated having to raise the tip chute when moving to the main hold.

This aerial view of Penarth Docks and Ely Harbour was taken circa 1951-52. The four tips on the River Ely are in the centre of this picture, with No. 1 the nearest to the sea. The Oil Wharf is just downstream of this, with its attendant tank farm on the spit of land beyond. Either *Rockleaze* or *Downleaze* can be seen moored at No. 3 Tip. The derelict piers of five more tips, Nos. 5 to 9, can be seen upstream of the four still in use when this photograph was taken. These had closed in the 1920s. Still in use nearest the camera was the Victoria Wharf and warehouses of the South Wales Public Wharf & Transit Co Ltd. The large wooden jetty was originally built to handle the import of iron ore. The two German square riggers *Pamir* and *Passat* can be seen moored in Penarth Dock, which was originally opened in 1865 and extended at the top end in 1884. At one stage, there were eleven coal tips in operation in this dock but just three remained in use by the time of this photograph, Nos. 2, 8 and 10. The railway lines serving the dock branched off from the main line at Cogan Junction, far right centre of the picture and Penarth town can be seen top right. Penarth Dock closed completely in 1963. The remains of a derelict jetty can be seen jutting out from the right bank of the River Ely near its mouth and it was just adjacent to this that *Lunan* was lost in 1941, after hitting a German mine.

Courtesy National Museums & Galleries of Wales

MOORING WITH THE BOAT

Mooring at Ely was the most likely source of problems. Because of the distance involved, by the time that we got there, it was always well past high water and there would be a considerable ebb tide flowing down the river which, at times of heavy rain, was made worse by an increased fresh water flow. It also meant that we arrived when the available width of the river was diminishing as the tide receded, which added to the problems of turning the ship in the river. Usually by the time we got there, the river was not much wider than the ship was long.

The ship had to be turned straight away so that she could leave as soon as possible when the water returned on the next tide. In a loaded state, the vessel could not be turned before high water without her bow and stern grounding on the steeply sloping banks, whilst to wait till then would have meant fighting the ebbing tide all the way back to Portishead and so not getting there in time to lock in. In any case, with so little room to spare, the risk of the ship grounding across the river in fully loaded condition could not be contemplated. With the steep banks, the ship would have broken her back as the water ebbed away underneath her.

There was no lighting at Ely Harbour whatsoever, so a night arrival and moor up had to be carried out in pitch darkness and, as often as not (almost always it seemed!) in driving wind and rain. It was a tense time for the Skipper, as for much of the operation his ship was virtually

This circa 1925 photograph of Ely Harbour illustrates the extent to which the water ebbed away on the bottom of the tide. On large tides, it would recede even further, leaving just a small stream formed by the river water. The mooring ring on its chain can just be made out on the nearest corner of the tip. It has the bow rope of the small sailing ship, whose bowsprit can be seen at the extreme left, attached to it. If the ring was under water when you arrived in the workboat to secure the stern rope, there was no option other than to secure it around the leg of the tip pier. The two tips in view are Nos. 1 and 2 and, coincidentally, loading at No. 1 Tip when the picture was taken was O&W's *Ferric*, with her workboat just off her bow. Beyond can be seen some of the oil storage tanks and a portion of the Victoria oil wharf, which was originally built to handle iron ore. In the left background, a rake of Ebbw Vale Steel, Iron & Coal Company wagons can be seen waiting to be unloaded. The harbour and the tips were still exactly the same during the 1950s and 60s and this photograph illustrates how much simpler they were than the taller hydraulic tips at Newport, which had to cater for the loading of larger ships. *Courtesy National Museums & Galleries of Wales*

out of control, and it was a difficult, physically very demanding job for the Sailor in the workboat, upon whom getting matters back under control rested entirely.

Approaching the tip upstream of the one at which we were to load, the ship would begin to make her turn with the last of the steerage way. After that, she was helpless until the crucially vital stern rope was secured and that was up to the workboat. It was the responsibility of securing this rope and the dangers involved in scrabbling in the dark, alone in the workboat in bad conditions, which had long troubled me about Ely Harbour but now, I was going to have to deal with it.

The Ely Harbour tips were of a much simpler design and constructed almost entirely of wood. Railway wagons were simply run onto the tipping platform at ground level, with no provision to raise the platform or the chute. The picture of *Ferric* at No. 1 Tip (*opposite*) graphically illustrates how far the drop could be from the mouth of the chute into the ship's hold once the tide had ebbed away and which, when loading dry coal, kept ship and crew almost permanently enveloped in a dense cloud of choking black dust.

These tips were served by parallel pairs of railway lines, each running over a weighbridge, one for loadeds and one for empties, which were operated from a single weigh hut. Nos. 1, 2 and 3 Tips were at such a sharp angle to the rail lines that the tipping platforms were accessed by means of wagon turntables. These were hand operated, using capstans. Nos. 4 and 5 Tips were on a straighter alignment to the tracks serving them. With these, both tracks ran onto the wooden pier leading to the tip, meeting at a turntable one wagon-length short of the tipping chute. Empties could thus still be trundled off along a separate line to the loadeds. In the view of No. 2 Tip on the left, the weighbridge can be seen at the landward end of the pier, with loaded wagons

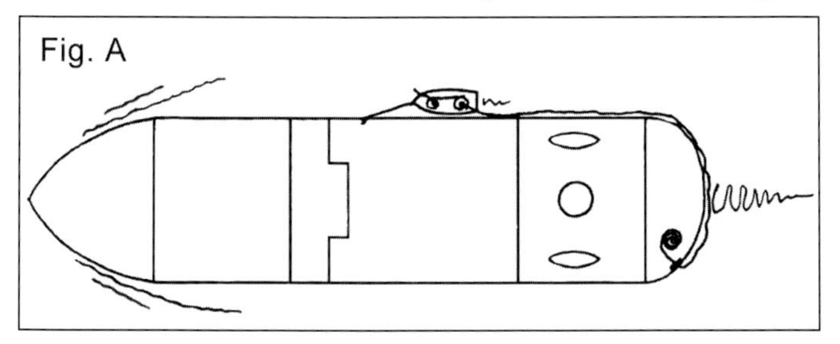

being weighed before they were turned onto the tip.

Soon after entering the mouth of the River Ely (which, incidentally, in conversation was nearly always referred to the other way round as "*the Ely River*"), the workboat would be put over the side from the forward hold and allowed to drift back towards the ship's stern. It was at this point that the ship would be hailed and told which tip to go to. In the diagram sequence which follows, this is No. 2 Tip.

A five-inch rope, with no eye at its end, would be taken from the port quarter and fed around the stern, outboard of all obstructions, with the end lowered to the Sailor, who had by now gone down the rope ladder and into the workboat. In the boat, the rope would be coiled first at the stern and then an equal amount, right up to the end of the rope, would be coiled at the bow. The very end of the rope was placed on the top of the coil, immediately to hand on the boat's side, where it could be found quickly in the dark if necessary and picked up immediately and surely (*see Figure A, below left*).

Going upstream and passing No. 2 tip, the ship would be almost alongside No. 3 tip as she began to make her turn. The Sailor in the workboat would judge when to let go the ship and would then set off for No. 3 tip, sculling the boat against and across the strongly ebbing tide. The shorter the distance the better. Too little rope let out from the ship would hold the boat back. Conversely, too much fed out would result in a large bight of rope streaming down the river on the ebbing tide, again impeding the boats progress. At this stage, there was virtually no control over the ship and she would begin to drift sideways down the river on the ebbing tide (*see Figure B, below*).

The quicker the stern line could be made secure (and with a very long eye), the better. It was vital that this rope held securely to stop the ship's sideways progress downstream. There was no time to secure the boat to the tip leg, it was up to the skill of the boatman. After judging exactly when to stop sculling, he pulled the oar inboard before scrabbling to the forward end of the boat. Then, balancing right at the forward end of the boat and with nothing to hold onto except the slimy wooden pile, he had to hold the boat there in position whilst feeding the rope around the tip leg and tying the Bowline knot. He also had to insert a piece of wood, referred to as a toggle, into the knot so that it could

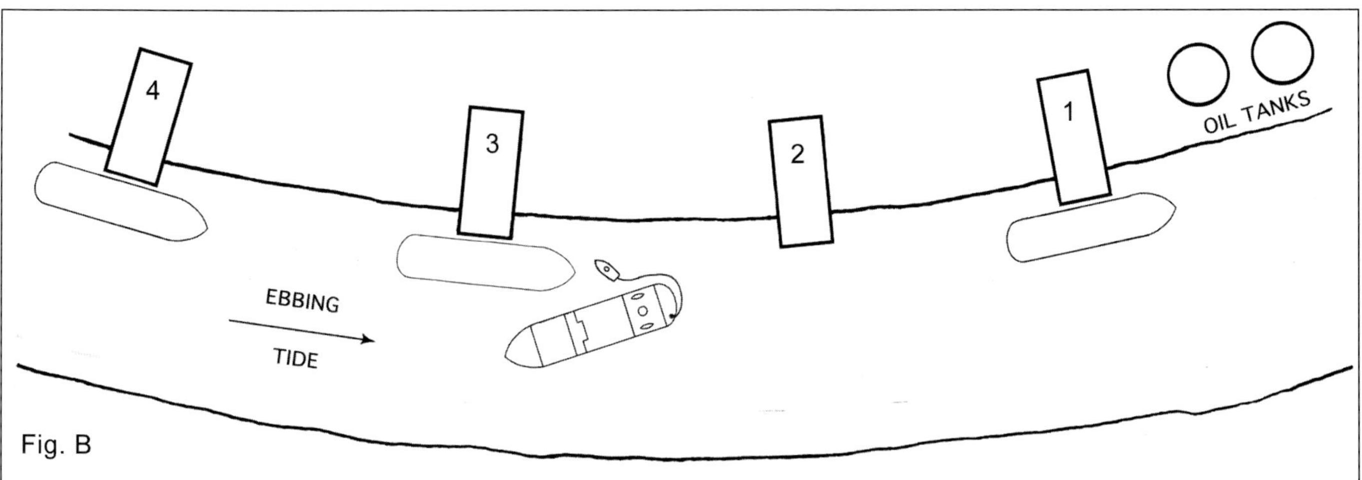

be readily undone later on. He would then feed the rope round the leg of the tip, to give an equal length to both sides of the eye formed by doing all this. And all the time he was doing this, the ship itself was still drifting sideways down the river. Furthermore, all too frequently it was all carried out in the dark, and in wind and rain (*see Figure C, below*).

When he had finished, the Sailor would shout out to the ship that all was secure and the stern rope would be winched in as quickly as possible to hold the ship in the tideway. With the stern rope now secure, the ship would be checked from further sideways progress down the river. Instead, she would hang on this rope and begin to turn very rapidly on it. The rope, meanwhile, would be bar tight and creaking with the strain. Streaming down the river on the end of the rope, the ship would be sweeping towards the bank and the tip at which she was to load. If it seemed she might hit the tip too heavily, very often an anchor would be dropped to check the rush (*see Figure D*).

With the ship now alongside her appointed tip, the Sailor in the workboat would now pick up the other ropes, and take a headrope to the tip immediately downstream and springs to the ship's own tip. She was now secure and the boat would be sculled round to the rope ladder for the Sailor to come back on board (*see Figure E*).

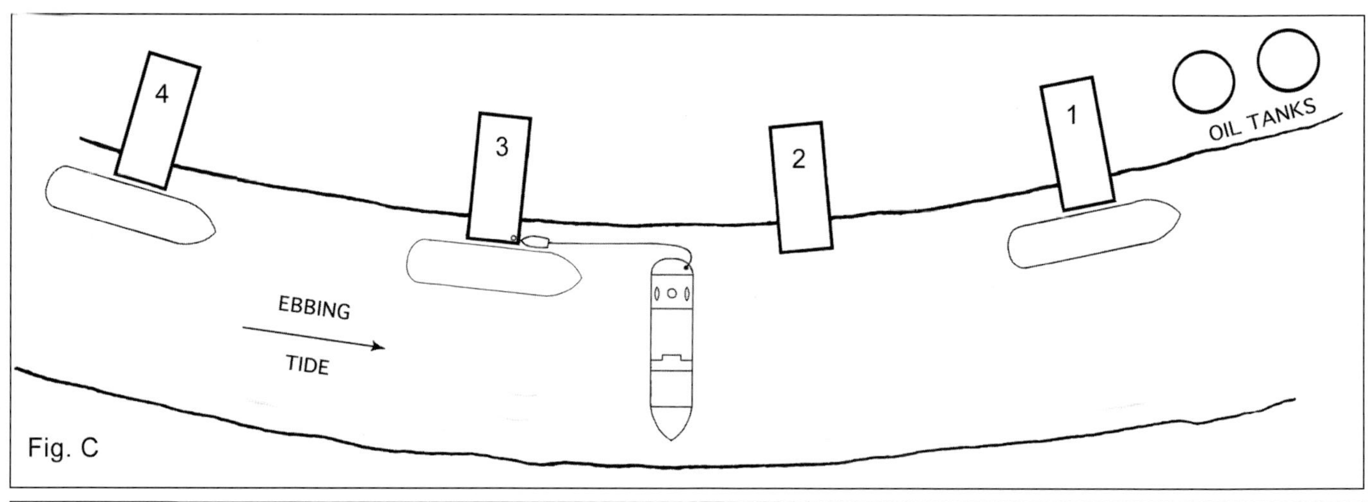

Fig. C

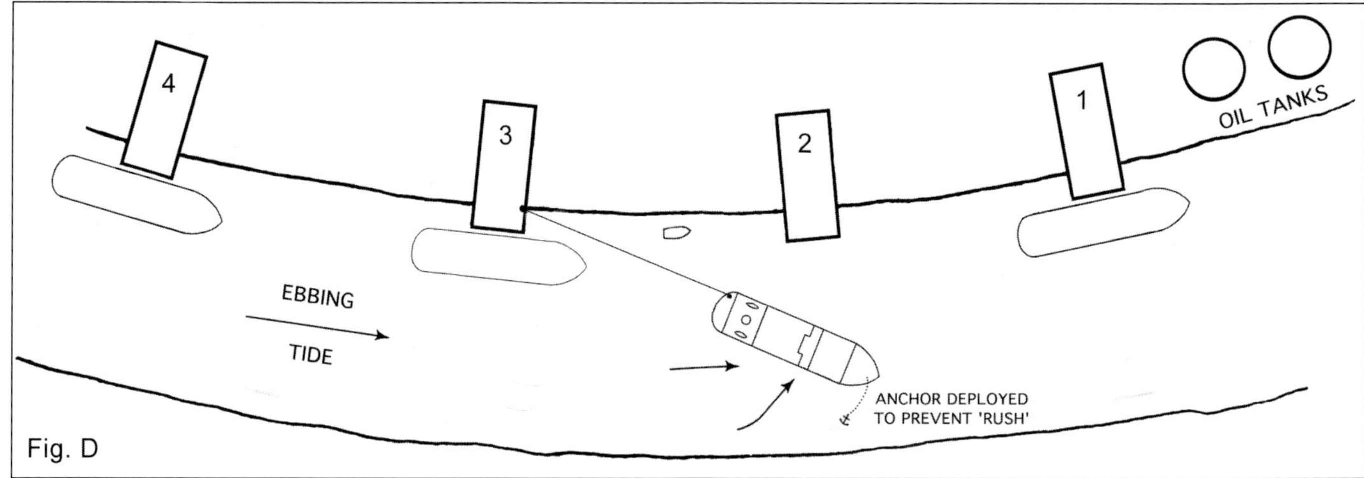

Fig. D

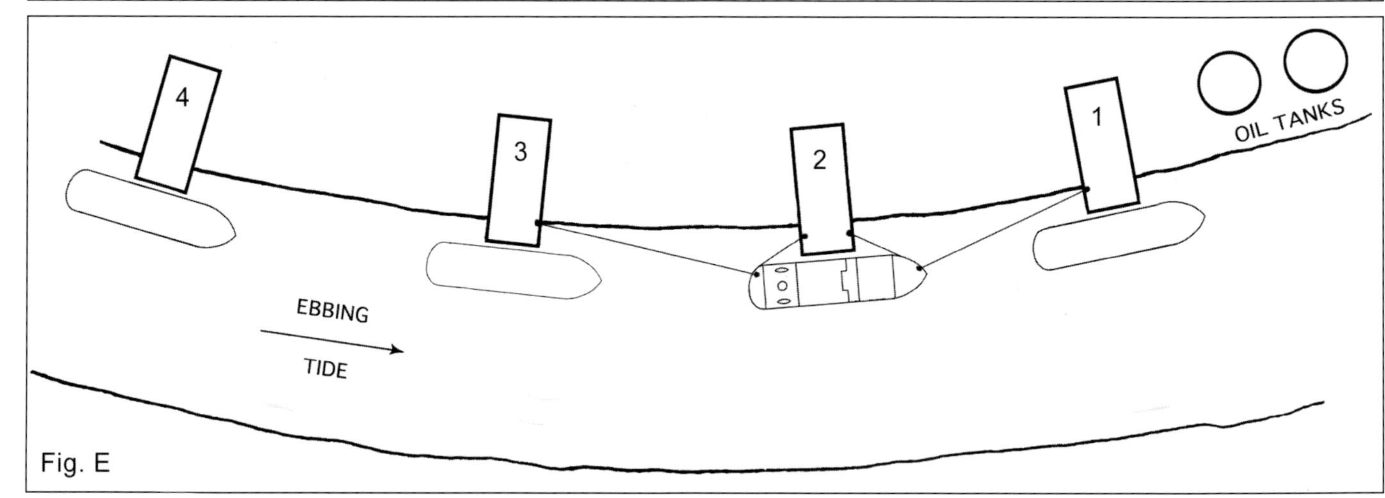

Fig. E

Left: *St. Vincent* prepares to swing into position for loading at one of the Ely Harbour tips by means of the rope. As can be seen, there was not a lot of water to play with.
Bottom: A few minutes later, the vessel nestles safely alongside the tip and awaits loading. *Both author*

Below: This sketch illustrates the predicament *Druid Stoke*'s Sailor found himself in, after looping the stern rope through the lifting strop on the workboat. *Author*

Everything about Ely Harbour was hard work and, after a short while, a trip to Newport was looked upon as a treat, especially the luxury of having trimmers come on board to do the shovelling, as well as the easy mooring facilities. There was also undoubtedly a considerable potential for accidents, especially for the workboat. Life jackets were far too cumbersome to wear in the boat but, fortunately, apart from a couple of minor incidents, nothing serious ever occurred.

One of the minor incidents involved ***Druid Stoke*** and her workboat one dark night while mooring up at Ely. Everything seemed to be going according to plan, with the all important stern rope having been taken in and made fast around the leg of the tip, as one of the mooring rings was too high to reach and the next one down was under water.

Hearing a shout from the Sailor in the boat, the man on the stern started to heave the stern rope in, the capstan making its usual clattering noise at full speed, whilst issuing forth its customary cloud of steam, so that all contact with the workboat was lost for a moment.

With the stern rope tight and all ready for the next rope to be taken ashore, there was no sign of the workboat but shouts could be heard astern of the ship. Fetching the big torch (the only electricity on the ship!), it could be seen that the workboat was hanging in the air! In the dark, the boatman had accidentally passed the heavy rope through the lifting strop and when the weight of the ship was abruptly taken by the rope, the workboat, together with its crewman, had been plucked aloft and was now hanging several feet above the surface of the water. Luckily, the small ship moored at the next tip upstream heard the commotion and sent its boat to run another rope in, so that the first one could be let go to free the suspended boat and its red-faced occupant.

As with so many things in life, he had carried out the operation hundreds of times before without incident but just this once, in the dark, when taking the rope forward in the boat to make the second coil, he failed to notice he had ducked it under the strop – easily done and surprising it didn't happen more often!

With the last of the cargo aboard and still in a heap, it would be shovelled down to allow the hatches to be put on if necessary, a quick bite to eat taken and, maybe, a couple of hours sleep until the time came to leave. Of course, if the weather conditions warranted it, the hatches would have to be put on, which virtually did away with any chance of proper sleep for the Sailors. A cat-nap was all there was time for in those circumstances. It also meant that any sleep on the trip back would be curtailed by the need to take the hatches off again when approaching Portishead.

The return of the tide meant that, once afloat and given a suitable safety margin, the ship could leave. However, sometimes she would suck into the mud and not lift as the water rose around her. Once this had happened, the workboat was retrieved and with it still slung from the derrick, it would be pulled rapidly from side to side in the hope that this would rock the ship a little to break the suction, at which she would bob up. The boat was then put back in

Left: *Hotwells* under No. 3 Tip at Ely in 1950. It can be seen that she has completed loading but there still remains a lot of work to be done, trimming that pyramid of coal down into the main hold before the vessel will be ready to sail on the next tide. *Chris Witts*

Opposite below: This photograph of *Druid Stoke* was taken in 1959, when she was nearing the end of her life. She was originally built without a wheelhouse and, by the time of this photograph, she had lost her second derrick. It can be seen that she still has her washboards, however. The hatchboards can just be made out stowed along the narrow walkway, the trampoline effect of which provided our only fun on board her in my day. *Chris Witts*

the water and the ropes let go. By this time, however, the water was nowhere near as high as it had been on arrival but the reason for the long eye tied in all the ropes would now become clear. Without it, the Bowline knot would be high above the boatman's reach on every rope but, as it was, the sag in the slackened rope brought it down to a reachable level. The toggles which had been inserted at the time of tying enabled the knot to be broken easily. These were usually short lengths of wood used as railway wagon braking handles ('sprags'), which could be found along the shore. Without them, even the easy release Bowline knot could tighten up to the point where, in a stiff five-inch rope, it would be almost impossible to break. With the toggle inserted, however, it would, when withdrawn, leave sufficient slack in the knot to enable it to be manipulated and let go.

Only a few months after I joined ***Downleaze***, she was sent to Hill's yard to have her now troublesome boiler removed and to have the reconditioned one recently removed from ***Sneyd***, before she was scrapped, put in its place. This was a major piece of work and it did not seem to make economic sense. ***Rockleaze*** was already tied up awaiting disposal for scrap and surely ***Downleaze*** was not going to be far behind. However, that was the programme and, with the prospect of a longish spell in dockyard hands and an unclear future for the ship, some of us were sent off relieving.

RELIEF ON COLSTON.

I was sent to ***Colston*** as relieving Sailor and had no objections to being back aboard my favourite, living in civilised conditions and running only to Newport for a while! She was in Osborn's yard when I joined her, having bought a cargo of coal to Bristol and she was due to sail the following day at midday.

We duly left the yard as arranged. The weather was very calm, warm and slightly misty but there were no problems making our way down the Avon Gorge following a sandsucker. By now, the ship had been fitted with her Decca Navigator gear and, as was routine, this was switched on and recording the position. Passing below the village of Pill, famous for its Bristol Channel Pilots, and getting towards the river mouth, a dense bank of white fog could be seen ahead and the sandsucker disappeared into it. We followed, the ship's bows being enveloped first and then the rest of the ship. It was like a wall. Outside it had been reasonably clear but, once inside, it was not possible to see even halfway along the ship, so dense was the fog. From the foc'sle, the edges of the water against the banks of the river could not be discerned. Suddenly, from ahead came the sound of rapid engine movements from the sandsucker, accompanied by three blasts on the whistle to indicate that she was going astern. The fog had totally closed in leaving us completely blind and the Skipper made the decision to anchor where we were, rather than just groping about.

The Decca was accurate to within sixty feet but we couldn't even see sixty feet, so any further progress would have been based on guesswork – foolish in such confined water.

So we anchored… and the fog didn't lift. We stayed there for the rest of the tide and Walton Bay Signal Station was advised by radio that we were anchored in the river below Pill. At the bottom of the tide, as it turned, the Decca plotted the small arc of crosses as the ship swung around her anchor… and still the fog stayed as thick as ever. Having planned to fill the freshwater tank when we arrived at Newport where the water was much softer than at Bristol, it was now pretty low, so the Skipper ordered no more washing, etc – the water was only for drinking. The top of the tide came and went with the fog as dense as ever and, again, the Decca plotted the swing. However, the concern now was that the tides were becoming bigger, with higher tops but an ever decreasing depth of water at the bottom. Eventually, the position would be reached when there would not be enough water for her to turn at the bottom of the tide. We needed to get away soon. Trapped for yet another tide, the Pill Ferry boat, having learnt of the situation, made its way down the river to us and advised that the whole river was closed in with dense fog and asked if we needed anything. It was decided that the Boy and myself should go back with the ferry to buy some necessities at Pill. So, unshaven and somewhat scruffy, I undertook my once ever shopping trip at Pill. Then, just as anxiety about turning the ship on the next tide was becoming acute, the fog eased sufficiently for us to make our way gingerly out of the river. By the time we reached Portishead, it was a perfectly clear sunny day. Looking back though, the pall of dense white fog could still be seen hanging over the river at Avonmouth and, even with us gone, the river remained closed to further traffic for another day.

After three weeks, the work on ***Downleaze*** was completed and she was ready to return to service. The new boiler settled in with no problems and we picked up our routine where we had left off, with a mixture of Newport trips and Ely Harbour runs. By now I was doing the boat work at Ely Harbour, taking it in turns with the other Sailor and, although I became accustomed to it, I recognised that I had been right to be respectful of that part of the job.

There were a couple of minor incidents, such as when the oar in the boat broke on one occasion and the ship drifted some way downstream, while the sailor in the boat (not me!) hauled himself back to the ship along the rope. Another oar was passed down to him and it was quite some time before the situation was bought under control, as he now had a considerable distance to scull back to the tip, towing a lot of rope behind him.

On another occasion, as he was taking the stern rope in, the drag on it from the tide pulled him in alongside the stern of a small ship that was moored at the tip ahead of us, waiting to load. He found himself pinned to the side of this ship by the combination of the weight of the rope and the stream of the tide – at which point she began pumping her ballast out, right into the boat. Such incidents were rare, though and, for most of the time, life was routine, wearisome and trouble free.

We were caught in the fog on our way back from Newport one day and the Skipper decided that our position was too unsure to allow us to continue by guesswork. The one thing that was certain and which would give us a true and safe position, was the English & Welsh Grounds Lightship, so he decided to make for the sound of its bellowing horn and then anchor nearby. In times of fog, the horn on the lightship could be clearly heard at Portishead, with its long, mournful note, followed by a grunt as it ended each blast. As we carefully made for the noise of the lightship, giving regular blasts on the ship's whistle, it was clear there were other craft that had had the same idea and each blast on the whistle would be answered by the anxious ringing of several bells. We stayed there for two days, during which time sleep was impossible so powerful was the lightship's horn. The air itself vibrated at each blast and, on occasion, plates on the foc'sle table vibrated and rattled. When the fog cleared suddenly, we found that we were one of five ships huddled around the lightship, while ***Hotwells*** was anchored at Walton Bay, having been on her way to Newport.

Despite her recent boiler change, after a couple more

months of running, the company decided to lay ***Downleaze*** up and she moored in the reserve position in the yard. We spent several weeks putting her to bed and painting her up. Then, another round of moves were made. I had thought that it couldn't get any worse, until I learned my fate… I was to be a sailor on ***Druid Stoke***.

MOVE TO DRUID STOKE

I was very uneasy about being sent to ***Druid Stoke***. Now it really couldn't get any worse and I was just grateful that the last of the barges had been scrapped a few years earlier! All of the steamers were primitive in their living conditions for the Sailors but the ***Druid*** was the worst by far. All the steamers were hard work for everyone in their crews but, again, the ***Druid*** was more so. She was readily acknowledged as the company's punishment ship, to which condemned souls were sent. She was also considerably slower than everything else. In a race for the locks to get in and dock in time to catch the last bus or train home, the ***Druid*** would always lose out.

Her accommodation was dreadful. She was similarly fitted out to ***Downleaze*** but her foc'sle cabins were smaller. Two Sailors occupied the starboard side, whilst the Boy occupied the port foc'sle cabin. The Skipper and Mate lived in what can only be described as a tunnel, across and through the superstructure under the wheelhouse. It was so confined that you had to pass through it sideways.

There were stories that her galley had actually been forgotten when she was originally designed, which seemed quite credible as it was literally the size of a telephone kiosk and consisted of a steel box hanging over one side of the ship's stokehold. A small black range filled the forward end of this cupboard and against the after bulkhead was a locker in which the coal for the range was kept, which also formed a seat on which you could sit while cooking. However, this meant that your knees were virtually touching the range and, after a few minutes, no matter how much you fidgeted and shifted about, the knees of your trousers were smoking and your legs were on fire.

There were no washing facilities anywhere. On ***Druid Stoke***, each and everyone, including the Skipper and the Mate, was issued with a general purpose bucket. The only running water was from a tap on deck, screwed directly into the freshwater tank. As with all the steamers, it was paraffin lighting and Bogey Stove heating. There was a basic – very basic! – toilet outside the port cabin door and the paraffin tank was outside the starboard one. However, at least the Sailors and the Boy did not have to trudge the length of the ship to reach the toilet as everyone at the stern did.

And all this in a ship operating in 1960 – not 1860!

She was horrible on deck as well. With almost no freeboard along the whole length of her cargo deck, any slight sea would come aboard. The walkway between the hatch coaming and the bulwarks along her side was very narrow, and her hatches had to be stowed in this space as well. So they were stacked on big blocks of wood against the coaming and one board would be placed on these blocks to make a continuous walkway along the deck. We foc'sle dwellers soon found that it was possible to trampoline your way along the deck, by bounding along and landing in the middle of the hatchboards forming the walkway. It made a rattling sound but it brought a bit of light-heartedness into our otherwise miserable existences. Fun was in short supply on ***Druid Stoke***. Work, on the other hand, there was plenty of!

Her Skipper was a man of many moods. He was a good seaman and very reluctant to admit defeat in fog. The ***Druid*** would sail when others wouldn't and, to be fair, we almost always got there. He could, in a good mood, be very chatty and good company but then, for no apparent reason, the mood would change and he would become very withdrawn and quiet. There was often an air of tension aboard her, with everyone wondering what mood the Skipper was in today. The ship herself didn't help. We had to do whatever the Skipper felt necessary and we often had to put all the hatches on, even when it seemed likely to us that it was going to be a balmy trip back.

The ***Druid*** had hinged washboards all along her sides on the cargo deck when I joined her. These covered large square holes in the bulwarks, the idea being that they would be closed shut by water on the outside pressing against them to keep the sea out but they would flap away from the bulwark to let any water that did manage to get aboard back over the side. A sort of crude one-way valve. However, they were seized solid and had been for a long time. Then, during her survey, one young keen Board of Trade Inspector decided that he didn't like this situation and ordered that it be remedied. The cheap and easy answer was to cut the washboards off altogether and simply weld bars over the resulting large holes in the bulwarks. Now the sea could get in just as easily as it could get out and was to cause we two Sailors even more work and loss of sleep.

The Skipper having initially decided that we didn't need the hatches on for the trip back, the two Sailors would turn in for a couple of precious hours sleep before discharging at Portishead. Very often though, it wouldn't be long before a series of short toots on the whistle attracted our attention and we would be instructed to stack the hatchboards up on top of the coal "*so they don't get washed away if any sea should come aboard through the washboard holes*". Most trips would mean lifting every hatch up, either to get them off the deck, or to batten her down and if she needed any hatches on at all, she needed them all. Having no well deck like the others, her whole length of cargo deck was vulnerable.

As explained, the Sailors were left to trim the cargo at Ely Harbour and if it seemed to be likely that the hatchboards would have to be secured due to the weather, we would do this as well, to avoid having to do it whilst on the way back. We would be working for an hour or more after everyone else had turned in. However, stowing the hatchboards was a noisy task and our well intentioned activities were not always appreciated by the Skipper and Mate as they tried to get some sleep. Not unreasonably, after the work we needed a wash and something to eat and drink, and that meant hot water from the galley, another cause of friction as we crept about trying to be quiet. And, having secured the hatchboards,

The *Druid* photographed at Newport circa 1961, after the removal of her washboards. Note the lack of freeboard which, combined with the holes where the washboards used to be made her very hard work for her deckhands. The hatchboards had to be lifted up onto the cargo almost every trip, to prevent them being knocked about by the water coming aboard and this meant she was decidedly tiresome to sail in. Her forward mast derrick is being used to swing the workboat back on board. Why the purposeless second mast was left in place, blocking the view from the wheelhouse, remains a mystery. Captain 'Bill' Butler is on the bridge.
Chris Collard

our sleep would be shortened by the need to get them all down on deck again before we reached Portishead.

For her size, the ***Druid*** had an enormous whistle with a very deep and resonant tone. It was commonly held that the reason that she made her way so successfully through fog, was because the deep blasts from the whistle used to convince other ships that ***Queen Mary*** at least was bearing down on them and they would shrink back to one side to give this mighty vessel (whatever it was) room to pass. Her Fireman used to swear that the boiler pressure gauge could be seen to drop whenever the whistle was sounded. As we groped our way through the murk, the other ship would slowly emerge from the gloom and both vessels would become visible to one another. Then, just to make sure that the other ship knew who it was that she had taken such pains to avoid, the Skipper, with a huge grin on his face, would give another blast on the whistle.

Her Mate was a born tinkerer, ever seeking to make little improvements to her to ease the workload and her Chief Engineer was a steam man to the core. His brother had been the sole survivor from the explosion which wrecked ***Lunan***. He knew and fussed over his engine as if it were his own. Good company at any time.

Her Second Engineer (Fireman) was an outstanding character. Elderly and single, he lived on the ship. He never ever compared or commented upon the differences that we young 'uns benefited from – he was still a young 'un at heart himself. Ever ready for mischief and a leg pull, water bombs were his favourite terror weapon and it was necessary to watch yourself when he was around. At other times, he would help gladly, particularly when the ship was at full stretch, whenever there was work to be done on deck and whatever the weather. He was a true gentleman and I am glad to have known him. It was the crew that made life on the ***Druid*** bearable and I am surprised to find that I have fond memories of her.

The other Sailor with whom I shared the foc'sle, was an ex-Royal Navy man with a passion for motor bikes. He owned and rode an old but hugely modified 600cc Ariel, which was barely legal.

With the Boy also living up forward, we had our own little gang and between us we made the most of the situation. It would have been very easy to despair of working in ***Druid Stoke***. There was nothing about that ship that was easy and a sense of humour was vital to be able to put up with the old thing. We became used to being the butt of ridicule from the other crews and simply knew that we would always lose out. The strange thing is though, even today, when speaking to any old Portishead inhabitants and asking if they remember 'The Coal Boats', they will always recall the name ***Druid Stoke*** – indeed, she seems to be remembered with affection.

The foc'sle was very similar to that of ***Downleaze***, in terms of its fixtures and fittings, including the large anchor chain pipe right in the middle of the cabin. Our washing water was obtained in the same way, by draining condensed water from the two deck winches into our buckets.

We became very ambitious, however, with our cuisine. From the day we went aboard her, it was clear that the galley was completely out for cooking purposes, since it meant queuing up one at a time. We had our Bogey Stove, so we improvised around that. As I had been told on ***Colston*** while learning to cook "*If you can eat it raw, you can eat it half cooked!*" The Bogey was only small but we eventually learnt to cook a two-veg meal and potatoes on it, with whatever meat we fancied and we managed to keep the food warm. Once cooked, the saucepans would be stood all around the bottom of the stove until the last one was ready. The meat meantime would be sizzling on the top in a frying pan. Sometimes we would combine forces with the Boy next door and cook everything together on the two Bogey's.

For a quick, ready hot meal, however, we had our own speciality. With the kettle always on the boil, we always had a supply on board of Symington's Soups. Purportedly in various flavours – ham and pea, tomato, oxtail – they all tasted the same, although the colours were different. They came looking exactly like large billiard cue chalks, with about the same texture and consistency. They would (eventually) partially dissolve in boiling water and although a bit gritty at the bottom of the mug, would at least be hot and (we liked to think) nourishing on a cold night.

Even more than on the '***Downer***', because the work was so much more difficult on the ***Druid***, the foc'sle was a welcome haven from wind and rain – cosy, warm, dimly lit, smelling of cocoa, paraffin and drying socks, not to mention the occasional back draught of evil green smoke from the Bogey Stove.

Her engine room was a spectacle in itself at night. With her back-to-front boiler, it presented that same dark and gloomy cavern, with the same sounds and smells as the other steamers. But the masses of metal that were her machinery would suddenly became bathed in a lurid red glow as one of the fire hole doors was opened to attend to the fire within. The crank-shaft, the connecting rods, the eccentrics would all be seen dancing their regular movements, accompanied by the rythmic snorts of steam, and would all be lit up in this fierce red glow giving the whole place a surreal look and atmosphere. It was always fascinating to stand on the grating spanning the two doors, one on either side, giving access to the engine room, to watch and look down upon this spectacle. I always liked diesel engines but it was easy to see how an engineer could become involved with this machinery, despite the dirt and the difficulties and the hard work that the engine room entailed; snorting and moving, it seemed almost alive.

Druid Stoke had been built with two masts and two big derricks. Between them, the derricks were able to reach every part of the hold. It was never quite understood why this had been so, as she was built solely as a coal transport where loading and discharging facilities were provided. The main mast was always a nuisance to visibility from the wheelhouse and the derrick had long been removed by the time that I joined her. The now purposeless mast and winch was still in place with no function to serve, not even to carry a second navigation light, as the ship was two feet below the length at which this was compulsory.

However, at the same Board of Trade survey which had seen the removal of the washboards, it was decided to remove the mainmast's redundant winch. This was done very quickly at Hill's yard, leaving a large expanse of open deck which became known as the 'wheelhouse ashtray' since, being flanked on all four sides by either vertical, or sloping plates, it made a natural trap for the many cigarette ends flicked from the wheelhouse windows. For some reason, even with the derrick gone and now the winch, the purposeless mast was left *in situ*, hindering the view from the wheelhouse. It could so easily and beneficially have gone at the same time.

The rest of the survey work was carried out and, after several more days, we sailed from the dockyard on a late evening tide bound for Newport. After reaching Avonmouth, we found ourselves in fog, which became progressively thicker as the night wore on, until it became necessary for the Sailors to be stationed on the foc'sle. In view of the extra distance involved in travelling down the Avon from Bristol and the lateness of our trip, the Skipper decided to go across the sands, instead of going all the way down around via the English & Welsh Grounds Lightship. This meant that there were no navigation marks to look for until we picked up the buoys on the approach to Newport itself. The trip across the sandbanks was nothing new. It had been done many times before, and the courses and times to make the voyage safely were all known to the Skipper. Not expecting yet to see anything, we two Sailors on the foc'sle were suddenly surprised to see a periodically regular lightening of the fog and this soon became a faint flashing light dead ahead. A quick shout back to the wheelhouse started the ship on a hard swing to port and the flashing was soon identified as the warning light on Goldcliffe Point, several miles upstream of Newport. We had been heading straight for it.

The Skipper rightly prided himself on his skill and reputation for being able to get the ***Druid*** about in fog and such a wide error seemed unexplainable. However, the Mate had a sudden realisation – "*Taking that winch out has removed about three tons of iron from within about ten feet of the compass.*" He was absolutely right. No one had given a thought to the effect on the ship's compass and it was indeed way out. It was duly reset and compensated for the new conditions before the next trip.

Her Skipper's only aid to navigation in fog was his trusty note book, giving the times and compass courses, and an alarm clock, which he would reset after passing each navigation mark to the number of minutes before the next one was expected to show up. Strange as it might seem, ***Druid Stoke*** very rarely failed to complete a trip in fog.

The ***Druid*** was not the easiest of ships for the Skipper either. Alone of the three steamers, she had total steam loss to the winches, so that instead of returning the used steam to the engine room for condensing and back to the boiler – a relatively clean system – the ***Druid*** exhausted her winch steam over the side in billowing plumes. In wet weather, when evaporation didn't occur quickly and with the wind in the right direction, the fore end of the ship could become invisible from the wheelhouse and all forward vision lost. This was not the best of situations and was much aggravated at Ely Harbour, where there was a long lift with the winch to get the workboat up out of the hold and over the side.

Many were the times that, having begun this operation, the Skipper, invisible behind a cloud of steam, would be heard shouting "*Shut that bloody winch off, I can't see a thing!*" In due course, the steam would clear, and normality would be resumed, at which point the task of lifting the boat out would restart – only to go through the same cycle three or four times, by which time, the advice from the wheelhouse would be to "*Hurry up and get that damn boat over the side, we're nearly there!*"

Getting steam on deck for the winches was a pretty fraught exercise for the Sailors too, whose task it was. It was very dark and gloomy in her fiddley at the best of times and pitch dark at night. The deck steam valve was fitted to the boiler some way down from the crown, so it was necessary to step off the grating, having ducked under the handrail and take a couple of steps down the curve of the boiler top, before groping about for the invisible valve. Had there been a slip or missed footing, the unfortunate Sailor would have slid down the boiler, presumably to end up in the stokehold.

So life on ***Druid Stoke*** was a pretty grim affair but, luckily, the Second Engineer, the two Sailors and the Boy all got on well and we made up for the drudgery with a bit of light relief when we could.

One genuinely unintentional incident caused quite a frosty atmosphere on the ship for a few days. Due to sail for Ely one morning at about 4 o'clock, we had the opportunity for a few hours sleep before leaving and, by chance, the other Sailor and myself met as we were walking along the quay wall to the ship. We decided to have a quick cup of cocoa. One of us would light the Bogey in the foc'sle, the other prepare the drink. Then we decided that it would be quicker to use the hot water from the galley kettle.

Unusually, the galley fire had gone out. The Second Engineer, who lived aboard the ship and kept the fire going for his own domestic purposes, had been ashore for the evening. All that was left of the fire were the hot ashes and a couple of red embers, The lighting wood that we threw in did not catch fire, so taking the paraffin lamp from the bulkhead, we tipped some fuel onto the wood, all that happened was a dense white cloud of paraffin vapour came billowing out… but no flame. Being non-smokers, neither of us had any matches, so the other Sailor volunteered to go down to the stokehold with a rolled-up paper and get a light from the boiler.

Just as he left on this errand, the Skipper, dressed in his long black coat and black trilby hat, emerged out of the gloom and seeing me standing there at the Galley door, asked what I was up to. Having explained, he said that he wanted to get his head down and did not want us fiddling about next door. He then stated that he had some matches and, telling me to get out of the way, he stepped in over the storm sill. I heard the sound of money jangling in his pocket as he found his matches, followed by the rattle of the matchbox being opened and then just the start of a match being struck… followed by a huge BROOMPH! as the paraffin vapour ignited. The other Sailor emerged from the engine room clutching his flaming torch, just in time to see the Skipper, preceded by a cloud of ash, staggering from the galley in a momentary ball of flame. He was livid and the air was blue for several minutes. His coat was grey from the ash which had erupted out of the stove and, to make matters worse, a couple of hot cinders burnt their way through the rim of his trilby. We decided that perhaps we would make the cocoa in the foc'sle after all.

When we saw the Skipper the next day, we noticed that his eyebrows were badly singed as well. He was not in a very good mood for several days afterwards.

About every fourth trip, the ship would need bunkering. It was a joy if this occurred on a Newport trip but more often than not, it was done at Ely. At Newport it took place in still water. At Ely, after loading the forward hatch, the ship would be allowed to move forward on her ropes with the ebbing tide, so that the tip chute could be lowered to where the bunker hatch was located, immediately behind the wheelhouse.

The hatch was very small and not as wide as the mouth of the chute, so, inevitably, more was going outside the hatch than in it and would have to be shovelled in when the chute was lifted up out of the way after bunkering. This was a good quality, dry and dusty steam coal, so it meant a lot of dust as the coal poured down the chute and into the bunkers.

The really difficult part of this operation arose from the fact that the bunker hatch was located between the wheel house and the funnel, and the chute would just, literally only by about two feet, lower between them. My station for working the ship was on the stern and when ready to take the bunker coal on board, the ship would be pulled well back against the ebbing tide by the stern capstan, after which the rope would be hastily taken from the capstan drum and secured on the pair of bitts fitted on the deck. By now, with a very strong run on the ebbing tide, the capstan could not be relied upon to hold the ship, so the bitts it had to be. However, the only appropriate route for the rope from the bitts was via a fairlead on the top of the bulwark, which meant that it rose steeply between the two. Consequently, as the rope was slackened to allow the ship to be carried forward, it would ride its way up the bitts, leaving only a couple of turns to hold the ship against the strongly ebbing tide.

Little by little, the ship would be eased forward in accordance with the Skipper's shouted instructions and the chute would be tentatively lowered into the narrow gap between the wheel house and the funnel. If the ship was allowed to go too far forward, it would mean having to put the rope back on the capstan to heave her back and that would require the chute to be raised because the instant the rope was let go, the ship would move rapidly forward with the tide bringing the chute into collision with the funnel. So, it was an inch-by-inch process of dropping her forward by easing the rope and letting the tide take her down. However, with only a couple of turns of rope on the bitts, this was not easy. I would try desperately to just ease it gently, until with a sudden crack it would slip and travel that bit more towards the top of the bitts, making it ever

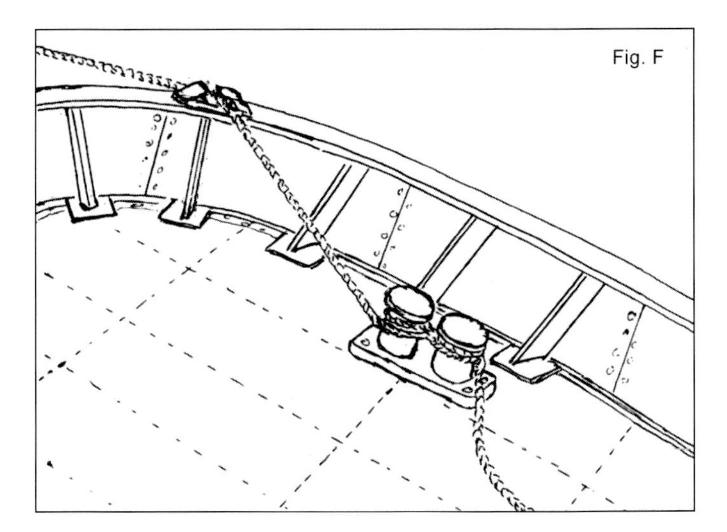
Fig. F

more difficult to secure it when told to. The Skipper would be shouting to "*Hold on to her, you'll have the bloody funnel out of her in a minute!*" – easier said than done.

Bunkering her was always a nightmare. The coarse sisal rope invariably inflicted nasty cuts on your hands as you struggled to hold onto it, a situation made worse by the fact that, as this rope was so important, it was always new or almost new and not yet softened by use (*Figure F, above*).

For all her faults and the hard work that she was for her crew, ***Druid Stoke*** is fondly remembered. Her Skipper was a good seaman and, despite the mood swings, we had total confidence in him. He was quite frequently in buoyant mood and when he was, he was good, knowledgeable company.

Her Mate – the tinkerer – was a happy fellow and served as a good buffer between the Skipper and ourselves. He became Mate on ***Colston*** later on when she was on the Yelland run. One day, arriving at Portishead on her way to Bristol for a visit to Hill's, ***Colston*** was seen to be sporting a beautiful white line all around the bridge front, with white painted port hole rims and, in all fairness, it looked quite well and suited her. However, when she arrived in Bristol and was seen by Mr. Osborn, there were immediate instructions to get rid of these unnecessary decorations!

Her two Engineers were good sports too and it was only the crew that made life aboard her tolerable. If everyone had been miserable, she would have been a dreadful ship to work on. As it was though, we got used to her, took no notice of the hard work and the deprivations she created, and just got on with the job, making a bit of light heartedness when we could. And at least I knew now that any move to another ship would be an improvement.

After spending about eighteen months aboard her altogether, ***Druid Stoke*** was instructed to go to Bristol to lay up. We took her to the yard, destored her, put a cover over the funnel and there she stayed until sold. Her faithful Second Engineer was allowed to continue living aboard her as watchman.

MOVE TO SALCOMBE

After a couple of weeks in ***Druid Stoke*** laid up in the yard, another shuffle of employees and ships took place. The Chief Engineer of ***Salcombe*** had reached retirement

A nice study of *Salcombe* taken in September 1965 as she departed the lock at Newport Docks. Captain Don Windows is at the wheel, George Payne, Sailor, is on the port bridge wing and Jack Baker, her other Sailor, can be seen walking aft along the hatchboards. *John Clarkson*

age and her Second Engineer would take his place. I was asked if I would be prepared to join her as the new Second Engineer. I would have much preferred to go aboard one of the Ruston-engined ships instead of another of the fleet's eccentrics but, given that the number of options were beginning to reduce, I readily accepted. Having sorted out my belongings, I went to Portishead the next day to join ***Salcombe***. Oddly enough, she was the one ship in the fleet that I had, as yet, not worked aboard in any capacity.

Amongst the Company's motorships, ***Salcombe*** had the same oddball status about her as the ***Druid*** had with the steamships. Apart from the obvious differences arising from her origins and her appearance, she always seemed to be something of a loner. At that time, I would have preferred to have gone to one of the other motorships, one of the four built by Hill's, which had the quite unmistakable family lineage. However, by the time I left ***Salcombe***, this had all changed and I was very happy aboard her. This was very much due to the good relationship between her new Chief and myself. We got along extremely well and he gave me a free hand regarding the cleaning and routine maintenance. Her outgoing Chief had become somewhat frail in his later years and had not been able to contribute much in the way of physical work in looking after her engine room. Consequently, everything had been left to the Second Engineer, now her Chief, so between us, we set about the catching up that was necessary.

Because of her design, her engine room seemed cavernous. Its sole access was directly from the main deck via the same pair of doors (one each side) that provided access to the accommodation. Access to the engine rooms on the other motorships was via a comparatively short ladder from a door at the accommodation level. Looking down into ***Salcombe***'s engine room from the main deck, it seemed that the machinery was a very long way down and there were three ladders, via two landings, to get down to it. It was like an echo chamber and rather dark as well.

Her machinery was unlike anything else in the firm. The other four motorships had six-cylinder main engines built by Ruston & Hornsby, all turbo-blown and basically similar apart from age-related variations. The auxiliary engines in these vessels were also by Ruston & Hornsby. Consequently, moving from one ship to another, for relieving for instance, was straightforward.

Salcombe, however, had a straight, eight-cylinder engine of German manufacture. The Ruston engines developed more than 520 bhp, whereas ***Salcombe*** only managed 400 bhp. However, despite being very heavily built and carrying almost the same cargo weight as the two biggest ships and nearly 100 tons more than the two smaller motorships, she was just as fast as the others. This was largely accounted for by the fact that the propeller was coupled directly to the engine, instead of being driven through a gearbox as was the case with the Ruston engines. With the latter, a good proportion of the power output from the engine was absorbed by the gearbox. The other benefit of this direct coupled system was that the engine revolutions were much less. ***Salcombe***'s main engine turned at only 210 rpm for nominal full speed, while the Ruston engines ran at 500 rpm. Wear and tear was, therefore, greatly reduced, hence the longevity of the engine.

The engine appeared to be very squat, with the highest part of it, as seen from the engine room deck, being only about head high. With its considerable physical length, resulting from its eight-cylinder configuration, and with no valve covers fitted, it was quite an impressive piece of machinery when running. It was in fact proportionally as tall as the Ruston & Hornsby engines but the deck level was simply built up around it and all the other machinery fitted and mounted appropriate to this deck level. This was to prove a difficulty when the two-yearly survey of the main engine came round.

The matter of her broken crankshaft has been explained earlier and it was this, together with her discarded mast and two derricks that I had discovered in the yard when I first joined the company.

Although very efficient in concept, the direct coupling of the propeller had considerable operating drawbacks and it became problematic during cold weather because of the inability to run the engine without the propeller turning. There was, therefore, no opportunity to warm up the engine – the first start-up of the day would be for an active move of the ship.

The engine was started with compressed air and there were two large receivers for this, each of which would hold sufficient air for about five starts in quick succession, before the pressure became too low to turn the engine. The bottles were pressurised by an air pump driven by one of the auxiliary engines – itself started by hand. The control lever for engaging the compressor was located close to the engine's controls. It thus formed an integral part of the operation of the engine, the compressor being engaged each time a start of the main engine took place, to ensure that the compressed air receivers were always up to maximum pressure. Once the engine had been running and was warmed up, starting it would be no problem, no matter how cold the weather but the initial cold start in these conditions was often reluctant. It could take four or five shots of air, especially if the ship had been laying quiet for a couple of days. It was the practice to have both air receivers fully charged before attempting a start but to have only one of them on line at any time, thus ensuring that if the first bottle became feeble, the second could be opened to give a full-power blast of air.

The most difficult situation was if just a short kick of power was needed, when moving the ship, followed by a stop. The air bottle would now be low on pressure, especially if the engine had needed a few starting attempts and it would not have run for long enough to get itself warmed up. By now the compressor would be struggling to get some air back into the bottle. A no start from the main engine could create difficulties if the next engine movement asked for was an astern move, to stop the ship hitting something! We never had that happen but the first few start-ups in cold weather were always a bit tense. Despite its out-of-sequence firing order, explained earlier, the engine was totally reliable and extremely smooth in operation.

Another oddity with *Salcombe* was that she had no repeat facility on the engine control telegraph from the wheelhouse. Thus the Skipper had to assume that the 'underground department' had responded with the engine move he had actually asked for.

Her two generators were two-cylinder Paxman Ricardos and these too could be temperamental when starting (by hand) in cold weather. However, there was a long-established aid to this, in the form of a curved hook bent to shape and on which a piece of rag was tied. Taking the air intake filter off the engine, the hook was hung directly under the intake, some diesel poured on the rag,set alight and then the engine swung again – it worked every time! Even the most reluctant of engines couldn't fight against it when forced to ingest actual flame.

However, the killer piece of machinery aboard *Salcombe* was the smallest and it wasn't in the engine room. Located in the foc'sle, it was the little ten horsepower, single-cylinder diesel engine which powered her forward windlass. This little engine was in a most inaccessible position and was hand started. And it was not a willing starter, meaning that often several attempts had to be made. The starting handle was not fitted to the crankshaft and had to be placed onto the starter dog very loosely, in order that it could be disengaged easily once the engine started; consequently, it was the easiest thing in the world to disengage the handle accidentally, just when it was being whirled round prior to knocking the decompressor lever in. So you were working in extremely confined conditions, off balance, using both hands at once, cranking this thing over, with your knuckles skimming past the hard edge of the steel tray in which the motor stood. There were more smashed knuckles aboard *Salcombe* than all the other ships put together. The other likelihood was the handle disengaging and coming up under your chin, which happened to me a couple of times. That seemingly lethal little engine was given the utmost respect. Only one person on board was not afraid of this little motor and that was one of her Sailors. He had the starting of it off to a fine art. Luckily, he was kind and willing enough to start it when needed, rather than wait for the Second Engineer to come along to get it going, so I tried to keep in his good books. It was worth it. Once started, this little engine drove the windlass through a large chain drive.

I had my own cabin on board and soon fitted in, getting on well with the Chief Engineer, who was a long serving O&W man with a lot of interesting anecdotes from the past. I was just getting used to the intricacies of using the ship's machinery, the electrical switchboard, etc, when, after a few weeks on board, we were told that *Salcombe* would be going to Bristol to lay-up for a month. The Chief booked his fortnight annual holiday to be taken during this time and we went to Bristol's Baltic Wharf to tie her up. The Chief instructed me to do a bit of painting and cleaning, to run the generators everyday and generally keep myself occupied in his absence.

He had been away only two days when the Superintendent visited the ship and said that the plans had been changed, and that we had orders to sail on the evening's tide, in a couple of hours time. The Skipper reminded him that the Chief was away and that I had only been aboard for a very short time, with just a couple of trips, so the Super came to see me and asked how I felt about taking the ship away. He explained that, for insurance purposes, there would have to be a Chief Engineer on board and that they had arranged for *Hotwells*' Chief to come with me. The only small problem was that he had never been in *Salcombe* at all, so her machinery was completely unfamiliar to him. In essence, that meant it would be me running the engine room. Luckily, I had already made my crib sheets about ballast pumping and the switchboard, and I had been handling the engine, so providing nothing untoward happened, I felt that it would be alright. However, I did make one proviso. If I was going to be responsible for it all, I wanted to make sure that everything was alright and that included running the main engine (which meant double mooring ropes, as the propeller would be trying to drive the ship), testing the steering gear, the firefighting pumps and hoses, etc.

All of this meant the ship would not be able to make the evening tide that day but we would be alright for the evening tide the next day. The Skipper was very understanding, thanked me for being willing to take it on and went back to the office to report that sailing would be delayed by twenty four hours. (We could, in fact, have sailed on the morning tide but the loading could not be rearranged in time.) That was the only occasion while I worked for the Company that a ship did not sail on the instructed time.

We spent the next morning making the tests I wanted, during which the Chief of *Hotwells* came aboard and it soon became clear that he was very uneasy at the position he was in, made worse of course by the fact that, as he knew, I was almost as strange to the ship as he was. He was not at all relaxed.

Came the time and we set off into the darkening night. The wind was fresh, there was rain about and the conditions worsened during the trip to Newport. By the time we got to the entrance to the lock, it was dark, gusty and wet. The Skipper had kept the power steering on all the way over, which of course meant that one of the generators had to be kept running. I had decided to change the generators over for the crossing, to spare the one near the engine controls which powered the all essential compressor. Once we were approaching Newport, I started the compressor generator but instead of transferring all the electrical services to this one, I left the electrical supply on the one which had been running for the crossing. Meanwhile, the Chief was uneasy about me being away from the engine controls for too long, while I changed the electrical switches over on the main switchboard.

As we got near the locks, it could be seen that a large ship was locking out. There were already a couple of other ships milling about outside waiting to be locked in and we added to their number, making the occasional shuffling movement to keep clear of them as the wind blew all of us about.

We had been dodging about in this fashion for about half an hour, by which time the big ship and her tugs were making their way out of the locks, whilst all we small fry outside had backed reverently away to give her plenty of room in the windy conditions.

Suddenly, there was an almighty bang and the engine room was plunged into pitch darkness. Immediately, the voice tube whistle blew and the Skipper, having heard the noise, was enquiring as to what was going on – all the navigation lights had gone out and, worse, he had no power steering. All this just at the wrong time. I replied that at that moment I didn't know what had happened. I could hear the Chief Engineer also asking and I just told him to keep still and stay where he was. Luckily, as part of my preparations for the trip, the emergency torch had been charged up and I knew exactly where it was. Feeling my way along the length of the engine in the dark I reached the work bench, felt into the corner and found the torch. Switching it on I went straight to the switchboard and, thinking slowly and carefully, changed all the switches over, so that all services were now coming from the compressor generator which was, of course, now running. The lights came on, order was restored and I don't suppose that the emergency had lasted more than half a minute but it felt like a lifetime. I couldn't leave the engine controls until we were safely moored in the lock and then went round to investigate what had happened. It had been a spectacular failure! The engine and crankcase of the generator was split wide open, and a piston and con-rod was dangling out of the hole. Water and oil was everywhere. There had been no indication of imminent failure while it had been running and both oil pressure and temperature had remained normal.

By the time we moored at the tip, it was too late to phone anyone and tell them of the calamity but, in any case, no one could do anything, so I left it until the morning before phoning the Super at home to tell him what had happened. He asked whether I wanted him to come to Newport, or would we be alright to make the return crossing. I couldn't see why not, so told him that we would come back. He agreed and having done that, I told the Skipper of the decision. I stressed strongly, though, that now we were completely dependent on just one generator, it was going to have to be hand steering for the return trip.

The return trip went normally and the Super met us on the quay wall, passing the Chief leaving the ship after his stressful trip. The oil and mess had been cleaned up but everything else was left as it was. Having looked at it carefully, he came to a conclusion, which agreed with what I had suggested in the telephone call, that one of the big end bolts had failed.

Once discharged, we went to Hill's yard, where the surviving original auxiliary engine was moved to replace the wrecked one and a brand new, three-cylinder Ruston & Hornsby auxiliary engine was fitted in the vital compressor station. As the damaged engine was being stripped out, I asked if I might have the remaining piston from it as a souvenir of my first grey hair! I made it into a table lamp. It had been a bit of a baptism of fire after so little time and experience aboard the ship.

The surviving piston from *Salcombe*'s destroyed auxiliary engine, still in my possession today. *Author*

After his fortnight's holiday, the Chief sauntered back aboard wondering why we were in dockyard hands and asking "*What have you done in my absence*" to need dockyard assistance. He wasn't at all sorry, though, to have got rid of one of the by now fragile original auxiliary motors. Later, the other original generator was removed and replaced with another of the three-cylinder R&H units.

Also in regard to her engine room, another matter arising from ***Salcombe***'s origins affected her two-yearly survey. For their surveys, the other ships fitted with Ruston & Hornsby machinery would have a squad of three Ruston engineers come aboard and they would do the technical work in checking the engine over, including the auxiliaries. In the case of ***Salcombe***, however, George Henry (O&W's 'Mr Fixit') would come aboard and he, the Chief and myself would dismantle everything and prepare it for the Lloyd's Inspector. Once satisfied, we would have the task of rebuilding it all. It was here that the high deck plates became a nuisance. It was of course necessary to get into the crankcase to work on the big ends and the main bearings but where the Ruston engines had their crankcase access doors above deck level and it was therefore comparatively simple, on ***Salcombe*** it was necessary to lift the engine room plates and to get down amongst the framework to remove the crankcase doors and to get inside the engine.

We had to do all the maintenance on the engine ourselves, including cleaning and servicing the injectors, and for this we were unique among the ships in having a stock of Jeweller's Rouge on the engine room inventory. The other ships just carried spare exchange injectors supplied by Ruston's. ***Salcombe*** was a good ship to learn on.

She was fitted with an electrically-driven reciprocating ballast pump instead of a centrifugal one and this would thump away regularly while pumping. However, it would suddenly go quiet when all the water had gone from whichever tank it was pumping out, giving good audible indication that it was time to change to the next tank.

Because of her engine's out-of-order firing sequence, the ship would develop a rhythmic bounce if she became too light at the stern and that this would begin to occur when the weight of fuel oil in her bunkers fell to just below six tons. As a consequence, it had become accepted operational procedure that ***Salcombe*** would order fuel before this situation arose. Although the Super was aware of this, the General Manager was not. One day, the Chief Engineer who, as an 'old hand' (with a fairly short fuse!) could be very forthright when put out, had telephoned the office to order bunkers. The General Manager questioned this and said that she shouldn't be low on fuel yet and asked how much she had on board. On being told '*About six tons*', he huffed and puffed and said that he was not going to have ***Salcombe*** refuelling with six tons still on board in the upper part of the Channel, when ***Colston*** and ***Brandon***, running down to Yelland as they were by now, didn't order fuel until they were down to four tons.

In reality, it made not a jot of difference to the operational efficiency, since the difference did not amount to any increase in cargo that could be carried.

The Chief bristled at the reaction and stated quite bluntly that until he got the fuel, the ship was staying alongside the wall! It became quite a heated exchange and when asked to explain, the Manager was told to ask the reason from the Superintendent. Presumably these enquiries were made, because our fuel was delivered that afternoon and the matter of her bunkers was never questioned again.

There were one or two such instances which highlighted the unwillingness of the Skippers and Chief Engineers to have the running of their ships dictated to them by the Office. Quite rightly, the Office had to decide the overall pattern of work which was governed by the needs of the power stations and this was never challenged by the ships' crews. If it was uncomfortable or pressured and meant unreasonably long hours, it was simply accepted as being part of the job but what was not acceptable to them was to have the Office try to interfere with the day-to-day running of their vessels. Decisions as to whether to sail or not in fog for instance, were never questioned by the Office. They were told, not asked. Mr. Osborn had complete confidence in the decisions made and no pressure was ever exerted by him.

During the very hard winter of 1963, the two power stations came under great demand and were using coal at maximum rates throughout the twenty-four hours, for day after day and it developed into a several week-long crisis. This demand impacted on the ships and the urgency for coal supplies became paramount. The same weather that was causing the crisis also created its own difficulties, as the loading became a very protracted affair and the ships were being told to come back to Portishead as soon as they had the bulk of their cargo of coal on board.

Discharging was curtailed and the business of hobbling out every bit of the cargo was dispensed with if it meant that the ships could catch the tide to go and fetch some more coal. The stockyards at both stations were virtually empty and they were running on what the ships could deliver. The crews of the ships worked for extremely long hours, often away for four or five days while loading and then, on arrival at Portishead for immediate and urgent discharge, having no opportunity to go home at all before leaving on the next tide, to return to South Wales for another cargo. No one complained though, it was just part of the job. It also meant, of course, that while these conditions prevailed, one trip a week was the norm, so no trip pay and large purchases of food supplies (by the beleaguered Boy) to stock up for the next four or five day trip.

Through all this, the power stations got their coal and maintained their maximum load.

A few months later, the ship had to go to Hill's for her survey, during which the mainmast was removed from its position forward of the wheelhouse and a new mast with two supporting legs, similar to the arrangement on ***Colston*** and ***Brandon***, was fitted instead, located well aft. The engine was stripped as described earlier and found to be in good order. On completion of the survey, the ship was ordered to return to Portishead but would lay up for several weeks. By now, larger vessels from other companies were beginning to take an increasing share of the work fuelling the power stations. With the older 'A' Station running only very occasionally and the overall amount of work decreasing with the reduced summer loading on 'B' Station, the Osborn & Wallis ships were being subjected to lengthening periods of inactivity. It was becoming apparent that this situation could not continue indefinitely.

Meanwhile, ***Colston*** and ***Brandon*** were being kept busy on the Yelland and Hayle power stations work and deployment of the Portishead ships crews to these two became a regular feature of our lives as various crewmen were relieved.

It was during one of my spells in this relieving, as Second Engineer in ***Colston***, that we left Barry one evening in bad weather. Going against wind and tide, the trip to Yelland was expected to take between seven and eight hours. As soon as we cleared Barry, it became obvious that it was going to be a rough trip. The Chief Engineer had arranged that I should look after her during the trip down (when there shouldn't be much to do) and he would then take over when we arrived off Bideford, looking after her during the discharge and ballasting. Recognising the weather conditions, he told me that I could, if asked, take the engine up to 530 rpm but to keep an eye on the temperatures. However, if still further revs were asked for, he was to be called. The ships were not overpowered and, consequently, it was necessary for the Skippers to use their experience to make the most progress they could when the weather was bad. They had to make a judgement as to how close inshore they could safely go in an effort to cut the tide effect, without getting too close to the shore onto which the wind was blowing.

All went well (though rough!) until we reached Ilfracombe, at which point the ship could make no further progress and, as expected, the Skipper twice asked for increased revs. Despite this, no progress was made until the run of the tide began to ease - only then did the ship slowly begin to forge ahead again.

On approaching Yelland, the Chief Engineer came down into the engine room and took over, so that I could get some sleep after a long and tiring night. I decided that I wanted some fresh air before turning in and, in any case, I wanted to see her going across the notorious Bideford Bar sandbank across the mouth of the river. This was always a tricky situation but even more so when the long rolling waves, straight from the Atlantic, were coming in under the ship's stern. Standing under the wing of the bridge and looking across towards Clovelly, I thought I saw a red light which hung in the air for a few seconds and then disappeared.

An aerial view of East Yelland Power Station circa 1970. It was situated on the tidal River Taw, further up which lay Fremington Quay (1 mile) and Barnstaple (4 miles). On the southern bank of the river estuary, a mile and a half to the east (left in this view) was Appledore, where the River Torridge came down from Bideford to join the Taw. East Yelland Power Station was built in the late 1940s and coal for its boilers was delivered both by ship and rail. The site was served by a narrow gauge railway system, the tracks of which can be seen radiating around the building. In the right foreground is the standard gauge line from Barnstaple to Bideford. Note the conveyor system which carried the coal from the jetty to the power station. Like the two stations at Portishead, East Yelland has also now gone, closing in the 1980s. Across the Taw in the background can just be made out the buildings and runways of RAF Chivenor. *Author's collection*

Not sure whether or not I had imagined it, I watched in the same area, more or less on our beam and, sure enough, another light rose into the air, and drifted back down. Certain now that I was not imagining it and aware of the fact that the Skipper on the wheel may not have seen it with his attention devoted wholly to the ship crossing the Bar, I hurried up to the wheelhouse and described what I had seen. Giving the wheel to the Mate, the Skipper used the Aldis lamp and aimed it at the position I gave him and, after questioning the source, got a faint reply that there was a yacht ashore on the rocks with three men on board, one injured. An immediate call to Ilfracombe Radio, advising them of the situation, brought a request that the ship stand-by to help if called upon. That meant turning her round in the breaking water on the Bar. Having begun this operation, the radio station called back to advise that the Appledore lifeboat had been alerted and was on its way, and that we should proceed as normal.

We learnt a little later that the yacht had got into difficulties in the bad weather and, whilst trying for shelter in Appledore, had been blown ashore on the rocks at Clovelly. It was the only incident that occurred while I was involved in the Yelland run.

In due course, I returned to ***Salcombe*** and to the increasingly long periods of laying up waiting for work. Clearly this situation could not carry on and whilst the two Yelland ships were secure enough in their employment, those of us in the older and smaller motorships began to realise that our prospects were becoming bleak.

So it was, with much sadness, that I decided to leave the company and seek other employment. I duly handed my notice in as had several others by now. I was asked to come to the office and was told to see Mr. Osborn. He said that he quite understood my anxieties but then, knowing of my soft spot for ***Colston***, he reminded me that her Chief Engineer was due to retire in less than a year, when her almost equally elderly Second Engineer would be promoted to Chief. He would need a new Second, who in turn, following his retirement soon after, would then become her Chief Engineer and that I had been lined up to join this ladder of succession.

However, the prospect of being virtually permanently away from home was not acceptable to me for family reasons, so I reluctantly held fast to my decision and duly left. It was not an easy decision. It had been my first job and I had this feeling of belonging with the company and the ships. This remained to the extent that despite having no further official contact with them, I continued to take an interest and it was not long afterwards that the company ceased operations and the ships were disposed of.

London & Rochester Shipping Co's *Jubilence* discharging at Yelland in 1964. She was smaller than the O&W ships and, when this photograph was taken, must have been standing in for either *Pertinence* or *Quiesence*, the two L&R heavyweights which usually fuelled Yelland together with *Colston* and *Brandon*. *Author*

Larger ships became the order of the day at Portishead. The London-registered *Corbrae*, built in 1952, of 2,002 grt and owned by William Cory & Sons Ltd, is seen here in the late 1960s discharging coal for 'B' Station. The coaster ahead of her, with its light coloured hull, is probably one of Everard's vessels. *Author*

OUSTED BY BIGGER SHIPS

It was to be larger ships, such as those of William Cory & Sons Ltd and the London & Rochester Shipping Company, which brought O&W's work supplying the power stations to an end after so many years. Osborn & Wallis had worked through many changes in governance of the electricity industry through the years, from the old Bristol Electricity Department up until it became the Central Electricity Generating Board but when these bigger ships arrived O&W were pushed aside and the little ships had to seek work elsewhere.

Loyalty did not come into it, for although this was a commercial operation, it was also part of a dying trade. In the 1960s, nuclear power was going to be the way forward, with the construction of new stations such as that at Hinckley Point, near Bridgwater. As nuclear power swiftly fell out of favour, however, amidst concerns about safety and the environment, the so called 'dash for gas', the construction of a new generation of gas-fired power stations, began in the 1980s. Today, the few remaining coal-fired power stations are supplied by rail and ship-borne coal, apart from a small amount delivered along navigable waterways in Yorkshire, is a thing of the past.

SUMMARY OF MY TIME WITH THE COMPANY

I worked for Osborn and Wallis for only eight years and, of those, the last years marked the beginning of the Company's decline.

I had permanent positions on five of the ships, as Deck Boy on ***Colston*** and ***Brandon***, as Sailor on ***Downleaze***, then as Sailor on ***Druid Stoke*** and finally as Second Engineer on ***Salcombe***. However, at times of holiday and sickness relief, I worked on ***Rockleaze***, ***St. Vincent*** and ***Hotwells*** at one time or another. Most of us spent periods of time in other ships of the Company during holiday relieving.

My time with Osborn & Wallis therefore, was little more than a very brief snapshot of experience but, probably because I was so young when I was first employed, it made a great impression on me such that, although I never again had a job where ships were involved in any way, I have retained a profound sense of attachment to the job, the men and the ships. Indeed, I have tried ever since, with varying degrees of success, to remain aware of the whereabouts of the old O&W ships.

I have fond memories of each of my five permanent ships and, of these, ***Colston*** is the very special one for me. At the time of writing, she remains as the last surviving O&W vessel and I am grateful that by great good fortune, I have, up until the time of writing, been able to keep in touch with the ship despite the immense distance that separates us. From the information available, it would seem that she is being maintained to a good standard and at some expense, so she hopefully has some years of life to come yet.

I count it as a privilege (though it did not seem it at the time!) to have worked in the three steamships as Sailor. Although our voyages were so short as to spare us the true rigours of foc'sle life in ships of the early part of last century, it certainly gave us a fair impression of what it was like to be self sufficient, to make do with the most basic facilities or, in the case of ***Druid Stoke***, with virtually no facilities other than those which we could improvise ourselves. The contrast in lifestyles which I experienced between the new motorships and ***Druid Stoke***, vessels belonging to the same company, was almost beyond belief but I wouldn't have missed it for the world.

What I experienced was as nothing compared with what those of an earlier generation, fully-fledged coasting seamen, had to cope with but so it has always been and always will be. There is no doubt that much of the work we did on the little ships, under the conditions in which it had to be done, would not be tolerated or expected today and quite right too. But at the time, it was simply the job and the discomfort and risks were part of it. It was quite normal and most of us were happy doing it.

I was told as a lad on ***Colston*** "*In my day, we had wooden ships and iron men, now we've got iron ships and wooden men.*" It was a fair observation. The job in my time was a soft and cosseted existence compared with what the seamen of earlier years had to endure. Long may the progress continue.

But the Company, its ships and its men, despite all the difficulties and discomforts and, sometimes, even the dangers, never failed in their task of supplying the power stations with the coal they needed. When the good people of Portishead could sit in their homes in front of their electric fires during a winter night, with wind and rain hammering against their windows, or when they were wrapped in thick enveloping fog as they groped their way home from lamp post to lamp post after a days work, somewhere out there in the Bristol Channel were the little black and brown ships, struggling with the same conditions to do their bit to make sure that the lights never went out.

Modest and insignificant little vessels, doing an important job well and, above all, doing it faithfully and reliably.

POSTSCRIPT

It will be remembered that my working life with Osborn & Wallis began without my father's permission. I had engineered and cheated my way out of school and a good education at the age of 15, whilst my father was serving with the army on the far side of the world. He had hoped that I would make good use of the opportunity that my education offered and he must have been very disappointed (appalled even!) to learn what I had done. I would not have tried to or ever have got away with it had he been at home and I knew that, at sometime, I would have to explain myself. Eventually, came the day when we met him at Bristol Temple Meads Station on his return after three years away and, whilst I was very happy to see him again, I was also extremely apprehensive at the thundercloud that I felt sure was gathering over my head.

However, no mention was made of my transgression that day, nor during the next day and the times that I was at home between trips. The tension was becoming too great for me and I just longed to get the reprimand over and done with. It was not until his fourth day at home, having let me stew for a good time, that he said quite unexpectedly and quietly "*Any chance of looking over this ship of yours sometime?*" And that was it. He never expressed any anger or discontent at what I had done and I shall ever be grateful for the wisdom he showed in accepting that the damage was done and that nothing was to be gained by creating bad feeling over the matter. With hindsight, I am certain that I did the right thing for me and I would do the same again if I had the opportunity. They were the happiest days of my life.

Above: *Hotwells*, always smart, at Portishead 'B' Power Station berth, having completed unloading. The well-stocked 'B' Station coal store can be seen behind her. 'B' Station itself is out of sight to the right; the chimneys and buildings belong to 'A' Station. The photograph was taken circa 1960 and the right hand chimney still sports its wartime camouflage paint. The second chimney was built after the war. *Author*

Right: A rather fuzzy view of *Salcombe* unloading at 'B' Station berth, with the bulk of the power station dominating the background. The unidentified ship ahead of her is one of the larger vessels which forced the O&W boats out of the Portishead trade in the early 1960s and on the long runs down Channel to East Yelland and Hayle power stations instead. *Author*

Overleaf: The eight ships of the Osborn & Wallis fleet during my time with the company. From a painting by Edward Paget-Tomlinson. *Author's collection*

M.V. BRANDON, BUILT CHARLES HILL, BRISTOL (YARD No 407), 1957, FOR OSBORN & WALLIS, 586 GROSS TONS.
M.V. HOTWELLS, BUILT CHARLES HILL, BRISTOL (YARD No 358), 1950, FOR OSBORN & WALLIS, 499 GROSS TONS,
OSBORN &
S.S. ROCKLEAZE, BUILT GOOLE SHIPBUILDING, 1924, AS GLYNCONWY. BOUGHT 1939 BY OSBORN & WALLIS, RENAMED ROCKLEAZE
486 GROSS TONS.
M.V. SALCOMBE, BUILT LEKKERKERK, HOLLAND, 1938, AS CAMROUX IV. BOUGHT 1942 BY OSBORN & WALLIS, RENAMED SALCOMBE
590 GROSS TONS.
SCALE 0 10 20 30 40 50 60 70 80 90 100 FEET

COLSTON
M.V. COLSTON, BUILT CHARLES HILL, BRISTOL (YARD Nº378), 1955, FOR OSBORN & WALLIS. 586 GROSS TONS.
M.V. ST VINCENT, BUILT CHARLES HILL, BRISTOL (YARD Nº 276), 1940, FOR OSBORN & WALLIS, 484 GROSS TONS.
WALLIS LTD
TOL
DOWNLEAZE
S.S. DOWNLEAZE, BUILT GOOLE SHIPBUILDING, 1924, AS SOUTHWELL. BOUGHT 1938 BY OSBORN & WALLIS, RENAMED DOWNLEAZE
486 GROSS TONS.
DRUID STOKE
S.S. DRUID STOKE, BUILT CHARLES HILL, BRISTOL (YARD Nº 174), 1929, FOR OSBORN & WALLIS, 486 GROSS TONS.
E.W. PAGET-TOMLINSON MAY 1993

COLSTON and BRANDON

Colston is seen in-bound with her cargo of South Wales coal, while *Brandon* heads down Channel. Uskmouth 'A' and 'B' power stations can be seen in the background, both on load. It is a bright but blustery day and the ships are seen in their original condition before the fitting of the Decca Navigator equipment, or the radar. *Colston*'s bell and her builder's plaque are shining brightly, and the workboat is sitting on the forward hatch. Capt. 'Sammy' Taylor, in his trademark white roll neck sweater, gives a wave from *Brandon*'s bridge as the ships pass. The degree of detail accuracy which Robert Blackwell adheres to is indicated by the fact that he rang me one evening to enquire whether the lifting strop on the workboat was linked by a shackle or a closed ring. He visited Portishead sea front to paint the South Wales backdrop accurately, whilst the colour of the water and its movements are exactly right for the weather conditions shown in the painting.

HOTWELLS and DOWNLEAZE

Hotwells has just made the turn down off the English & Welsh Grounds lightship whilst coming from Newport and is passing *Downleaze* heading for Ely Harbour. The coastal sailing schooner *Irene*, in her final form, can be seen cutting across the sands heading for Newport. *Downleaze* just rolls very gently responding to the wind and the slight chop on the water and, when I look at this painting, I can feel myself bracing and waiting for her to roll gently back the other way. *Rockleaze* and *Downleaze* were handsome little ships from any viewpoint and these paintings illustrate their good lines nicely. The funnels of the three steamers were always pink, since they were painted with standard red-lead paint which soon turned pink with the heat. Again illustrating his attention to detail, Robert Blackwell contacted Trinity House to ascertain exactly which type of Lightship was stationed at the English & Welsh Grounds.

ROCKLEAZE and SALCOMBE

Salcombe heads out light ship, with *Rockleaze* in-bound, loaded. A light mist is covering the flat, almost oily, water and *Salcombe*'s bow wave is the only disturbance on its surface. Bits of rubbish, seaweed and flotsam float on the water, as the gulls wheel around *Rockleaze*'s stern. With not enough wind to disturb the smoke from *Rockleaze*'s funnel, both ships have a look out stationed on the foc'sle head, each being careful not to stand directly under the drops of condensation dripping from the mast stays. *Salcombe* is shown here with her mainmast in its final form.

DRUID STOKE and ST. VINCENT

Under a lowering sky, *Druid Stoke* proceeds towards Portishead, passing *St. Vincent* on her way to Newport, whilst Rea's *Kingsgarth* beats her way down Channel to pick up a freighter bound for Avonmouth. There is a nasty little squall of rain about to engulf *St. Vincent* and she is emitting her usual bit of blue smoke from her funnel, indicating that her engine will be getting new piston rings during her next survey at Hill's dockyard. Capt. Bill Butler can be seen on the '*Druid*'s wheel and the sailors will soon be emerging from the foc'sle to get the hatches stripped off ready for discharging. *Kingsgarth* was built for King's of Bristol but was taken over by Rea's shortly after completion. She was lost during 1964 while acting as bow tug to *Port Launceston* when leaving Avonmouth and all but two of her crew went down with her.

Above: A rare colour shot of *Druid Stoke* in the early 1960s, moored just outside the company's dock and officially in reserve. The red lead on her funnel and hull has faded to a very pale pink, almost white. *Author*

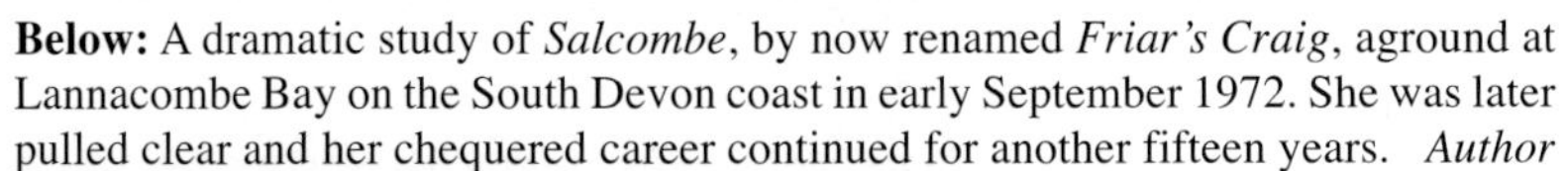

Below: A dramatic study of *Salcombe*, by now renamed *Friar's Craig*, aground at Lannacombe Bay on the South Devon coast in early September 1972. She was later pulled clear and her chequered career continued for another fifteen years. *Author*

Salcombe's watery grave is just outside Bridgetown Harbour, Barbados, where she was scuttled in 1985 as a diving wreck. Pounded by hurricanes, she soon began to break up and these photographs, taken during 1994, show the extent of her destruction. **Above:** The main engine can be seen in the centre of the picture. In the mid-distance is the bedplate and generator from her port auxiliary but note that the engine itself is missing. **Right:** The main engine with its flywheel and thrust bearing. **Below:** Her bow and foc'sle section, with its chain driven windlass, remains intact.

Right: *Empire Townsman*, one of the ex- Ministry of War Transport ships which O&W had been given management of from 1943-46, seen here in one of her later guises as *Sir Cedric* at Truro in the mid 1970s. She was last heard of in northern France in 1990. *L. Robinson*

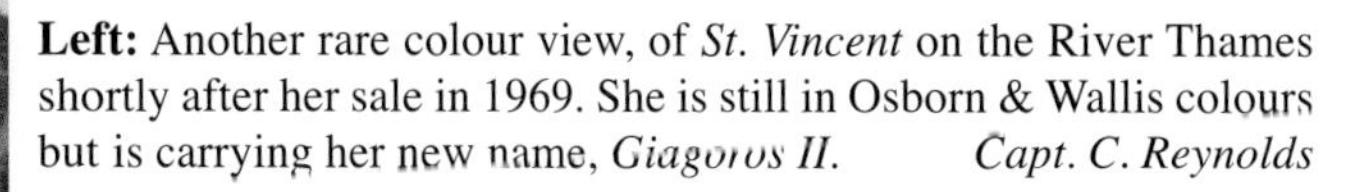

Left: Another rare colour view, of *St. Vincent* on the River Thames shortly after her sale in 1969. She is still in Osborn & Wallis colours but is carrying her new name, *Giagoros II.* *Capt. C. Reynolds*

Below: Various studies of *Hotwells* lying in Osborn & Wallis's dock at Bristol awaiting sale in June 1970. As usual, she was in immaculate condition and was destined for new owners in Scotland, where she spent the next seven years. *All Capt. C. Reynolds*

Above: This final colour view of *Hotwells* awaiting disposal in June 1970 is included for the detail of the company's yard and wharf. As well as the large crane, the stone-built offices can also be seen in the background. Alongside *Hotwells* is a very interesting little vessel, *Nigel*, very distinctive with her flat stern. She was built on the Clyde in 1915 as a landing craft and used in the Dardanelles campaign during the First World War. Afterwards, she was adapted for cargo carrying and despite only having about 18 inches of freeboard when laden, worked down Channel and round the tip of Land's End to ports on the south Cornish coast. She operated out of Lydney for many years and I remember seeing her quite often pottering around the Channel, although she could be very difficult to spot when loaded, lying so low in the water. *Capt C. Reynolds*

Above: Now renamed *Rosewell* and, after a second change of ownership, re-registered at Lerwick, *Hotwells* is seen at the port of Leith in the colours of the Voe Shipping Company on 21st August 1977. She had just been sold to new Greek owners and, a few hours after this photograph was taken, her new Greek name, *Myrsini*, was painted on her stern. She continued to fly the Red Ensign for a short while, as a courtesy flag. Note that both her lifeboats had been removed, although the davits for the port boat remained in place. *R. Jolliffe*

Left: *Myrsini* enjoying the sunshine at an unidentified Greek port in 1988. Despite her new colours, the removal of her lifeboats and addition of the crosstree on her mainmast, she remains unmistakable as O&W's old *Hotwells*. *Capt C. Reynolds*

Above: *Colston* moored at Portishead in the mid 1960s, during a quiet time on the Yelland run. She is on the opposite side of the dock to the power stations and, as the decade wore on, quiet periods like this were to become more frequent. *Author*

Right: An historic photograph as *Colston* arrives in the River Usk at Newport on 26th August 1970 as she is delivered to W.E. Dowds Ltd. She looks very smart, with her band of red boot topping all on show in her unladen state. This was her final voyage in Osborn & Wallis colours.

Right: In March 1987, *Colston* arrived at Gloucester Docks with a cargo of fertilizer and, on hearing she was heading there, I drove up to reacquaint myself with my old ship. The first job I ever had on her way back in 1955 was polishing the bell and her crew very kindly allowed me to recreate a moment from my maritime career.
Far right: After one offer to sell me the bell was turned down – for which I kicked myself for years – I was finally granted a second opportunity and *Colston's* bell is today one of my most treasured possessions. The bell lanyard was made for me by my old ex-RN fellow sufferer aboard *Druid Stoke*. It very cleverly incorporates the O&W funnel colours. *Both author*

Left and below: I have always regretted that I had not taken more photographs during the years I worked on the coal boats so when I went to see *Colston,* whilst she was unloading at Gloucester in March 1987, I took as many photographs of her as I could. This was just as well because by the end of that year, she had departed for the Caribbean. These two views show her being unloaded and her rather garish Corveda Marine livery – in comparison to the old days! Further views depicting this voyage up the Gloucester & Sharpness Canal to the docks at Gloucester and back to Sharpness can be found on pages 169-71. *Author*

Above centre: At this time, her engine room was little changed from when she was first built.
Below: The ship was in good cared for condition and the interior of the wheelhouse was also almost unchanged from O&W days. *Both author*

Left: *Colston*, by now renamed *Stengard*, is seen moored at St. George's, Grenada, in the mid 1990s. She looks smart and tidy, with even the midships crane sheeted down. Her bright new livery suits her well and she sits comfortably in her new environment. *Capt. C. Flanagan*

Above: Her engine room is clean and tidy.

Above right: In comparison with the picture on the previous page, it can be seen that her wheelhouse has been completely upgraded and modernised. Even the deck head has been panelled. Capt. 'Sammy' Taylor would have been proud of her.

Right: This selection of views of my old ship is closed with an almost eerie coincidence. In 1955, *Colston* had been built as a slightly enlarged and modernised *Hotwells*, which in turn was a direct descendant from O&W's first ever motorship, *St. Vincent*, built in 1940. How strange therefore that, today, *Colston* carries the name 'St. Vincent' on her stern as her port of registration. Seen here at Barbados, she has been fitted with an awning over her after deck. She also keeps more elegant company these days, with the P&O cruise liner *Arcadia* in the background.

Right: *Brandon* in drydock at Hill's yard in preparation for her sale to W.E. Dowds Ltd of Newport in 1970. Charles Hill's shipbuilding yard is also now just a memory, although one of the dry docks is today home to the restored *Great Britain*. *J. Hill*

Below: *Brandon* at Avonmouth Docks in the early period of her Dowds' ownership. She retained her Bristol registration for only a few months after purchase. Her new livery, whilst smart, was not quite as striking as her old O&W colours, despite the red lifeboats! The massive Spillers warehouses and grain silos make for an imposing backdrop which dwarves the boats. *J. Hill*

Below: Again in Dowds' colours, *Brandon* is seen departing Liverpool Docks in the 1970s. The crew were obviously anticipating some inclement weather out in the Irish Sea because the hatchcloths have been battened right down and even the big mid-ships ventilator has its cover on and is facing aft. *Neil Burns*

Brandon and *Colston* locking out of Gladstone Dock, Liverpool, on 26th January 1978, both loaded with grain. This fine view shows the pair together again, as occasionally happened. Brandon still retained the brown upperworks (apart from the bridge structure) of her O&W days, eight years after changing hands. Perhaps it was a way of being able to tell them apart. However, this photograph does illustrate two of the small recognition points that distinguished them. Most notable is the different position of the crosstree on the mainmast, the other being the slightly increased rake of the top of the funnel on *Brandon*. *Colston* had white superstructure but with all the ventilators, etc, painted in the same colour as the mast. The original docking lights on the mainmast are very prominent. The gap in *Brandon*'s handrails over the roller fairlead aft differed from *Colston*'s, which were extended and shaped so as to close the gap more and improve safety. *Neil Burns*

Left: A very rare colour photograph of *Brandon* in Franco British Chartering Ltd ownership. The ship is fitted with a life raft, carried on the top of the water tank at the stern. *Capt. C. Reynolds*

Below left: Another location, another livery. *Brandon* is seen here in Corveda Marine colours at Great Yarmouth in November 1986, with South Denes Power Station in the background. *Capt. C. Reynolds*

Below: *Brandon* at Dover, also in 1986. *Capt. C. Reynolds*

Above left and right: Changing times – changing places. This is Bristol's Floating Harbour from similar viewpoints in 1958 and 1998. In the 1958 picture, taken from O&W's yard, the RNVR ship *HMS Flying Fox* can be seen on the left, while one of the pair of salvage tugs (at the time, the most powerful tugs ever built in Britain), is being completed at Hill's yard. It was the birthplace of many fine ships but they were limited in size by the room available for launching. Within that limitation, however, Hill's-built ships were among the best in Britain and the loss of the yard and the skills it nurtured are to be regretted. The docks area is now a housing development and a marina, and only the square tower of Bristol Cathedral remains as a recognisable landmark on the skyline in the second photograph. *Both author*

Above: Newport Docks in the 1990s, with Fifoots Point Power Station in the foreground. Beyond, the piers guiding ships into the main entrance lock and part of the Alexandra Dock can be seen. The 'A' Station, to the left, is no longer generating. The docks are still busy today, although coal is no longer loaded here. The bases for the coal hoists can still be seen jutting into the dock. The power station is rail served for its coal deliveries. *Author's collection*

Above: This wooden jetty is all that remains of No. 1 Tip at Ely Harbour in 2005. It is not in use, so its continued survival must be in some doubt. There is little else to see. The land behind, where the railway lines serving the tips once ran, was being cleared when this view was taken, with the last few wooden sleepers in a pile just out of view to the left. In the background, the 21st century face of Cardiff gazes out over the bay. *Neil Parkhouse*

Left: With the entrance lock rebuilt and much reduced in size, Portishead Dock is also now a marina and almost completely unrecognisable from my day. This is the view today from the entrance lock. The power stations stood on the right. *Author*

Part Four
THE POST OSBORN & WALLIS YEARS

1. THE SHIPS

The lives of the five remaining ships did not end when Osborn & Wallis disposed of them in1969 and 1970. All of them survived, for varying lengths of time and went on to work in other waters, eventually in every case surprisingly far away. I have made efforts to keep in touch with them ever since, with varying degrees of success.

St. Vincent has had the least recorded about her post O&W activities and, in view of her eventual fate, this is perhaps not surprising. Consequently, little can be written about her activities.

Hotwells, likewise, vanished into obscurity a couple of years after O&W sold her. She did come to light again years later, though not in happy circumstances. Nothing is known of the major part of her life after leaving the Company and any information, sent via the publishers, would be very welcome.

Salcombe's later life is reasonably well documented. This unfortunate vessel was seemingly dogged by the effects of the German mine which had so damaged her right at the start of her career and was probably the cause of her eventual demise.

Colston is also quite well documented, although she too became invisible for a couple of years but a stroke of luck enabled renewed contact to be made with her. In this regard, I have been extremely fortunate in the way that luck has put the pieces into place to maintain contact with her. She always was – and remains – my favourite O&W ship.

Brandon's post O&W history is as well known as that of *Colston*. The two ships were twins and almost throughout their life they remained together, so that tracking one of them automatically meant that the other was around to be recorded as well.

Empire Townsman and *Empire Runner* also merit being covered. Although not strictly within the remit of this account, as the ships were not owned by O&W, they were managed by the Company for about three years during the Second World War. This being the case, there is a connection and a related interest in their post O&W years.

In the pages that follow, each of the ships and their lives after the Osborn & Wallis years are dealt with as far as it has been possible to keep track of them but, for the reasons stated, some of these sections will necessarily not be as comprehensive as others.

EMPIRE TOWNSMAN

During 1947, she was disposed of by the Government to W.D.Tamlyn & Co Ltd of Plymouth and renamed ***Roselyne***. In 1953, she was sold to the Fowey Harbour Commissioners, who changed her name once more to ***Lantyan***.

In 1964, she was again sold, this time to the Seaborne Aggregate Co Ltd of Southampton, who converted the vessel to a sand dredger and renamed her ***Pen Arun***. This company later changed its name to Amey Marine on becoming part of Amey Roadstone Corporation's quarrying empire.

In 1974, she was bought by Dale Sand & Gravel Co Ltd of Guernsey, who renamed her ***Sir Cedric***.

During 1976, she was again sold, this time to the Roselyne Shipping Co Ltd and in 1978, this company sold the ship to the Soc. Pte. Derrien-Bichue of France. She was last heard of working at Morlaix, France, in 1990.

EMPIRE RUNNER

In 1947, she was disposed of by the Government to the Zinal Steamship Co Ltd (J. Furness & Sons Ltd, London) and was registered at Goole. On 31st May 1950, while on passage from Barry to Hayle with a cargo of coal, she ran aground on Porthmear Beach, St. Ives, in dense fog.

During 1950, she was sold to the South Coast Shipping Co Ltd, converted to a sand dredger and was renamed ***Sand Runner***, retaining her Goole registration.

On 1st August 1967, she was sold to Pollock & Brown, of Mortham, Southampton and was broken up.

Lantyan, ex-*Empire Townsman*, circa 1960. *A. Sutcliffe*

ST. VINCENT

This ship, once the radical new departure for O&W and the pattern for all the Company's ships built afterwards, was sold during 1969 to M. Gigilnis & D. Kalkassinis of Greece and renamed ***Giagoros II*** (see photograph on page 153). In 1970, she was sold again to E.I. Koritsidis (and others) and registered at Thessolonika.

Nothing is known of her subsequent activities until 1981, when she was sighted by Italian Coastguards off Ponza Island at night, running without lights. The coastguard vessel gave chase and she was boarded. Contraband cigarettes and hashish were discovered. By this time the crew had set the ship on fire and she sank a few hours later.

Enquiries revealed that she had been re-registered several times using variations of her legitimate name. When caught, she was sporting a further shortened version of her name but was showing no nationality or port of registration. It was a sad and shameful end for this little vessel, which had been the pride of Osborn & Wallis just forty years before.

SALCOMBE

Salcombe was disposed of during late 1969. A South Coast owner was interested in the purchase of the ship and to this end, she was taken to Southampton for inspection and survey, where she was hauled out of the water and onto the slip at Husbands Yard. As a result of this, the ship was purchased by George Dupenios of Torquay, Devon, following which she was renamed ***Friars Craig***. However, she retained her Bristol registration.

On 3rd September 1972, she ran aground at Lannacombe Bay on the south Devon coast, which, ironically, is close to the resort of Salcombe (see photograph on page 152). The ship was undamaged, however, and was later pulled clear by the Brixham trawler ***Angelus*** and the local crabbing vessel ***Superfluous***, whilst the Salcombe lifeboat and the minesweeper ***HMS Kedelston*** stood by.

In 1974, she was disposed of and a series of rapid changes of ownership followed, all apparently linked to one another. She was first sold to Yieldbrace Ltd of Rochdale in 1974 but was immediately sold again to Red Rose Shipping Line, also of Rochdale.

In 1978, she was again sold, this time to Yieldbrace Ltd of St. Vincent in the West Indies. During 1980, she was bought by John Grace and Charles Peterkin of St. Vincent.

Finally, in 1983, she was purchased by Captain Shamir Khan where she lay in Bridgetown, Barbados, and where

Opposite page top and bottom, and this page top: These three views show *Salcombe* on the slip at Husbands Yard, Southampton, where she was taken in 1969 for inspection by new owners. *All Capt. P. Tamblin*

Right: Ex-*Salcombe*, now renamed *Friars Craig* and looking quite different back in the water, making for the entrance lock at Preston Docks in 1973. Seen here unladen, she had also undergone what looks to be a partial repaint, to the rear of her hull and superstructure. *John Clarkson*

she had been lying unused by the various previous owners for at least five years.

Captain Khan was unable to carry out the work needed to make her seaworthy after these years of inactivity and, by 1985, there was considerable anxiety from the Harbour Authorities concerning her condition. Indeed, it was thought likely that she might sink at her moorings, thereby creating considerable difficulties for the port. They therefore instructed that the ship be made seaworthy within a limited time or she should be disposed of.

On 2nd July 1985, after having her masts cut off and having been stripped of anything useful, she was towed to sea for the last time. She was taken just 200 yards offshore, to a spot where she would not interfere with traffic and sunk, to form an artificial reef and to be used as a diving wreck for scuba tuition. However, insufficient allowance was made for tidal currents and, even worse, the hurricane conditions which occur in the area. As a result, the ship very quickly broke up and lay in pieces on the bottom in seventy foot of sunlit but gloomy water.

Having successfully made the Atlantic crossing, her subsequent lack of use, which led directly to her demise, seemed odd. Contact was made with one of her previous owners in Barbados, which resulted in the information that after having purchased the ship, it was suggested that there was 'something wrong' with the crankshaft in the main engine. A reply was made recounting the whole story of the broken crankshaft and its consequences, and the fact that the engine had been totally reliable for the whole of the ship's life thereafter. It still seems inexplicable that, because of this rumoured problem, never properly investigated and despite having just completed the long voyage to the Windward Islands, the ship was never to trade again. Instead, she was allowed to lie and deteriorate to the point where she was condemned – a sad and wasteful end.

Could it be that the German mine which injured her forty years before had secured her demise after all?

Information concerning the ship when she was stripped prior to being sunk, included the details that her two Ruston & Hornsby auxiliary motors started immediately and ran without any difficulty despite having been untouched for years. These were removed before she was sunk.

The ship did not survive intact for very long. Pounded by hurricane seas, where the strength of the incoming waves had their most powerful effect in such shallow water, the old *Salcombe* was soon torn apart (see colour photographs on page 159).

Top, above and left: Three views of the old *Salcombe* at Bridgetown, Barbados, where she sat for five years awaiting repairs which were never carried out, whilst deteriorating further all the time. It is thought the crane was fitted for her work in the Caribbean. In the view left, her spare propeller can be seen in front of the superstructure. *All R. Jolliffe*

Salcombe's deadlight. *Author*

Having spent three years aboard *Salcombe* as her Second Engineer, I still find this picture of her scuttling, just outside Bridgetown Harbour upsetting. *Author's collection*

HOTWELLS

Hotwells was sold to W.N. Lindsey of Leith, who renamed her ***Rosewell*** and re-registered her at Leith. She was later sold to the Voe Shipping Company and her port of registry was changed to Lerwick. At some time during this period, she lost the typical Charles Hill cylindrical freshwater tank. It was replaced with an ungainly square tank, which did nothing for her appearance.

She remained trading chiefly around Scotland and the north of England until 1977 when, after major repairs to her engine, she underwent a further change of ownership. Whilst lying at Leith that August, she was sold into Greek ownership, being purchased by Panagiotis Maidonis, who renamed her ***Myrsini***.

Nothing is known of her subsequent activities until she came to light during 1992, by which time she was virtually unrecognisable. Her well-deck had been filled in and she had been given a midship mounted crane. She now had a 'soft-nose' bow and her bridge area had been entirely rebuilt. Only from the funnel aft could the original ***Hotwells*** still be discerned.

By 1995, she was in very poor condition and she was reported as having been in difficulties in heavy weather in the Adriatic Sea on 26th December 1996. In an effort to shelter from the weather, she made for the port of Ancona in eastern Italy but while trying to enter she struck a pier and began to take in water. She discharged her cargo and was beached in shallow water where temporary repairs were made. However, the damage proved to be more extensive than at first thought and the ship was eventually given up as a total loss during 1999.

Top: *Hotwells* in 1972, after purchase by W.N. Lindsey, who renamed her *Rosewell* and changed her Port of Registry to Leith. *Author*
Middle: Photographed at Rhodes in June 1992, *Myrsini* (on the right) is now completely unrecognisable. Her well-deck has gone and she has a 'soft nose' bow. The whole bridge and wheelhouse structure is completely different. She is fitted with a midships crane and only at the stern can the original *Hotwells* be recognised. *Ron Baker*
Bottom: During 1995, again at Rhodes, *Myrsini* was seen in this very run down condition. From this view, the original *Hotwells* is a little more obvious. *P.J. Anderiesse*

COLSTON

During 1970, ***Colston*** was sold, with her sister ***Brandon***, to W.E. Dowds Ltd of Newport, South Wales. Both vessels were, however, to be managed by James Stewart of Glasgow.

Colston first went to Charles Hill's dockyard, where she underwent inspection before purchase and to have some work carried out for her new owners. The most significant change to her appearance was the extension in height to the freshwater tank aft, which rather spoiled the previous line of the sloping tank top as she was built. The funnel was also painted green but the black top was retained. The original galley funnel had been removed several years before, with the conversion of her cooking facilities to gas when she went on the Yelland run while in O&W ownership.

She left Bristol on 26th August 1970, still in Osborn & Wallis colours and wearing the O&W house flag for what should have been the last time. However, as certain of her crew members were 'bought' with her, there are reports that she continued to fly the O&W house flag on occasions, something which her new owners turned a blind eye to. She did, though, lose her Bristol registration adopting the home port of her new owners, Newport.

Almost immediately after the transfer of ownership, her superstructure was painted white and her masts were painted a sand colour. This change suited her well, although she retained the black hull and red band of boot topping. Later still, the masts became white in colour and this improved her appearance still further.

Whilst with W.E. Dowds, ***Colston*** (and her sister) traded all around the coast of Britain. After ten years with the company, in 1980, ***Colston*** and her sister were sold to the Franco British Chartering Co Ltd, of London. In 1983, they changed ownership again, still as a pair, coming under the control of Invicta Shipping (Thames) Ltd, this company being an associate of Corveda Marine Ltd. They were re-registered in Gibraltar. Corveda Marine eventually took control of them and apparently had plans to change ***Colston***'s name to ***Wolf Rock*** but this never took place.

Corveda Marine made considerable modifications to the pair shortly after taking control of them. This included eliminating the foc'sle door closures, which had previously been merely stout boards fitted into slides and locked in place, there being one such closure on the port and starboard sides of the foc'sle. These large apertures were completely plated in and replaced by one small steel access door, on the port side.

Fore and aft views of *Colston* spruced-up and ready for inspection at Hill's yard in 1970. *Both J. Hill*

A lovely aerial study of the little coaster whilst in Dowds' ownership, out in the English Channel on an almost flat calm day. *Courtesy Fotoflite*

The funnel encasing the engine room exhausts was radically altered and replaced with a more modern structure, physically joined to the after end of the bridge and wheelhouse. There was no technical necessity to make this change, it was simply a clever cosmetic alteration, well executed, to improve and modernise the appearance of the two ships. It suited them well.

In 1985, ***Colston*** was laid up at Rochester on the River Medway and remained there for nearly a year. She was soon joined by her sister, although ***Brandon*** went back to work slightly earlier and so suffered a shorter lay-up. During March 1987, I visited the ship while she was at Gloucester Docks, and found her to be in good, cared for condition.

Shortly afterwards, sometime between the end of August and the end of December 1987, ***Colston*** made the long voyage to the Windward Islands. She had been bought by Naviera Colston S de RL, one of the many small 'one ship' companies that abounded in the Caribbean at the time.

Looking very smart, *Colston* is seen here unloading at the small port of Whitstable, in Kent, again during her time with W.E. Dowds. *Capt. C. Reynolds*

She was again on the move in 1995, when she was bought by another 'one ship' company, Stengard Ltd of Belize. Having kept her original name for forty years, she lost it at last when her name was changed to ***Stengard***. Her colours became even more garish than in her time with Corveda Marine, her hull becoming bright blue, upperworks white,

ESTABLISHED 1924

J. GIBSON JOHNSTON LIMITED

DIRECTORS: E. R. GORE W. H. GORE

TELEPHONE:
HULL (0482) 224028

AFTER OFFICE HOURS:
W. H. GORE (0482) 43519

REGISTERED IN ENGLAND NO. 276745

SHIP SALE AND PURCHASE BROKERS
SHIPPING VALUERS — INSURANCE

TELEGRAPHIC ADDRESS:
GIBSONJOHNSTON HULL

TELEX NO. 52148
ANS. BACK 'GIBJON'

REGISTERED OFFICE:
ST. MARY'S CHAMBERS, LOWGATE, HULL HU1 1PL

WE CAN SECURE FOR SALE THE SINGLEDECK VESSELS - "BRANDON" AND "COLSTON" - DETAILS OF WHICH APPEAR UNDER OUR FOLIOS C/4367-4368(B1)

BUILT: 1957/1955 by Charles Hill & Sons Ltd., Bristol.

CLASS: Both vessels have been extremely well maintained by first class British owners and are offered for sale with Lloyds Class (+100A1 and LMC maintained) with special surveys passed November, 1979. D of T Class VIII.

FLAG: British.

TONNAGE: 586 GRT/297 NRT.

DIMENSIONS: Length overall: 51.51 m, Beam: 9 m, Summer Draught: 3.7 m (loaded)

HOLDS/HATCHES: These exceptionally well maintained sister vessels are excellent sea ships, soundly built to withstand the rigours of coal trading around Lands End, and offering two holds (No. 1 approx. 44'9" x 27'3" x 9'10" height. No. 2 approx. 53'2" x 27'10" x 13'0" height) and two hatches (No. 1 approx. 35'9" x 17'0" No. 2 approx. 39'4" x 17'0").

DEADWEIGHT: With a total deadweight of about 790 tonnes, on summer marks, the vessels can load a deadweight of about 740 tonnes of cargoes stowing at up to 53 cubic feet per tonne, and in practice it has been found that cargoes said to stow at 55/56 are well accommodated because of the self-trimming facility.

CAPACITIES: m.v.'s "Brandon" and "Colston" provide the combination of the ease of self-trimming for bulk cargoes with the ease of cleaning offered by steel hold ceilings.
GRAIN cubic cap: 1098 cu.m. (39,220 cub.ft.)
BALE cubic cap: 1044 cu.m. (37,760 cub.ft.)

MAIN ENGINE: Both vessels are fitted with a Ruston and Hornsby main engine, situated aft, developing 540 bhp.
(The Engine rooms are under Lloyds Continuous Machinery Survey)

SPEED/CONS.: Service speed of about 9.5 knots, when fuel consumption is excellent, at approximately 1.3 tonnes per 24 hours steaming.

AUXILIARY MACHINERY: The auxiliary machinery on each vessel comprises of:-
2 Ruston Diesels of 22 kilowatts and 1 Ruston Diesel of 19 kilowatts reducing 220 volts D.C. Current.

ACCOMMODATION: The crew accommodation comprises separate Messrooms for Officers and Rating and the vessels presently operate with a complement of 4 officers and 4 ratings, all in single berth cabins.

SAFETY EQUIP.: Safety equipment comprises of 2 Lifeboats and 1 Liferaft on each vessel together with the requisit number of D.T.I. firesuits, hoses and extinguishers.

NAVIGATIONAL EQUIPMENT: Navigational equipment on rental/maintenance includes Decca Navigator and Marconi Radio Telephone and V.H.F. and Kelvin Hughes Radar (Type 17), which is the vessels own equipment.

IMMEDIATE INSPECTIONS OR PRELIMINARY VIEWING CAN BE ARRANGED WHILST THE VESSELS ARE LOADING/DISCHARGING AT SOUTH COAST OR NEAR CONTINENT PORTS.

PRICE: Owners are inviting offers for the two ships, either singly or en bloc and would put forward offers at around £45,000 each vessel.

Two views of *Colston* at Sharpness in 1983, when she was in the ownership of Invicta Shipping (Thames) Ltd. In the top view her bell is missing, although her plaque is still in place. Presumably the bell was in safe storage at this time. In the bottom view, the vessel is seen turning into the docks from the Gloucester & Sharpness Canal, having discharged a cargo at Saul, part way up the waterway. The original route of the canal carried on to the left, where there was a lock out into the River Severn. This was replaced by a new entrance when Sharpness Docks were built in the early 1870s. Just behind *Colston*'s wheelhouse can be seen the sole surviving pier of the old Severn railway bridge, damaged in an accident in 1960 and demolished in 1967-69. The pier supported the swing section over the canal.

Top: Author's collection
Bottom: Photomarine

In 1987, following her long spell tied up in the River Medway, *Colston* made her first commercial voyage since 1985. She was sent across the English Channel to Antwerp, to pick up a load of fertiliser bound for Gloucester Docks, where she arrived on 14th March after traversing the Gloucester & Sharpness Canal. This selection of views show the vessel at various stages in her journey along the canal. *All Chris Witts*

On her return from Gloucester, *Colston* is seen exiting the canal and passing through the swing bridges into Sharpness Docks, a few miles up the River Severn from Avonmouth. Sharpness still handled a substantial amount of grain traffic at this period and in the right background can just be seen part of the tall grain elevator built onto the old Severn Ports warehouse. *Chris Witts*

Seeing double! Both looking trim in Corveda Marine colours, *Brandon* and *Colston* are seen here when laid up in the River Medway at Rochester in 1985. *Colston* stayed for nearly a year. By this time, both had been extensively rebuilt and, in particular, the new funnel arrangement, a cosmetic enhancement to modernise their appearance, should be noted. *Bernard McCall*

and with her funnel becoming blue, with a white band and a red top. Mr Osborn would have been horrified! However, a little more decorum was established later when, although retaining the dazzling upperworks, the hull colour was changed to a deeper navy blue.

When comprehensively photographed in 1995, the vessel appeared to be very run down and shabby, and it seemed certain that her life was nearly over. It was in consideration of this and the fact that the ship had undergone a name change, that her bell was bought.

However, in 2000, following an inspection, she changed hands again. A dry docking and a thorough examination had shown that, despite the outward appearance, she was fundamentally very sound, with her hull still in excellent condition. Her new owners then set about refurbishing her and a considerable amount of money was spent on the ship, since when she has been well cared for by her crew. She is currently (2004) engaged in transporting a variety of cargoes, including cement, and Banana boxes, throughout the Caribbean and regularly makes trips to South America. Built in Bristol, originally for the muddy waters of the Upper Bristol Channel, the warm and clear Caribbean water, coupled with her runs to South America, are a remarkable change for the little ship, now fifty years old.

That there must be confidence for her future is shown in the reports that she was due to be drydocked during 2004, for extensive repairs and maintenance of her hull, and for the renewal of her tank tops. Her present crew confirm that she is an excellent sea boat in the waters of the Atlantic and the Caribbean, and she is well liked by them. There is considerable pride in their little fifty year old ship. She is the smallest unit in a fleet of charter vessels and is useful for carrying cargoes which would be less economically carried by the larger ships in the fleet.

Colston at Bridgetown, Barbados in 1993. *Capt. C. Reynolds*

BRANDON

Having been sold to W.E. Dowds Ltd of South Wales, together with her sister, ***Brandon*** worked in that fleet for ten years. Then, during 1980, Dowds decided to dispose of the pair and they were purchased by the Franco British Chartering Co Ltd of London.

Franco British Chartering Ltd sold the pair during 1983 to Invicta Shipping (Thames) Ltd of Gravesend, an associate company of Corveda Marine, based in Kent, and this company took the two ships over completely during 1983. Some modifications were made to both ships, including plating in the two foc'sle doors and most noticeable, the complete re-shaping of the funnel structure, which now became a unit with the bridge and wheelhouse. Although somewhat angular, the new funnel suited both ships admirably and improved their appearance considerably. Charles Hill had already been using this styling motif for some time before building the pair for O&W. They would doubtless have wished to do something similar for ***Colston*** and ***Brandon*** but a curved bridge front, a tripod mast and a sloping top to an oval funnel was as futuristic as Osborn & Wallis was prepared to go!

On taking the pair over, Corveda Marine planned to change ***Brandon***'s name to ***Racebank*** but this was never carried out. However, the port of registry was changed to Gibraltar and her hull painted a bright orange.

Corveda Marine sold both ***Colston*** and ***Brandon*** during 1987 and at last the pair were separated, having been bought by different Caribbean-based concerns. ***Brandon*** sailed from Casablanca in July 1987, to cross the Atlantic bound for Houston, Texas, to her new owners, a company named Trans Orient Ltd. However, 400 miles out, she suffered an engine failure and was towed back to Lisbon, arriving there on 27th July 1987. There she remained while her mechanical problems were investigated but, after two years of indecision, it was eventually decided that she was beyond economical repair. She was then arrested for non-payment of harbour dues and was promptly sold to Baptista Y Iramos Ltd on 11th November 1989, who broke her up during December of that year.

Above: *Brandon* in Jeffries' dry dock at Avonmouth in the 1970s. Somewhat dwarfed by her surroundings, timber packing has been used to keep her upright whilst being worked on. *Capt C. Reynolds*

The demise of ***Brandon*** in 1989 and of ***Hotwells*** during 1999 leaves ***Colston*** as the sole remaining ship that once flew the Osborn & Wallis house flag.

Conceived only as Bristol Channel traders, the four motor ships which Charles Hill & Sons had built for the Company had 'flown the flag' far beyond the bounds that they had been intended for. One had gone to the West Indies, two of them had emigrated to the Mediterranean and they had all made long distant voyages on a regular basis. At the time of writing, the fifty year old ***Colston*** still trades far from her birthplace and in deep waters.

Little Bristol Channel colliers, stoutly built in Bristol, for a Bristol Company. They served long and they served well, and they can justly claim the accolade ...

'SHIPSHAPE AND BRISTOL FASHION'

Below: In calmer surroundings, an unladen *Brandon* shows off her lines and colours well in this late 1970s view. *K. Byass*

A fine study of *Brandon* in tip-top condition and ploughing across the English Channel once more in blustery weather, all battened down and with her big ventilators facing aft. *Fotoflite*

2. THE PLACES

This final short section documents and illustrates the changes that have occurred over the last thirty years to some of the places that were significant in the lives of the Osborn & Wallis ships and men. Time waits for no man and, in the name of progress, many of the places that we used to visit or which we called home have now changed almost beyond recognition.

ELY HARBOUR, PENARTH

Ely Harbour today is now completely unrecognisable from the place where we used to load coal. All of the heavy industry has disappeared and the coal tips have long since been dismantled. The River Ely is now fronted on its west bank by modern houses and apartments, much sought after for their views across Cardiff Bay. The river itself is used for mooring small yachts and pleasure craft, and can now only be accessed by passing through the Cardiff Barrage, built right across the bay a decade or so ago. Amidst all this modernity and rejuvenation, it is perhaps surprising to find that the wooden pier of No. 1 Tip still stands in the river, as does part of the old iron ore jetty. The bridge carrying the A4232 dual carriageway now spans the river just beyond where we once loaded coal and where a young Deck Boy went in trepidation of being out on the tidal waters of the Ely in the workboat, especially in poor weather in the dark.

Although accessed from a separate entrance lock and never visited by us, the adjacent Penarth Dock is now an upmarket marina development and part of the landward end of it filled in and built on. There is no sign of the myriad of railway lines which served the coal tips, although the bases of a couple of them still remain. New housing surrounds the dock completely, built to within feet of the dockside.

The modern world has erased the old Ely Harbour, as this 2005 view shows. This is almost the exact spot where *Lunan* met her end (see page 52) and the mud banks have been covered with stone for the benefit of those who live in the new development along the watefront. *Neil Parkhouse*

NEWPORT DOCK

Although trade through Newport Docks is today just a fraction of what it was fifty years ago, it remains one of the busier of the South Wales ports. Now owned by Associated British Ports, Newport's deep water berths and range of facilities has seen tonnages through the docks increasing over the last decade. Traffic handled include steel, scrap metal, timber, ore, sand, clay, agricultural products, coal and coke, as well as general goods, and specialised cargoes such as cars and railway locomotives. The docks are still rail served as well as by road, the dry dock in the North Dock remains in use and W.E. Dowds are also still in operation here.

What has changed is the way much of this traffic is dealt with and the number of ships calling. Fifty years ago, the port would constantly be crowded with ships waiting their turn to load coal for export, with vessels even moored at the buoys in the middle of the dock. In addition, general cargo was an important feature of the work of the dock, all of which, because of the nature of traffic handling at the time, provided hundreds of jobs. With modern cargo handling methods, fewer but bigger ships and the reduction in the rail network around the docks, many of these jobs have gone. New warehouses and cargo terminals have also replaced much of the infrastructure that existed in the 1950s and 1960s, whilst the coal hoists disappeared along with the South Wales coal industry, apart from a handful of the stone jetties on which they stood. Nevertheless, most of the dock area from the days when the Osborn & Wallis boats used to call regularly still remains in use (*see photo on page 160*).

OSBORN & WALLIS'S YARD AND DOCK HOTWELLS, BRISTOL

The yard, with its telfer crane, was used for the importation of sand for a number of years after Osborn & Wallis left but eventually that industry too left Bristol and the whole area became part of a housing development. Unlike the historic

Its previous incarnation as a dry dock always made O&W's dock at Hotwells slightly awkward to work due to its stepped sides, as this circa 1925 view illustrates. The company's steam barge *Ferric* is here dwarfed by an interloper, *River Fisher*, part of the fleet of James Fisher & Sons Ltd of Barrow-in-Furness. Of 457 grt and built by John Fullerton & Co of Paisley in 1899, *River Fisher* worked for Fishers until 1928. After a few months with a Cardiff owner, she was sold to France and as *Sainte Elme* had various owners based in Marseilles. On 8th April 1936, *Sainte Elme* was wrecked on the eastern tip of Ile Saint Honorat, off Cannes, when her steering gear failed in heavy weather during a voyage from Marseilles and Cannes to Nice, with a cargo consisting of about 60 tons of bran, flour and empty barrels. The crew were rescued by a boat from a monastery on the island. During the night the vessel floated off and was blown across the Bay of Cannes, coming ashore at Pointe Saint-Marc near Theoule. The wreck was partly demolished *in situ*, although remains can still be seen. *Author's collection*

Left: The dock in 1998, from a similar viewpoint to the picture on the previous page.

Below: A ghostly echo of O&W days, when the ships would moor up in the yard and the crew would carry out some 'over the side' painting from the convenience of the steps. Someone from *St. Vincent* cleaned his paint brush out at the end of the day by daubing the ship's name on the drydock wall. The stepped sides are now quite handy for yachtsmen and pleasure boaters. Note how close the houses have been built to the edge of the dock. *Both author*

Below: Looking in the opposite direction, with the old O&W office surrounded by scaffolding whilst in the process of renovation. Although ringed by modern housing, this little haven and the company's office are welcome survivors in the Osborn & Wallis story. *Author*

Merchants Dock close by, which was filled in and built upon, the O&W water basin, the old G.K. Stothert's dry dock, has had to remain as a feature of the area. The office building is likewise protected and has undergone extensive renovation.

PORTISHEAD DOCK

Whilst the tiny Hotwells Dock was Osborn & Wallis's base, the dock at Portishead was the hub around which the lives of the ships and their crews revolved. Indeed, following commissioning of the first power station in 1929 and the building of 'B' Station after the Second World War, Portishead became almost the sole reason for the company's existence. The company had grown in the business of transporting the fuel for Bristol's electricity industry from its slender beginnings right through to the fuelling of these two plants. Although small by today's standards, both were major undertakings in their day. 'A' Station had the two largest generators in Britain when it was first built, whilst 'B' Station was a key element in the supply of electricity to the South West of Britain. Both stations were the concept of Bristol's own Electricity Department, and were planned and designed by the City itself.

In the late 1940s and early 50s the British Electricity Authority (BEA), as it was to become after nationalisation, made several attempts to use their own collier fleet to supply the two stations with coal but continual difficulties were encountered by their less experienced crews. The strongly flowing tides and the consequent currents swirling around the pier, caused all sorts of problems as the bigger ships tried to run across them to enter Portishead Dock. The wooden pier was hit several times and in the end these attempts were quietly abandoned and it was left to the 'experts', who were used to the vagaries of the Bristol Channel to maintain the supply of coal to the two stations. It is true that in later years larger ships did eventually oust the O&W vessels but, to do so, they had to employ tugs and the services of a Pilot. The Bristol Channel, with its huge range of tides and the consequent speed with which the water races in and out of the estuary, cannot be treated lightly.

With the closure of the power stations and the other industries surrounding the dock, the whole area was left looking like a barren waste land for a number of years. A temporary steel barrage was built across the dock end of

The Telfer-type cranes provide a striking backdrop to *St. Vincent* at the power station coaling wharf at Portishead in the early 1960s. She rides high in the water having been discharged. *Author's collection*

Part Five
THE MEN

Dennis Shone, Sailor, Freddy Sharp, the Boy, and Frank House, Mate, posed on *Druid Stoke* in the mid 1950s, before I joined her. Dennis was ex-Royal Navy.

The following is by no means a complete list of all those who worked for Osborn & Wallis but rather a collection of those names I remember as having been part of 'the job'. Some are shore staff, from the O&W yard at Hotwells and from the docks and the power station coal unloading plant at Portishead. The ships crews are generally as I remember them, although reminiscing with other ex-O&W men has filled in a few gaps. To anyone who has been missed out, or to their relatives who may be looking for their names, I can only apologise. Fifty years has passed now since I started on board *Colston* and over forty years since I left the company. Time is not kind to the memory and all records of the company's staff have long since disappeared.

The first section of the list, the crewmen, has the names in alphabetical order. Each name includes a short note to indicate what they did, nicknames (in brackets) and some other brief details.

CREWMEN

Jack Adair Canadian. Chief Engineer on *Downleaze* while I was on her.

George Allenby Skipper of *Rockleaze*.

Arthur Anderson Second Engineer of *Colston* when I joined her. Died about a year after.

Geoff Anderson Boy on *Druid Stoke* while I was with her (Arthur Anderson's son).

Jack Baker Sailor on *Salcombe* while I was on her

Walter Barling ('Wally') Second Engineer (Fireman) on *Druid Stoke*. Lived aboard.

Bill Base Chief Engineer on *Druid Stoke* while I was on her. (His brother Fred was the sole survivor of the *Lunan* explosion.)

Jackie Beard Second engineer of *St. Vincent*. Second Engineer on *Colston* on Yelland run. Then Chief Engineer on *Colston*.

Len Bennet ('Wiggy') Skipper of *Downleaze*, then Skipper of *St. Vincent*.

Harry Brunt ('Trigger') Mate on *Druid Stoke* while I was with her. Mate on *Colston* on Yelland run.

George Burden Second Engineer on *St. Vincent*.

Bill Butler Skipper of *Druid Stoke* while I was with her. Mate on *Brandon* on Yelland run.

Colin Campbell Chief Engineer on *St. Vincent*, *Hotwells* and then *Colston*, when I joined her. Moved to *Brandon* as Chief Engineer when she was delivered.

David Caple Sailor on *Hotwells*.

Jock Clark Boy on *Hotwells*, Sailor on *Druid Stoke*.

Tom Colcombe Senior Skipper until retirement. Skipper of *St. Vincent* when she ran ashore in fog off Black Nore Point. Never really got over it.

Alf Coles	Ex-RN. Skipper of *Rockleaze*, then *St. Vincent*, then *Colston* on Yelland run.
Micky Cooling	Boy on *Sneyd*. Boy on *Downleaze*. Sailor on *Downleaze*. Sailor on *Hotwells*
Stan Cooper	Sailor on *Rockleaze*.
Dave Corner	Boy on *Salcombe*, then Sailor in *Druid Stoke*.
Bill Derrick	Chief Engineer of *Rockleaze*.
Tom Derrick	Mate of *St. Vincent*. (Tom Derrick's older brother. Drove blue Ford Zephyr 1, then Ford V8 Pilot.)
Robert Edbrook	('Jiggy') Boy on *Downleaze*. Sailor on *Downleaze*.
? Fishlock	('Bunny') Sailor on *Rockleaze*. Sailor on *St. Vincent*.
Tony Gale	Sailor on *Druid Stoke*. Sailor on *Colston*.
Bill Greer	Skipper of *Hotwells*.
Ted Haskins	Chief Engineer on *Downleaze*. Second Engineer on *Brandon* on Yelland run. Chief Engineer on *Brandon*.
Ronnie Hayman	Boy on *Colston* when new. Second Engineer on *Hotwells*.
Brian Holder	('Gladys') Boy on *Salcombe* while I was on her.
? Hood	('Hoody') Chief Engineer on *Salcombe*. 'Bought' with the vessel, then named *Camroux IV*, in 1942.
Frank House	Sailor on *Druid Stoke*. Mate on *Druid Stoke*, Mate on *St. Vincent*.
William Humphries	('Barry Bill') From Barry, S. Wales. Mate of *Hotwells*. Then Mate of *Colston*. Sold with her to W.E. Dowds Ltd. Became her Skipper with Dowds.
Fred Knight	Sailor on *Colston* while I was her Boy
George Lindholm	(Estonian) Sailor on *Downleaze*. Sailor on *Hotwells*.
Fred Maull	Mate on *Downleaze* while I was with her.
Kenny May	Mate on *Rockleaze*. Mate on *St. Vincent*
Robert McCallion	('Mac') Mate of *Salcombe* while I was with her.
Pete Miller	Second Engineer (Fireman) on *Downleaze*. Second Engineer on *Brandon* on Yelland run.
Frank Murphy	('Spud') Boy on *Rockleaze*. Sailor on *Rockleaze*.
Denis Parsons	Sailor on *Downleaze*.

Above: On a sunny day circa 1957, the crew of *Downleaze* take a break from loading operations at Ely Harbour. Chief Engineer Ted Haskins is at the back, with Robert Edbrooke, Sailor, Pete Miller, Second Engineer, and Micky Cooling, the other Sailor, in front.

Above: Pictured here on *Colston* are Jimmy Wong, Sailor, and Alfie Coles, who was then Captain of *St. Vincent*. Alfie took over as *Colston*'s Skipper when Sammy Taylor and the entire crew were transferred to *Brandon* in 1957.

Left: Micky Cooling, Sailor, Frank Rosewell, Sailor, and Ron Hayman, Second Engineer, on *Hotwells*.

George Payne	Sailor on ***Salcombe*** while I was on her. (Along with Jack Baker, the pair of them were known as 'Bill and Ben'.)
Bobby Pine	Boy on ***Hotwells***. Boy on ***St. Vincent***.
Trevor Phillips	('Popeye') Chief engineer of ***Hotwells***.
Ronnie Pring	Second Engineer of ***Colston***. Replaced Arthur Anderson.
Bill Rendle	Chief Engineer of ***St. Vincent***.
Gordon Richards	Deep sea man. Mate of ***Colston*** when I joined her. Then ***Brandon***. Always wore old cap that he had worn through two torpedo sinkings during the war and a wreck prior to that. Skipper of ***Sneyd*** until laid up. Skipper of ***Downleaze*** while I was on her.
Frank Rosewell	Sailor on ***Hotwells***.
Tommy Scarrett	Chief Engineer of ***Salcombe*** while I was her Second Engineer.
Freddy Sharp	Boy on ***Druid Stoke***.
Dennis Shone	Ex-RN. Sailor on ***Druid Stoke***.
Sam Strickland	Boy on ***St. Vincent***.
Sammy Taylor	Senior Skipper. On ***Colston*** when I joined her. Then ***Brandon***. Went on Yelland run with ***Brandon***. Skipper on ***Druid Stoke*** during my childhood trip.
Bobby Villis	Boy on ***St. Vincent***. Sailor on ***Downleaze*** with me.
Don Windows	Skipper of ***Salcombe*** while I was with her. Previously Skipper of ***Downleaze***.
Jimmy Wong	Sailor on ***Colston*** while I was her Boy.

Above: Frank Rosewell enjoys a 'fag break' aboard *Hotwells* whilst moored alongside the power station wharf at Portishead.

Left: A few moments later, Frank has now swapped hats with the other seaman, who has not been identified and may not be an O&W man.

Right: Frank 'Spud' Murphy, Sailor, Pete Miller, Second Engineer, and Micky Cooling, Sailor, posing on *Downleaze*.

The next two lists are the staff at O&W's Hotwells yard and the names of those men we got to know at Portishead Dock. Both lists are presented in order of seniority, with a note of each person's position.

HOTWELLS YARD

Denis Osborn	Managing Director of Osborn & Wallis.
Frank Skuse	Manager of Osborn & Wallis.
R. G. Paynter	Marine Superintendent (departing as I joined the company – fearsome reputation!)
Max Goodacre	Marine Superintendent while I was with the company.
Jack Allen	Senior Clerk.
Rodney Herman	Clerk.
Bill Snell	Yard Foreman.
George Henry	Fitter (ex-Charles Hill).
?	('Clemmy') Crane driver.

Above: Some of the company's men on the occasion of the Queen's visit to Bristol in 1956. On the left with the beer glass is Frank Rosewell (Sailor, *Hotwells*), with Mr Dennis Osborn standing next to him and Ronnie Pring (Second Engineer, *Colston*) visible just behind them. Behind Mr Osborn to his left is Ted Haskins (Chief Engineer, *Downleaze*). The next three in line I have not been able to put names to. Glass in hand is Jock Clark (Boy in *Hotwells*) and on his left with the quiff is Micky Cullen (Boy in *Downleaze*). The older chap with the glasses behind I don't know but standing on the right is Bobby Villis (Boy in *St. Vincent*). In front with Frank 'Spud' Murphy (Boy on *Rockleaze*) is Shirley McCallion, Robert McCallion's daughter. Frank and Shirley were later married.

Top right: Taken on the same occasion, the two men are Alf Coles, who was then Skipper of *St. Vincent* and the Mate, Kenny May.

PORTISHEAD DOCK

? Davis	('Docky'). Portishead Dock Master.
Capt. ? Turner	Later Dock Master.
Jack Jelly	Assistant Dock Master.
Hector Hamer	Lockgateman.
Ken Cutland	Coal Foreman, Power Station.
Denis Jones	Coal Foreman, Power Station.
Arthur Tudgay	('Taffy') Coal Foreman, Power Station.
Cliff Brown	Crane Driver, Power Station.
George Coles	Crane Driver, Power Station.
Dave Corner	Crane Driver, Power Station.
Toby Cross	Crane Driver, Power Station.
Trevor Hill	Crane Driver, Power Station.
Tommy Irvine	Crane Driver, Power Station.
John Quick	Crane Driver, Power Station.
Bert Skerm	Crane Driver, Power Station.
Charlie Sulley	Crane Driver, Power Station.
Eddie Bessant	Hatchman, Power Station.
Albert Villis	Hatchman, Power Station.
John Bence	Dock Maintenance Man.
Harold Buckland	Dock Maintenance Man.

Above: One of the coal handling gangs at Portishead Power Station circa 1960. The only one I can put a name to is W. Edbrooke, third from left, front row, who was my uncle.

Left: Mr Denis Osborn, Managing Director of the company, making a presentation to Bill Rendle, Chief Engineer of *St. Vincent*, on the occasion of the latter's retirement. Mr Osborn's involvement with Osborn & Wallis dated back to its incorporation as a limited company in 1921, which was undertaken in conjunction with his father William, one of the founding partners in 1880. The Wallis connection had lapsed around the time of the First World War, probably with the death of Humphrey Wallis, the other founding partner.

CREWS OF SHIPS

This final list groups the men with the ships on which they served. Ship names in bold indicate those on which I had a permanent posting. Names of crew in bold are those serving on the ship at the same time as myself (my name is also included where relevant). Where there is more than one name against a particular rank, they should be in the order of serving on the ship but some of these men were either before or after my time with O&W.

BRANDON

Skipper	**Sammy Taylor.**
Mate	**Gordon Richards.** Bill Butler.
Chief	**Colin Campbell.** Ted Haskins. Jackie Beard.
Second	**Ronnie Pring.** Ted Haskins. Pete Miller.
Sailor	**Fred Knight.**
Sailor	**Jimmy Wong.**
Boy	**Mike Winter.**

COLSTON

Skipper	**Sammy Taylor.** Alf Coles.
Mate	**Gordon Richards.** Harry Brunt. Bill Humphries.
Chief	**Colin Campbell.** Ted Haskins. Jackie Beard.
Second	**Arthur Anderson. Ronnie Pring.** Jackie Beard.
Sailor	**Fred Knight.** Tony Gale.
Sailor	**Jimmy Wong.**
Boy	Ronnie Hayman. **Mike Winter.**

HOTWELLS

Skipper	Bill Greer.
Mate	Bill Humphries.
Chief	Colin Campbell. Trevor Phillips. Ronnie Hayman.
Second	Ronnie Hayman.
Sailor	Frank Rosewell. George Lindholm.
Sailor	Micky Cooling. David Caple.
Boy	Jock Clark. Bobby Pine.

ST. VINCENT

Skipper	Tom Colcombe. Alf Coles. Len Bennet.
Mate	Colin Campbell. Tom Derrick. Kenny May.
Chief	Bill Rendle. George Burden.
Second	George Burden. Jackie Beard.
Sailor	Frank House. 'Bunny' Fishlock.
Sailor	Frank Murphy.
Boy	Bobby Villis. Bobby Pine. Sam Strickland.

SALCOMBE

Skipper	**Don Windows.**
Mate	**Robert McCallion.**
Chief	'Hoody' Hood. **Tommy Scarrett.**
Second	Tommy Scarrett. **Mike Winter.**
Sailor	**George Payne.**
Sailor	**Jack Baker.**
Boy	Dave Corner. **Brian Holder.**

DOWNLEAZE

Skipper	Don Windows. **Gordon Richards.** Len Bennet.
Mate	**Fred Maull.**
Chief	Ted Haskins. **Jack Adair.**
Second	**Pete Miller.**
Sailor	**Bobby Villis.** George Lindholm. Denis Parsons .
Sailor	Robert Edbrooke. **Mike Winter.** Micky Cooling.
Boy	Robert Edbrooke. **Micky Cooling.**

ROCKLEAZE

Skipper	George Allenby. Alf Coles.
Mate	Kenny May.
Chief	Bill Derrick. Bill Rendle.
Second	
Sailor	Frank Murphy. 'Bunny' Fishlock.
Sailor	Stan Cooper.
Boy	Frank Murphy.

DRUID STOKE

Skipper	Sammy Taylor. **Bill Butler.**
Mate	**Harry Brunt.** Frank House.
Chief	**Bill Base.**
Second	**Wally Barling.**
Sailor	Frank House. **Dave Corner. Denis Shone.**
Sailor	**Mike Winter.** Jock Clark. Tony Gale.
Boy	**Geoff Anderson.** Freddy Sharp.

SNEYD *(Laid up at time I started. Didn't work again)*

Skipper	Gordon Richards.
Mate	
Chief	Joe ?
Second	
Sailor	
Sailor	
Boy	Micky Cooling.

Left: Captain William 'Bill' Greer. During my time with the company he was Skipper of *Hotwells.*

Right: Fred Knight, Sailor on board *Colston.*

Above: Bill Rendle and Jackie Beard, Chief and Second Engineer respectively of *St. Vincent*.

Above: Dennis, Freddy and Tony Smith, *Druid Stoke*'s other Sailor, snapped at Ely on the same day as the view on page 181.

Below: Bill Rendle and Jackie Beard relax in their accommodation aboard *St. Vincent*.

Above: Walter 'Wally' Barling, Second Engineer, Freddy and Jock Clarke, Sailor, on *Druid*'s stern. Wally, here indulging in a spot of the grand old Somerset sport of 'gurning', was a pleasure to work with, ever ready for a joke and a laugh. He never grumbled, whatever went wrong and was always willing to help out on deck. He was single and lived aboard *Druid*. When he died in the 1980s, Dennis Shone was Mate in one of the ARC Sandsuckers and having stopped the ship, he scattered Wally's ashes into the Bristol Channel as requested.

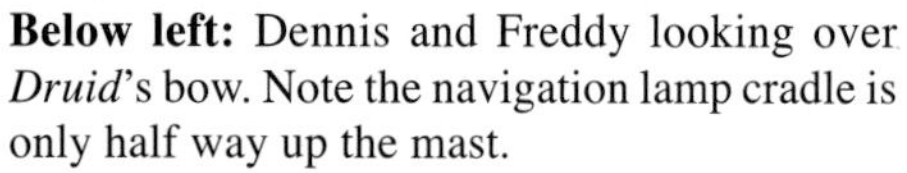

Below left: Dennis and Freddy looking over *Druid*'s bow. Note the navigation lamp cradle is only half way up the mast.
Below right: Dave Corner, Sailor, and 'Spud' Murphy, Sailor on *Rockleaze*, on *Druid*'s bridge.

Above: Jock Clarke and Dennis Shone. Jock took my place as Sailor, with Dennis, on *Druid Stoke* when I left her to become *Salcombe*'s Second Engineer.

Above right: Bobby Villis, Boy on *St. Vincent.*

Right: Dennis on *Druid Stoke*'s forehatch, in the Old Berth right at the top of Portishead Dock. Dennis was the other Sailor with me in my time aboard the ship. Note the coal grab descending into the hold.

Below left: David Caple, on the right, Sailor on *Hotwells.* He joined just after I left the company.

Below right: Chief Engineer Bill Rendle in his domain, *St. Vincent*'s engine room, operating the main engine controls.

Index

VESSELS
A1 42
Agra 31
Alpha 42
Alverton 23, 25
Angelus 162
Ardeola 34
Bengo 31
Blanche 24, 31, 33, 34, 37
Brandon 8, 9, 21, 79, 81, 82, 83, 89, 93, 99, 100, 106, 108, 113, 116, 117, 118, 119, 120, 123, 141, 144, 161, 166, 167, 173
Camroux 66
Camroux IV 66, 67, 71
Carley Float Liferaft 56, 60
Charlotte 23, 27
Cigale 37
Clifton 36
Colston 8, 9, 21, 74, 75, 76, 77, 78, 79, 80, 81, 82, 83, 87, 89, 91, 92, 93, 95, 98, 99, 100, 106, 113, 116, 118, 119, 123, 130, 134, 136, 141, 143, 144, 161, 166, 167, 173, 179
Crestville 55
Devonia 24
Dolcoath 25, 40
Downleaze 55, 56, 57, 60, 61, 66, 70, 73, 79, 82, 88, 99, 106, 119, 120, 121, 122, 123, 130, 131, 132, 134, 144
Druid Stoke 7, 10, 21, 46, 47, 49, 61, 70, 71, 82, 88, 99, 129, 132, 133, 134, 135, 136, 138, 144
Eclipse 26
Empire Runner 70, 161
Empire Townsman 70, 161
English & Welsh Grounds Lightship 131, 135
Enterprize 11, 23, 24
Esso Chelsea 116
Esso Fulham 116
Esso Lambeth 116
Esso Wandsworth 116
Eugenia 26
Eureka 25, 38
Euterpe 15, 25, 26, 40
Farleigh Combe 55, 60
Ferric 40, 41, 70, 88, 126, 127
Floating Crane 24
Fredavore 26
Friars Craig 8, 162
Geeststar 8
Giagoros II 162
Glanoventa 53
Glynconwy 57, 59.
Goldcrest 57
Governor Albuquerque 28, 31, 33
Governador Albuquerque 31
Herschel 24, 34
Horsham 53
Hotwells 21, 71, 72, 73, 75, 79, 82, 88, 98, 99, 131, 139, 144, 161, 165, 173
Hudson 56
Inchbrayock 48, 49, 50, 51
Itchen 27
Jantar 113
Kedelston, HMS 162
Kingsgarth 63
Kingswear Castle 8
Lantyan 161
Lunan 21, 49, 51, 55, 66, 67, 70, 134; Loss of 51-53
Marion 33
Monkton Combe 57, 60
Morvah 42, 46, 47, 70, 88
Myrsini 165
Netham 15, 26, 28-31
New Zealand 36, 37, 38
Ocean 33, 36, 38, 70
Orb 15, 38, 39, 70
Pamir 124
Passat 124
Pen Arun 161
Perseveranza 26
Pheonix 27
Plumgarth 63
Racebank 173
Rockleaze 57, 60, 61, 66, 70, 73, 82, 88, 98, 99, 106, 123, 130, 144
Roselyne 161
Rosewell 165
Salcombe 8, 10, 66, 67, 68, 70, 71, 73, 79, 82, 99, 102, 106, 118, 136, 137, 138, 139, 140, 141, 143, 144, 161, 162, 164
Salcombe lifeboat 162
Sir Howard Elphinstone 36
St.Vincent (1) 15, 34
St.Vincent (2) 7, 21, 61, 62, 63, 64, 66, 68, 70, 71, 73, 82, 87, 88, 99, 118, 144, 161
Saltwick 26, 38
Samson 36
Sand Runner 161
Severn Collier (Class) 70
Sir Cedric 161
Sneyd (1) 27, 28
Sneyd (2) 53, 54, 55, 56, 70, 88, 129
Southwell 55, 57, 58, 60
Stakesby 22, 26, 38
Stengard 167
Sunshine 27
Superfluous 162
Thomas & Maria 25
Tornyvore 26
Vaarli 25
Vrouw Mary 26
Wolf Rock 166
Wye 24, 26
Yan Yean 27

COMPANIES & PROFESSIONAL BODIES
Abdela & Mitchell Ltd 42
Abercorn Shipbuilding Co Ltd 33
Alexandra (N&SW) Docks & Railway Co 102
Albright & Wilson 9, 115
Ald Shipping Co 55, 57, 60
Alverton Steamship Co Ltd 25
Amey Marine 161
Amey Roadstone Corporation 161
Associated British Ports 176
Baptista Y Iramos Ltd 173
Bartram, Haswell, & Co 34
Batchelor J. (Cardiff) 34
Board of Trade 7
Bristol Corporation Electricity Dept 14, 18, 66, 143
Bristol Tramways & Carriage Co Ltd 14
Bristol Tramways Generating Station 33
British Electricity Authority (BEA) 177
Brown-Boveri 71
Brown. T.R. & Sons 31
Cardiff Coal & Shipping Exchange 11, 23
John Cashmore & Co 31, 33, 36, 38, 40, 42, 55, 88
C.D. Holmes & Co 55
Central Electricity Generating Board 143
Chapman & Co 36
Charles Hill & Sons Ltd 7, 8, 9, 21, 40, 42, 46, 47, 61, 66, 68, 71, 75, 81, 87, 93, 95, 113, 116, 117, 173, 179
Cigale Ltd 37
Clwyd Steamship Co 57
Cochrane, Cooper,& Schofield 36
Congo & Central African Co 31
Corveda Marine Ltd 9, 166, 173
Cory. William & Sons 143
Dale Sand & Gravel Co Ltd 161
Day, Summers & Co 27
Decca 79, 82, 99, 101, 130
Deutz 66
Dodgin C.W. 42
Dolcoath Steamship Co Ltd 25
Dominion Line 34
Dunsmuir & Jackson 34
Esso 115
Eureka Steamship Co Ltd 25
Euterpe Steamship Co Ltd 25
Finch E. & Co Ltd 27
Flinn, Main, & Montgomery 34
Fowey Harbour Commissioners 161
Franco British Chartering Co Ltd 166, 173
Geest 8, 9
Gloucester Power Station 21
Gloucester Railway Carriage & Wagon Co Ltd 24
Goole Shipbuilding & Repair Co 55, 57
Governer & Company of Copper Miners 36.
Grangemouth Steamship Co 49
Guernsey Coasters Ltd 55
Great Western Railway 33
Herschel Steamship Co Ltd 34
Holmes C.D. & Co 36, 55
Horsham Steamship Co Ltd 53
Hull Steam Fishing & Ice Co Ltd 36
Inchbrayock Steamship Co Ltd 51
Inglis A.& J. 31
Invicta Shipping (Thames) Ltd 166, 173
James Stewart 166
J. Furness & Sons Ltd 161
John Harker Ltd 70
John Harrison Ltd 53
John Lysaght Ltd 15, 23, 33, 38
John S. Monks Ltd 53, 55
Laing, James 25
Lloyds 7, 8
Lobnitz & Co 28
London & Rochester Shipping Co 79, 143
Mahe Steamship Co Ltd 37
Mahe Syndicate Ltd 37
Marshall, T.D. 36
Ministry of War Transport 21, 70
Miskin Manor Shipping Co 55
Mississippi & Dominion Steamship Co Ltd 34
Napier 61, 71, 75
National Maritime Museum 8
Naviera Colston S de RL 167
Neilson, I. & Son 40
Newcastle Coal Shipping Co 66
New Steam Tug Co Ltd 27
Newall & Co Ltd 31, 33
Orb Ironworks 15, 23, 38
Osborn & Wallis Ltd 7, 8, 9, 10, 11, 15, 18, 21, 23, 24, 25, 26, 27, 28, 31, 33, 34, 36, 37, 38, 40, 42, 46, 47, 49, 53, 55, 57, 60, 61, 66, 67, 68, 71, 75, 79, 81, 90, 100, 116, 117, 118, 120, 139, 141, 143, 144, 161, 162, 166, 173, 175, 176, 177, 179
Overton Steamship Co Ltd 51
P & A Campbells 7
Paxman-Ricardo 67, 139
Port of Bristol Authority (PBA) 121
Pilotage Authority, River Medway 9
Plenty & Sons 38, 40
Pocketts Bristol Channel Steam Packet Co 31
Prinz Hendrik Maritime Museum 8
R.& D. Jones Ltd 57
R.& W. Paul Ltd 57
Rees Shipbreaking Co 60
R.P. Care & Co 55
Richard Dunstan Ltd 70
Richard England Steam Ship Co 55
Riley Bros Ltd 42

Robert Taylor & Sons 51
Rollo, D. & Sons 34
Roselyne Shipping Co Ltd 161
Ross & Duncan Ltd 53
Ruston & Hornsby Ltd 9, 61, 68, 71, 73, 75, 113, 138, 140, 164
Saltwick Steamship Co Ltd 26
Samuelson, M. 27
Schermuly (Rockets) 113
Scriven & Reid 55
Sea Breezes (periodical) 28
Seaborne Aggregate Co Ltd 161
Seligmann 31
Ships Monthly (periodical) 8
Soc. Pte. Derrian-Bichue 161
South Coast Shipping Co Ltd 161
Pollock & Brown 161
Red Rose Shipping Line 162
South Wales Railway 27
Speedwell Ironworks, Coatbridge 57
St. Baldred Shipping Co Ltd 55
St. Vincent's Ironworks 15
Stakesby Steamship Co Ltd 26
Stengard Ltd 167
Stephen, A. & Sons 25.
Stothert & Co 36
Stothert & Marten 24
Stothert, G.K. & Co Ltd 18, 28, 34, 36, 42, 53, 177
Strand Slipway Co 25
T.van Duivendijk, Sheepswerf, N.V. 66
Tate, A. & Co 55
Thomas Walker & Co Ltd 53
Thompson, J.L. & Sons 26
Trans-Orient Ltd 173
United Alkali Co 11, 23, 24, 33
Voe Shipping Co 165
Walker, C.H. & Co 38
Walker, T.A. 33
Ware, James. A. 34
Water Transport Co Ltd 42
W.D. Tamlyn & Co Ltd 161
Weatherley, Mead & Hussey 31
W.E.Dowds Ltd 79, 82, 166, 173, 176
Whitecross Wire & Iron Co Ltd 34
Wilkie & Turnbull 34
William Beardmore & Co Ltd 57
Williamson, R. & Son 53
Wingate, T. & Co 31, 33
W.N. Lindsay 165
Yieldbrace Ltd (Rochdale) 162
Yieldbrace Ltd (St.Vincent, W.I.) 162
Zagury, Isaac (Liverpool & Loanda) 31
Zinal Steamship Co Ltd 161

PLACES

Ancona 165
Angola 31
Appledore 143
Adriatic 165
Avon, River 18, 23, 24, 34, 135
Avonbank Electricity Works 14
Avonbank Power Station 14
Avonmouth 135
Barbados 8, 162, 164
Barnstaple 21, 79
Barry 79, 141, 161
Bath 23, 24
Battery Point 7, 9, 118
Belize 167
Beverley 36
Bideford 141
Bilbao 25
Black Nore Point 7, 61
Bray 51
Bridgetown 8, 162
Bridgwater 42, 144
Brimscombe 42
Bristol 7, 11, 14, 15, 16, 21, 24, 28
Bristol Channel 7, 9, 10, 11, 23
Bristol City Docks 11, 12, 13, 23
Briton Ferry 28
Brixham 162
Cape Finistere 25
Cape Verde Islands 31
Cardiff 11, 16, 18, 23, 24, 33, 34, 42, 55, 79
Casablanca 173
Chepstow 26, 27, 33
Clevedon 121
Clovelly 141, 143
Cumberland Basin 95
Dublin 51
Dundee 36, 51
East Yelland Power Station 21, 142
Ely Harbour 7, 47, 61, 73, 79, 82, 98, 99, 100, 106, 119, 120, 123, 124, 125, 126, 127, 129, 131, 132, 135, 136, 175, 179
Feeder Canal 11, 14, 15, 23, 33, 46
Forest of Dean 42
Gibraltar 166, 173
Glasgow 28, 31, 33, 34, 40, 53, 166
Gloucester 9, 26, 70
Gloucester Docks 70, 167
Gloucester Power Station 70
Goldcliffe 28, 135
Goole 70, 161
Gravesend 173
Great Yarmouth 26
Greece 162
Guernsey 161
Hayle Power Station 21, 79, 100, 141, 161, 179
Hinckley Point 144
Holms Islands 79, 100
Hotwells 18, 20, 21, 53, 67, 88, 176, 177
Houston 173
Huelva 11
Hull 27, 36, 53, 55
Humberside 18
Husbands Yard, Southampton 162
Ilfracombe 141, 143
Immingham 18
Ipswich 57
Isle of Tudy 33
Krimpen 56
Lannacombe Bay 162
Lavernock Point 26.
Leith 165
Lekkerkerk 66
Lerwick 165
Lescoril 33
Lisbon 173
Liverpool 28, 34, 53, 57
Llanelly 60
Loanda 31
London 33, 36, 37, 53, 166
Lydney 42
Manchester 34
Middlesborough 26
Mauritius 37
Medway, River 167
Merchants Dock 177
Mersey, River 34
Monmouth 26
Montrose 27, 49
Morlaix 161
Mortham 161
Neath Abbey 27
Netham 11, 23
Newcastle 55
Newport 7, 15, 23, 33, 36, 38, 73, 79, 82, 91, 100, 101, 102, 103, 104, 105, 106, 107, 108, 122, 123, 129, 130, 131, 135, 136, 139, 140, 166, 176, 179
Normandy 21, 56, 60, 70
North Foreland 25
North Shields 34
Northam 27
Ouessant 27
Paisley 33
Palmeirinhas 31
Passage West 47
Penarth 21, 26, 27, 66, 175
Penarth UDC Cemetery 53
Pill 130, 131
Point House 31
Ponza Island 162
Port Louis 37
Porthmear Beach 161
Portishead 8, 9, 18, 21
Portishead Dock 9, 16, 17, 106-113, 114, 115 , 177
Portishead Power Station 7, 18, 19, 21, 46, 49, 65, 66, 70, 71, 79, 82, 89, 141, 177
Plymouth 161
Queens Square, Bristol 11, 14, 18, 24
Quimper 33
Rochdale 162
Rochester 167
Rotterdam 8
Salcombe 162
Sete 25
Severn, River 33
Severn Tunnel 33
Somerset 7
Southampton 27, 161, 162
South America 9
South Shields 36
South Wales 7, 10, 11, 15, 23
Spain 11, 23, 34
St. Ives 161
St.Vincent, W.I. 162
Stroud 42
Sudbrook 33, 38
Sunderland 25, 26, 34
Swansea 28, 79
Taibach 36
Taw, River 21, 79
Temple Back 11, 14, 24
Thames, River 66
Thames & Severn Canal 42
Thessolonika 162
Torquay 162
Trelleck 26
Usk, River 28, 102
Walton Bay Signal Station 101, 130, 131
Warrington 33
West Hartlepool 33
West Indies 162, 173
Whitby 26
Windward Islands 8, 164, 167
Workington 53
Wye, River 27
Yelland 10, 7, 82, 100, 119, 136, 141, 143, 166, 179

PEOPLE

Adair, Jack 122, 181, 185
Allen, Jack 184
Allenby, George 181, 185
Anderson, Arthur 181, 185
Anderson, Geoff 181, 185
Baker, Jack 181, 185
Barling, Walter 181, 185
Base, Bill 181, 185
Beard, Jackie 181, 185
Bence, John 184
Bennet, Len 181
Bessant, Eddie 184
Brown, Cliff 184
Brunel. I.K. 27
Brunt, Harry 181, 185
Buckland, Harold 184
Burden, George 181, 185
Butler, Bill 181, 185
Campbell, Colin 181, 185